Out of the Mud Grows the Wisteria

LIFE JOURNEY AND ESSAYS OF A JAPANESE AMERICAN JODO SHINSHU BUDDHIST MINISTER

BY LAVERNE SENYO SASAKI

To all my teachers from grade school, high school, colleges, institutes, seminars, lectures, and ministry, without whose guidance and support I would have not become what I am today.

Namu Amida Butsu

Book design by Michael Sherman
Back cover photo: LaVerne with grandson Odin and Sharon's dog, Koko
Back cover illustrations by Sasaki grandchildren
Edited by Mika Ono and Sharon Sasaki

Copyright © 2017, LaVerne Sasaki
ISBN 978-0-692-92318-4

Printed in the United States of America

TABLE OF CONTENTS

i. Foreword by Bishop Kodo Umezu
ii. Preface: Out of the Mud Grows the Wisteria
iii. Introduction: On Jodo Shinshu Buddhist Ministry

Chapter 1: My Roots.. **11**
- Sasaki Family *Mon* (Crest)
- Grandfather Senju's Global Ministerial Activities
- Another Grandson's Remembrance, by Fumihiko Sakow
- My Parents, Rev. Sensho and Kinuko Sasaki
- My Parents, Myself
- Five Brothers
- Remembering Sasaki-*sensei* and *Okusan,* by Kimi Hisatsune
- Remembering my first BCA *Sensei,* by Rev. Junjo Tsumura
- March Memorial Service: Reflecting on My Parents
- 'Goodbye, Sasaki-*sensei*,' by Sumi Uyeda
- A Personal Recollection of Mrs. Kinuko Sasaki, by Rev. Richard T. Schellhase

Chapter 2: Beginnings: Stockton, Tacoma, Penryn, Sacramento, and Tule Lake, 1930–1945............................ **27**
- Coming into the World
- In and Out of Penryn Elementary School
- Church Kid
- Pearl Harbor Day
- Tule Lake
- Tule Lake Camp Schooling

Chapter 3: Coming of Age: Sacramento, 1945–1953................... 35
- A YBA Kid
- Basketball: Team Players
- Learning on Summer and Part-Time Jobs
- The Greatest Weightlifter Tommy Kono
  and *Karate Kid* Pat Morita
- Sacramento Church Hosts Japanese Celebrities
- Transitions
- Decisions

Chapter 4: An Education: Tokyo, 1953–1958........................... 43
- Bon Voyage
- Settling In
- Tokyo University Students
- My Visit to Japan Medical College
- A Different Kind of New Year's Eve
- Japanese Expressions Are So Interesting and Funny
- The Hanayama Family
- Reflections, by Takaye Hanayama
- Many Excellent Teachers
- An Animal Memorial Service, Not a Pet Memorial Service
- Zen Training
- Wise Advice on My Graduate Thesis Selection
- Lady Kujo, Asoka Hospital and Sumo Grand
  Champion Chiyonoyama
- Traveling Fourth-Class on a Ship to Rangoon, Burma
- The World Buddhist Conference
- Sights and Insights from India, Nepal and Ceylon
- Lecture Tour of Japan

**Chapter 5: Launching Family and Ministry:
Stockton, 1959–1971**... 73
- A New Life

- My Two BCA *Senseis*
- University of the Pacific Studies
- Marriage
- Many Trips to the Maternity Ward
- City Redevelopment and Fundraising
- Impermanence of the Human Body
- Community Service
- U.S.-Japan Sister City Activities

Chapter 6: Carrying the Torch: Mountain View, 1971–1990.........85
- A Fortunate Move
- The Taste of a Japanese Rice Cracker Described by a Prison Inmate
- What Big Things After a Glass of Wine!!
- My Sports-Related Buddhist Karma: The Los Angeles Summer Olympics
- My Visit to Israel
- Mini-Sermon: Make Room for What is Important
- Mini-Sermon: Nembutsu in a Nutshell
- Haruko Muranaka—a Life of Inspiration and Challenge
- Lessons from Lady Eshinni's Life
- Living Amida's Light: A Life of Reflection
- The Mountain View Buddhist Temple: My Cultural, Social and Spiritual Home, by Dr. Kenneth Tanaka
- Rev. Sensho and Mrs. Kinuko Sasaki, by Hiroji Kariya

Chapter 7: On the Cusp of a New Century:
San Francisco, 1990–2000.. 105
- A Global City
- Young Adults
- Compassion: Heart of the Buddha (*Hotoke No Kokoro, Daijihishin*)
- The Growing Popularity of Buddhism

- Senior Citizen!?
- Personal Memories of Past Bishops of the BCA and Ministers of the Buddhist Church of San Francisco
- The Universal Buddhist Way of Life Is Not Confined Within the Walls of a Church
- Shin Buddhism is Neither a Religion of Ritual, Nor of Prayer
- Religion Should Be a Cause of Unity
- Gift of Amida Buddha, by Rev. Joen Amagishi
- Nirvana Day—What It Can Mean for Me
- Obon, Obon, It's Festival Day
- Bodhi Day Service: Its Buddhist Meaning
- *Okagesamade*: Into the 21st Century
- The Indescribable Power of Religion
- *Jinenhoni*: The Importance of a Life of Freedom and Naturalness
- Dharma Appreciation—What? How? When? Why?, by Della Bruens
- Thoughts on *Kazoe Doshi* (Age 70 by Japanese Age-Counting)

Chapter 8: Retirement: San Bruno, 2000–Present………….. 129
- Retirement
- Caucasian Senior Center Buddhist Services
- 21 Years Later, a Letter
- War: A Sign of *Mappo*
- A Wonderful Bishop: Kenryu T. Tsuji
- BCA in the 21st Century
- Unexpected Joy in Mexico
- The Unforgettable Earthquake
- Tule Lake Pilgrimage: A Meaningful Service
- Second Trip to India

- My Dharma Friend, Rev. Toshio Murakami
- Reflections on My 80th Birthday
- In Memoriam: Dr. Kenneth Inada, Buddhist Scholar
- Me with Cancer?? No Way!
- Surgery
- Going Home
- My Perspective on Good Health
- Suicide, My Personal View
- What a Relief! It Was Only a Nightmare
- Tell Me About My Monshu Father
- Shousei Hanayama's Farewell Message
- White Bones… So REAL
- "*Jabu Jabu Jiichan*" for 13 Grandchildren
- My Pleasant, Satisfying and Fulfilling Relationship with LaVerne Sasaki, by Rev. Richard T. Schellhase
- Traces of a Key Dharmaic Trait in the Life of Rev. LaVerne Senyo Sasaki, by Rev. Tetsuo Unno
- A Reflection on My Life

Acknowledgments……………………………………………… 179

Appendix: Grandfather Senju Sasaki…………………………… 180
    1. About the First Overseas Minister, Senjū Sasaki, by Rev. Shudo Takahatake
    2. Singapore Report by Senju Sasaki, translated by Dr. Nobuo Haneda

FOREWORD

by Bishop Kodo Umezu

Rev. LaVerne Senyo Sasaki is one of my senior Dharma teachers and friends. He has always stayed young at heart and full of energy and passion, even after retiring from the active ministry of the Buddhist Churches of America (BCA). His sincere desire to share his deep appreciation of the Buddha's profound teaching with everyone has not diminished. Rev. Sasaki's service to the BCA spanned 42 long years and I still see him at every event and program at the Jodo Shinshu Center in Berkeley, California.

The seeds of his work in this country were planted when his grandfather, Rev. Senju Sasaki, arrived in Canada in 1905 to start the Buddhist Mission of North America. Rev. Senju Sasaki came with his wife, Tomie, and son, Sensho (LaVerne's father, who later became a BCA minister).

It is customary for many Japanese parents to give their sons names containing a common character. The Sasaki reverends have the common character *sen*, which means one thousand, in their given names. The grandfather's name, Senju, appears in one of the hymns of Shinran Shonin, the founder of the founder of Jodo Shinshu Buddhism. The father's name, Sensho, means one thousand mighty elephants (the elephant signifies a great Dharma power). Rev. LaVerne Sasaki's parents gave him the name Senyo—one thousand great oceans—in the hopes he would have an ocean-like mind and actively engage in overseas missionary work. LaVerne Senyo did not fall short of his parents' aspirations for his contributions to his Hongwanji Overseas Missionary lineage here in North America.

In reality, the BCA was too small for him. He was always looking at the larger world. That does not mean, however, that he did not care about the members and temples that he served. He interacted with people from all walks of life and encouraged them to hear the Dharma, as he continues to do through these memoirs.

Today, he has a wonderful family supporting his work. He is a loving husband to Helen and a caring father to Brian Senshin, Stanton Senshu, Sharon Hiromi, Ellen Kyomi and Rina Emi.

It is my sincere wish that this book be read by many people, so his deep and passionate Dharma-loving heart can offer a guiding light.

Gassho,
— Kodo Umezu
Bishop, Buddhist Churches of America

PREFACE

Out of the Mud Grows the Wisteria

How to summarize my life, so far, of 87 years?

A wise Buddhist priest once summarized his life in one word: "dream." Less wise, I require seven: "Out of the mud grows the wisteria."

"Out of the mud grows the lotus" is a popular Buddhist saying. The late Rev. Hogen Fujimoto wrote a book of this title to describe his experience as a Buddhist chaplain with prison inmates who, by learning and accepting the Buddhist path, were able to find spiritual strength and joy. A similar metaphor was used by my friend and eminent Buddhist scholar, the late Dr. Taitetsu Unno, in his 2002 book, *Shin Buddhism: Bits of Rubble Turn into Gold.*

In the 1960s, San Francisco radio broadcaster Don Sherwood closed his KSFO morning show with: "This is Don Sherwood signing off. Remember folks, out of the mud grows the lotus." I was so thrilled to hear this quote that I once wrote him a letter, although he never did reply.

Mud represents the obstacles and pain that we face in human life. As a minister, husband, friend, father, grandfather and human being, I have my share of greed, anger and ignorance. My "mud" includes insensitivity and inattentiveness to others, boasting and self-centeredness. In Buddhism, we count 108 imperfections (faults). Upon hearing this at one of my talks, I remember a fourth grade student responding, "I know I have some faults, but not that many."

Buddhism is so truthful in exposing imperfections that we instinctively "cover up" with excuses and justification. Shinran, the founder of Jodo Shinshu Buddhism, continually reminds us how easy it is to find faults in others, but how we grope in the darkness about ourselves.

Despite my personal faults, I have been able to lead a happy and optimistic life. Buddhism is often misunderstood as pessimistic, because the first Noble Truth states that life is *dukkha* (suffering). I believe the opposite, that Buddhism is the most optimistic among all world religions because it emphasizes that the beautiful lotus grows out of mud, as opposed to clear, purified water.[1]

Similarly, the wisteria plant rises out of the earth's soil. It wasn't until I was a minister at Stockton in the 1960s that I saw a living wisteria. At the Marysville Buddhist Church minister's residence, I saw a purple-colored stem flower and asked the minister's wife, "What kind of flower is that?" She responded with surprise, "Reverend Sasaki, you're not familiar with the wisteria flower?! That is the symbol of our Jodo Shinshu teaching!" I should have been embarrassed, but I was not. I considered it a learning experience, as I was pretty ignorant about plants and flowers.

The Wisteria Crest is the official symbol of the Jodo Shinshu Hongwanji Buddhist temples: two wisteria blossoms form a circle with two intertwining vines in the center. The flowers are symbolic of brightness and the transitory nature of life and all things. The Wisteria Crest represents our Jodo Shinshu way of life in that the spiritual conclusion is like this flower, which blooms with its head down, symbolizing humility, a welcoming heart-mind, and sincere reverence to Buddha. Upon realizing our imperfect selves and receiving the light of Buddha's wisdom, we learn to "droop in spiritual humility," which leads to a life of joy and gratitude.

The title of this book reflects my interpretation that the wisteria, symbol of Jodo Shinshu, is spiritually equivalent to the lotus, symbol of general Buddhism.[2] A haiku poem that crystallizes this idea is in Takamaro Shigaraki's book, "Heart of the Shin Buddhist Path": *"Shibugaki no shibu ga sono mama*

---

[1] The best-known Buddhist scripture (sutra) that communicates this idea is commonly called the *Lotus Sutra* (the Mahayana sacred writing, "*Saddharma Pundarika Sutra*"). This writing was so highly regarded by the Prince Regent Shotoku (574–621 CE) that it is one of the three sutras he selected as the doctrinal basis of Japanese Buddhism.

[2] This is described in the "Koso Wasan," Shinran's hymn of praise of India's Vasubandhu (known as Seshin in Japanese; Seshin is the second teacher of the seven great teachers revered by Shinran), which, in part, reads: "of those who encounter the power of the Primal Vow, not one passes by in vain; they are filled with the treasure ocean of virtues, the defiled waters of their blind passions not separated from it."

amami kana." (Ah! How very sweet! Is the bitterness of the Bitter Persimmon.).

Dr. Hisao Inagaki, prominent Jodo Shinshu Buddhist scholar, described *shinjin* and *satori* with these words: "It is often asked whether *shinjin* and *satori* are the same or different experiences… They are different but not unrelated. *Shinjin* is awakening to Amida's wisdom, compassion, and power, while *satori* is realization of your Buddha Nature."

I believe the following four positive interpretations are the future of our Jodo Shinshu religion as it exists with other Buddhist schools and various world religions: a) *bonno soku bodai* (the Mahayana Buddhist principle of non-duality, that defilement in itself is enlightenment); b) the Jodo Shinshu idea of *kiho ittai* (that realization of an imperfect self is at the same time the realization of Amida Buddha's unconditional wisdom and compassion); c) the Jodo Shinshu idea of *shinjin bussho* (*shinjin* is Buddha Nature, an oft-overlooked expression); and d) the Mahayana Bodhisattva ideal given from a Jodo Shinshu perspective.

For me, the wisteria is expressed in the Japanese word *okagesama*, a realization of gratitude to the whole of life, with all the unknown and unseen causes and conditions (karma) that make it possible, good or bad. This realization has helped me to deal with life's problems with spiritual strength, gratitude and optimism. As his five boys grew to adulthood, our father constantly taught us the "four gratitudes," in other words, gratitude for: 1) the good karma given to us by parents and ancestors; 2) the many teachers and people who provided guidance and the necessities of life; 3) the country and world; and 4) the Buddha, for the wisdom necessary to live this difficult life with peace of mind, joy and gratitude.

In writing this book, my primary objective is to preserve and continue the Buddha Dharma legacy given to me from my parents, teachers, and ancestors. Secondly, this book allows me to share my past experiences with family and future generations. Thirdly, I seek to transmit the Buddha Dharma in countries outside of Japan and share the history of one minister within the Buddhist Churches of America organization.

— *Namu Amida Butsu* [3]

---

[3] The late Bishop Kenryu T. Tsuji translates *Namu Amida Butsu* as "I am one with Buddha."

INTRODUCTION

On Jodo Shinshu Buddhist Ministry

My story is intertwined with the Buddhist Churches of America (BCA) Jodo Shinshu Buddhist tradition in the mainland United States.[4] By way of introduction, I share some of my thoughts on this heritage—which is unique and often misunderstood.

Jodo Shinshu, a Pure Land Mahayana Buddhist school taught by our founder, Shinran (1173–1262), is a later historical development compared to early Buddhism. For this reason, our form of Buddhism is often misrepresented as being corrupted from Shakyamuni Buddha's teaching and even as being Christian-like.

The traditional view of a Buddhist priest is someone who is "sacred and holy," as it is popularly understood and as implied by the title "Reverend" given to us here in America. Traditionally, a Buddhist priest spends his entire life in a temple without a wife, family, home, automobile, money or any other so-called necessities of life. This form of Buddhism is called Theravada Buddhism and still actively practiced in Southeast Asia. Priests' lives are totally dependent on the gifts of lay followers.

Dramatically different from Theravada Buddhism is the BCA Jodo Shinshu Buddhist tradition. The BCA's mother temple is the Jodo Shinshu Hongwanji-Ha in Kyoto, Japan, and our spiritual leader, the Gomonshu, 25th Head Priest Kojun Ohtani. The BCA headquarters is at 1710 Octavia Street,

---

[4] Honpa Hongwanji Mission of Hawaii is older (organized in 1889), while organizationally and doctrinally the same.

San Francisco. Our practice and way of life are similar to the Jewish and Christian traditions in that priests have a wife and family, live on a residence separate from the temple or church, are given a salary, vacation and days off, have no restrictions on eating, smoking or drinking, are governed by a board of directors and possess automobiles, credit cards, etc. Our daily practice is not even meditation in the Theravada, Tibetan or Zen traditions. Rather, it is a practice called the Nembutsu path (a way of faith in the infinite Buddha (*amida nyorai* in Japanese), called Amida Buddha), where we live, work and play with Buddha constantly in mind. Our regular ministerial practice consists primarily of conducting Buddhist services (Sundays, funerals, family memorial services, wedding ceremonies), administrative duties, study sessions, lectures, home and hospital visitations, counseling and public activities.

As such, our ministerial practice is radically different from early Buddhists and current Southeast Asian Buddhist ways. And yet, this form of Buddhism possesses a deep historical connection to early sixth-century Buddhism in Japan when Prince Regent Shotoku Taishi (574–622 CE) laid the foundation of Buddhism in Japan with his commentaries on three important Mahayana Buddhist scriptures. One of the commentaries discussed *Vimalakirti-Nirdesa Sutra* (critique of Theravada Buddhist priests by a great lay Buddhist named Vimalakirti), which pointed to the importance of the laity in Buddhism.

Later, Shinran emphasized the laity even further. Upon spiritual reflection of his priestly life of discipline, meditation and intensive study, he realized it was futile for him to honestly and humanly fulfill the difficult way that Buddhism was traditionally practiced by priests. He, therefore, felt unable to call himself a priest. And yet, he was also not a layman, for he was blessed and shown the way of Buddhism by many great Buddhist teachers. So, based on his deep spiritual insights, Shinran called his path "neither priestly nor lay."

With this historical and doctrinal background, Jodo Shinshu ministers dedicate their lives to sharing and teaching this form of Buddhism as a way to attain Nirvana.

Although historically rooted with Japan, in the United States our form of Buddhism has departed somewhat from traditional Japanese practice. First of all, priesthood is not normally transmitted within a family as is in Japan. Our temples or churches have different ministers assigned to them like

Protestant churches. Our institutions are operated like a business or professional organization with a governing board of directors, membership dues, donations and pledges. Therefore, we ministers are not generational "owner/priests" as in Jodo Shinshu Buddhist temples in Japan. Although we do not like to be called "employees," we are actually hired by our "employers," the lay members, who ideally support the giver/teacher of Buddha's teaching with gratitude and joy.

Our ministerial functions are also different from the Theravada priests. It is a profession of many professions. We are expected to be teachers, organizers, fundraisers, counselors, visitor and public relations persons, all in the same body at the same time. Rarely can a person fulfill this kind of expectation. Further complicating the situation, ministers had been basically educated as teachers of Buddhist doctrine and not really as ministers of a church.

Some ministers leave the organization or are frustrated because success is often not measured by their success teaching Buddhism, but by their popularity. A successful minister is the minister who excels in human social relationships with his or her church members. As a sports fan, in some ways ministry is like being a baseball manager or football coach—social skills, rather than merely coaching, often determine success.

However, there are good sides of being a Buddhist minister here in America compared to being a priest in Japan. In the United States, the culture and history has led to respect for religion and its clergy, including Buddhist ministers. When I was studying in Japan, I saw Buddhist priests were in general not given similar respect. Due to the long history of Buddhism and some corrupt Buddhist priests, in Japan priests were often characterized—in popular culture and everyday conversation—as being concerned only with funeral ceremonies and their monetary compensation. Big temples in Japan were better financially, but in small temples many priests had to be schoolteachers or run a kindergarten for income.[5]

However, despite all the issues and problems confronting us as ministers, our work is most rewarding and satisfying. We are privileged to be the messenger of Buddha's teaching so that lives of many people can be made wiser and happier with the great Buddha's wisdom and compassion.

[5] In great contrast, I can still vividly remember traveling on a chartered train with the delegates of a World Buddhist Conference from Rangoon to Pegu or Mandalay. Burmese farmers, upon seeing the colored-robe Theravada Buddhist priests on our train, dropped their work tools and prostrated on the dirt to express their respect and gratitude. This is still the general Buddhist attitude to priests in Theravada Buddhist countries such as Myanmar (previously called Burma), Sri Lanka (formerly called Ceylon), and Cambodia.

We have had our frustrations and problems, but I ask, "What profession or occupation doesn't have human frustrations and problems?"

I can only quietly and sincerely recite in *gassho* (palms together in prayer position as a sign of gratitude and reverence) and gratitude for the lifetime work given to me by parents, teachers and ancestors.

MY ROOTS

Sasaki Family *Mon* (Crest)

Fumiya Sakow (Senju Sasaki's great-grandson and my cousin, the late Fumihiko Sakow's son) was kind enough to provide this information.

The Sasaki family emblem is *yotsume-bishi* (四つ目菱), or four-eyed diamond, which may have some relation with the famous warlord Takeda clan (Shingen Takeda 武田 信玄); the Takeda emblem (武田菱) looks like the Sasaki emblem, except without "eyes" on the diamond pattern.

The "eyes" refer to human ties or solidarity. Therefore, "four-eyed diamond" hearkens to strong ties and solidarity among family members.[6] Among many variations of *yotsume-bishi*, ours is specifically *sumitate yotsume-bishi* (隅立四つ目菱) or right-angled (square) four-eyed diamond.

---

[6] Most of the Sasaki families in Japan using this emblem trace their roots back to the original Sasaki clan, a medieval feudal warlord family headquartered in Shiga Prefecture. The Sasaki clan began to use this emblem when it helped establish the Kamakura Shogunate (1192–1333). The clan later moved to Shiga Prefecture (just south of Fukui) and served Oda Nobunaga in the 16th century.

Grandfather Senju's Global Ministry

I wish I had learned more about my grandfather, Senju Sasaki (1871–1944), while he and my dad were still living. I only hold sparse childhood memories—our grandfather would chase my brother Conrad and me after our pranks.[7]

In researching the life of Reverend Senju Sasaki, I was amazed by his ministerial dedication and global reach. A true visionary, he was known beyond Japan's Fukui prefecture as a leading progressive Jodo Shinshu Buddhist and one of the few globally minded Buddhist priests of his time. I feel small compared to him, especially considering that his work took place a century ago!

Senju Sasaki was born in 1871 in Fukui, Japan, a prefecture that produced many of the Buddhist Churches of America's early ministers.
Senju, at age 16, was sent to the best Honganji (one of the two prominent Shin Buddhist sects in Japan) school, the Bungakuryo, which had many prominent teachers including historically prominent scholars Mokurai Shimaji, Renjo Akamatsu, Kozui Ohtani, Lafcadio Hearn, Kotaro Sugimura, Junjiro Takakusu, Egen Sakow (Senju married his younger sister, Tomie) and Yemyo Imamura (who later became Hawaii's first bishop).[8]

In 1897, Senju was assigned by the Honganji to minister to a pearl divers' village on Thursday Island, Queensland, Australia. This village was made up of pearl divers from Wakayama prefecture. In 1899, he and his wife moved to Singapore, where Senju was the assigned Honganji minister to some 1,800 Japanese people. During his six-year stay there, it is reported that Senju, during this time of the Russo-Japanese War, notified Japan of an invading Russian naval force passing through Singapore, thwarting a major disaster for Japan.[9]

Senju Sasaki was a man of great compassion and many talents. He was multilingual in English, Japanese and even Devanagari, an ancient language of India. His proficiency with Devanagari even attracted Hindu people who needed help writing or deciphering letters. His wife, Tomie, who was also affectionately called *"Okusan," "Naishitsu"* and *"Bomori,"* taught Japanese

---

[7] See various photos of my grandfather's life.

[8] Rev. Shinjo Ikuta, Enkakushi: *History of the Buddhist Churches of Canada*; Japanese-language history book called *Hokubei Enkakushi* (1935), edited by Kenju Masuyama.

[9] Research by Rev. Shudo Takahatake (former Montreal, Canada Buddhist Church minister), which brought out more of my grandfather's illustrious history.

immigrants skills such as sewing, homemaking and etiquette.[10]

In 1905, Senju was assigned as the first Honganji minister in Canada (Vancouver).[11] He delivered the first Dharma talk in Canada on the steps of Vancouver City Hall on October 26, 1905, just two weeks after his arrival. This Dharma talk thundered like the lion's roar to the ears of some 500 persons in the audience. The Foundation Committee and Reverend Sasaki raised $5,668 in donations, and the first temple in Canada, on 32 Alexander Street, Vancouver, was founded December 12, 1905.[12] On April 21, 1909, the government of British Columbia granted official recognition to Buddhism.

In May 1909, Rev. Sasaki and former Abbot Komyo Ohtani (father of 23rd Abbot Kosho Ohtani) traveled to London via the Siberian Railroad to study the various religions of Europe and the world. He also visited Jerusalem, toured South Africa and payed homage to sacred remains in India.[13]

Senju returned to Fukui, where an Englishman named Thomas Kirby, who had met Senju in Vancouver, came to live with him at Kozenji Temple to study Buddhism and Jodo Shinshu under Senju's tutelage. After Senju introduced him to Hawaii Bishop Yemyo Imamura, Kirby became the first Caucasian Buddhist minister in Hawaii.[14]

In 1918, Senju was assigned to be a chaplain for the Japanese army in Siberia. From 1923 to 1925, he served as the acting bishop for Buddhist Churches of America and minister of the San Francisco, Stockton and Berkeley churches. In 1927, Senju was assigned to be *Rinban* to Otaru (Hokkaido) Betsuin Church.[15]

I was told he died on June 23, 1944, during World War II, deeply concerned about the fate of his son (my father), and his youngest daughter, my Aunt Masako Sakow, then interned in the "enemy country of United States."

These are only highlights of Senju Sasaki's illustrious career. I regret I was not able to learn first-hand of his great vision, dedication and worldwide experience.[16]

---

[10] The first English-language history book on Jodo Shinshu in Canada, *Bukkyo Tozen: A history of Jodo Shinshu Buddhism in Canada*, 1905–1995, by Terry Watada

[11] ibid.

[12] ibid.

[13] Rev. Shinjo Ikuta, Enkakushi: *History of the Buddhist Churches of Canada*; Japanese-language history book called *Hokubei Enkakushi* (1935), edited by Kenju Masuyama.

[14] *A Grateful Past, A Grateful Future: Honpa Hongwanji Mission of Hawaii 100 Year History* 1889–1989.

[15] Research by Rev. Shudo Takahatake

[16] For more information on Senju Sasaki, see the appendix in this book.

Another Grandson's Remembrance of Senju Sasaki
By Fumihiko Sakow

My cousin, Fumihiko Sakow, lived with our grandfather Senju Sasaki when he was still a child. He recorded these thoughts and memories years before passing away in a car accident in 2015. Fumihiko's son, Rev. Hitoya Sakow, is now the head priest of Jofukuji Temple, in Fukui, Japan.

My humble writing skills cannot do justice to my grandfather on my mother's side, Senju Sasaki. There is so much to tell about him and I cannot think of anyone else like him. He identified himself as "*Tembei Ronin* (天米浪人)" (*ronin* (浪人) means a person unsettled in one place; *tembei* (天米) means America), since he journeyed into India, Singapore, North America, Canada, Brazil and Argentina. Today we can go to anywhere in the world by airplane in hours, but in those days it took a few months to go from Japan to North America.

Why did such a young minister from the countryside born in Imadate (Kojiro's hometown) in Japan's Echizen Province entertain high aspirations and go to countries where people speak not only English but also Spanish, Dutch and other languages? It can only be described as a miracle. He had an impressive spirit of enterprise and open-mindedness. He went to foreign countries by steamboat, which would take a few months, to help spread the Nishi Hongwanji (Pureland Buddhism) overseas. I wonder if my grandfather accompanied the Monshu, Ōtani Kōzui, and took on his emissary task at the same time.

I don't want to use the word "spy," but I imagine that both Christian and Buddhist missionaries carried their national backgrounds on their shoulders when assuming their jobs. My grandfather never told us, his grandchildren, that he helped the intelligence agencies of Japan. However, I remember one incident during WWI when I told my grandfather that Singapore had been captured and renamed "Shōnantō (昭南島)." Upon hearing the news, he danced for surprise and joy. Recently, I came to realize that he was filled with emotion at that time.

I think back on the time I saw a group photo of my grandfather and Tōgō Gensui (東郷元帥).[17] In terms of my grandfather's companionship with the marshal, my grandfather should have been sitting close by. However, his

---

[17] Gensui is a rank of military, translated as marshal in in English.

face cannot be found. I became suspicious and looked at the picture again carefully. I found him looking back on the right side of the 50-person group and thought, "My grandfather avoided having his photo taken in order to hide his identity but was accidentally photographed." He never imagined his grandson would find him in the photo later on. As the phrase goes, "The foolish ostrich buries his head in the sand and thinks he is not seen." I myself think the bonds of kinship are quite mysterious.

My grandfather Senju passed away before the end of the Pacific War, but it was a blessing he didn't have to feel the chagrin of wartime defeat. I was raised by my grandfather for about three years. Even so, I wish he hadn't had to spend his last days inconvenienced by a lack of food; I would have liked him to drink coffee, his favorite drink, as much as he would like! I would say that he is smiling in the Pure Land now!

My Parents, Myself

My parents were the greatest influence on my life. Their lifetime example and dedication to the Buddha Dharma and Nembutsu (the recitation of the name of the Amitabha Buddha) convinced me to make Buddhist ministry my life's work. As I look back, I have a fuller appreciation of their influence, which has shaped me as a person, husband, father, grandfather, minister, friend and citizen.

My father, Reverend Sensho Sasaki, was born on July 16, 1903 in Fukui, Japan, the 25th generation of the family there. He was named Sensho, 1,000 elephants, because he was conceived in India, while his parents were visiting Buddhist sites. My mother, born Kinuko Hokyo, was a layperson in a devout Higashi Honganji Jodo Shinshu family, whose family home in Fukui hosted the Hoonko service for five to seven days each year. Sensho and Kinuko were married on May 20, 1929.

Both were actively involved in the ministry until the last day of their lives. The day before her accidental death, my mother served tea and refreshments to the Buddhist Church of America (BCA) Campaign for Buddhism in America Committee at the Mountain View Buddhist Temple. My mother actively served as a minister's wife (*okusan* or *bo-mori* in Japanese) for almost 60 years![18] Such a long record as active minister's wife will be difficult to challenge.

---

18 See "A Personal Recollection of Mrs. Kinuko Sasaki" by Rev. Richard T. Schellhase, p.25

My father and mother complemented each other in their service to a Buddhist temple. My mother, a memory whiz, not only recalled the many church members' names, but even remembered the telephone numbers of the many Sacramento church board members. My father was not like her. If my father tried to remember everything as my mother did, he would have been a nervous wreck. The "unattached, laid-back casualness" of my father was probably the right way to maintain his sanity.

My father was so casual, relaxed and friendly with the church members that he would, without any hesitation, visit a church member's home and even take a nap there. I could not do that. And it would never have crossed my mother's mind.

My parents showed me that meaningful or effective ministry is not all Buddhist knowledge or even skill in teaching or communicating the Buddhist message. Unfortunately or not, a large aspect of successful ministry rests on human relationships.

Five Brothers

Being the oldest of five boys, the minister's kids, was memorable. . . The five of us—myself, Senpo (Conrad), Senryu (Louis), Senmaro (Maro) and Senrey (Rey)—all grew up in the church parsonage, with parents truly dedicated to the work required of them at a most critical period of Japanese American history.

The church was the center of the community during the trauma of the hysteria before and especially after World War II, and our parents had to prioritize people who needed help with housing, counseling and other resettlement issues. It was an extra responsibility to take care of five growing boys. Having their children get a "good" education was not our parents' primary goal. In many ways, they sacrificed time with us for the larger good of the community.

We all turned out fine, but we were sometimes in the midst of a "gang" mentality while living in a "skid row" type area. Lunch often meant canned pork and beans or money to spend at fast food places to buy hot dogs, tacos or tamales!

Senpo

Senpo (which means 1,000 mountains)—later known as Conrad—was born on June 9, 1931, in Stockton. Conrad and I, being only 15 months apart, did most things together.

We were bedmates in the pre-war years when our family was in Penryn and Sacramento. I was irritated by his bad habit of eating crackers in bed. We often had other brotherly brawls, including an incident when he threw a dart that hit me in the leg when I was running away from him.

My brother took the name Conrad when we enrolled together at Sacramento High School in 1945, after we returned from Tule Lake Internment Camp. He was among six of us who decided to change our first names on the spot. Conrad and I chose our names from twin brothers we admired, Conrad and LaVerne Kurahara.

During that time, Conrad and I both played basketball for the Sacramento YBA (Young Buddhist Association) and had many mutual friends. Our team even won the Sacramento YMCA basketball championship one year.

Later, Conrad visited me in Japan. At the time, I was a graduate student in Tokyo and he was an American Army GI sent to Japan during the Korean War. I took him to our family Buddhist Temple (Kozenji) in Fukui. Looking at grandfather Senju's family album there, he saw that it showed photos of me at three months of age, six months, one year, two years, etc. Conrad asked, "Where's my picture?" Was this the traditional Japanese custom of oldest child favoritism?

In his adult years, Conrad was a very popular, well-liked fellow who worked at Aerojet in Sacramento. His wife, Joyce, and sons, Randy and Ricky, have always lived in Sacramento. Conrad enjoyed fishing, golf and outings with his many friends, as well as our favorite snack: Chinese ginger. Chinese ginger, in fact, was a favorite snack of all my brothers, as well as many young people in our crowd in the early days.

Conrad was also overall a compassionate person. He purchased the house next door to his own as a retirement home for our mother to live in during her later years. However, it turned out that Mom continued to live in Mountain View, where I was minister, even after our Dad passed away in 1971; she stayed to continue her "work" as *bomori* (minister's wife) to help Helen and me.

Unfortunately, Conrad eventually developed lung cancer, which spread to other parts of his body. He passed away on February 11, 2004.

Senryu

My second brother Senryu (1,000 dragons)—also known as Louis—was born April 30, 1935.

He was a smart kid and a good student. He even played on the Sacramento High School "B" basketball team until he was afflicted with infantile paralysis (polio) during its epidemic years. This polio surely took a toll on him as he had to withstand pain and suffering, not only physically but also socially when he was coming of age! Despite that, he was able to complete high school and then graduated from Sacramento State College to become a medical technician.

As I was away from my younger brothers during my graduate studies in Japan (1953–1958) during their teen years, I regret that I was not able to be or act as their "big brother" during their formative teen years. I miss the intimacy they had with my brother Conrad.

Louis lived in Marysville, Donner Lake, Dos Palos, Stockton and Gridley during his working years. He married Jeannie Richardson, and they had one child, Marcia, while also raising Scott, his stepson. Although Louis and Jeannie later divorced, they always stayed on good terms.

During the time Louis lived in Donner Lake, he developed a serious case of spinal meningitis, which caused him great pain. He was able to get back on his own and work again, but he did not stay in one place for a long stretch of time.

Louis did a lot of volunteer work as a medical technician, as well as in Buddhist churches and for service clubs. He even went to the US Virgin Island, St. Thomas, at his own expense to extend his expertise. A faithful Buddhist until the end, he set up his small *obutsudan* (home shrine) wherever he lived.

Louis was a very private person; I regret that I didn't have more talks with him about his innermost feelings. He passed away from complications from cancer surgery at Oroville Hospital on November 17, 2006, at the age of 71.

Senmaro

My third brother, Senmaro (1,000 perfections) was born on May 20, 1940, in Sacramento. I remember him as a very cute-looking child.

I was 23 years old and Maro was only 13 when I went to study in Tokyo. I missed seeing him play high school football and being drafted into the Army.

After attending Sacramento Junior College, he worked for the California Department of Motor Vehicles from 1959 to 1997 in many capacities. Maro was twice married, to Mabel Mizusaki and Winnie Evans, and has two sons, Mark and Robb, a daughter, Mara, whom he raised from age 7 to 18, and seven grandchildren.

For many years, Maro's favorite activity was deep-sea fishing for different species of tuna in the Pacific Ocean. He enjoys all kinds of food—especially spicy. He also enjoys creating verses of poetry to commemorate events.

Maro now resides in Long Beach.

Senrey

My youngest brother, Senrey (1,000 objectiveness) was born on June 9, 1942 in Sacramento, right before our family was sent to Tule Lake Relocation Center. Rey may have been the best athlete among the siblings. He was a star basketball player and even boxed in junior college.

Rey was a barber for most of his adult life with a shop in Gridley. He had many customers who farmed in the area, so he enjoyed hunting for ducks and pheasants in their rice fields. He also liked to play basketball and for many years served as a respected referee for basketball games.

Rey married Gladys Sasaki of Marysville in 1962; they subsequently divorced. He has three children: a daughter, Janelle, and sons, Blake and Brent. His children are all successful in their own right—Janelle in Tokyo as an activist for diversity in the workplace, and her brothers in California, working for sports teams.

Rey now has four grandchildren and lives in Yuba City.

Remembering Sasaki-*sensei* and *Okusan*
This article was written by the late Kimi Hisatsune (daughter of late Rev. Inshu Yonemura and wife of Dr. Clarence Hisatsune), frequent writer for Buddhist Churches of America (BCA) Wheel of Dharma and longtime family friend.

The late Rev. Sensho Sasaki, father of Rev. LaVerne Sasaki, was one of the BCA pioneers of the 1920s—when my father Rev. Inshu Yonemura (who died in 1949 at Enmanji Temple, Sebastopol, California) was also active. As is well known to many now, *Issei* [first-generation Japanese American] Buddhists of the time had huge economic problems as they tried to make a living in a strange country, so most of them were unable to build a special minister's home near the church and many young ministers had to reside patiently in a small part of the church building.

Just before WWII, we visited Rev. Sensho, who was living with his wife and five sons above the Sacramento Buddhist Church. Undoubtedly, it must have become increasingly difficult for them as the number of children increased!

My father highly respected Rev. Sensho for his intelligent approach to Buddhist propagation, so while he was discussing mutual ministerial problems with this gracious host, I would go into the kitchen to watch Mrs. Kinuko Sasaki's wonderful cooking. From her simple procedure of adding baking powder to the flour when preparing *tempura*, I learned for first time how to make a light coating for the fried shrimp! For some cooks, this would be a little thing, but, for this teenager, it was good advice that remained in my memory!

Since all the five boys' first names begin with "Sen," Mrs. Sasaki called each of Senyo's younger brothers by the latter part of their names: Ho! Ryu! Maro! And Rei! Surprisingly, they all snapped to attention when they heard their mother's vigorous but compassionate voice.

My sister, Julia, had the good fortune to stay a short period with the Sasaki family when she began her state work in Sacramento. Because of Mrs. Sasaki's genuine concern, Julia was treated like a real daughter in spite of her many shortcomings.

As the first son of this distinguished family, Senyo (LaVerne, later also Rev. Sasaki) never forgot his responsibility to the tradition of Buddhist priesthood that had been carried through 26 generations. Even in his youth, he led not only the assigned church groups, but also other communities, whether Buddhist or not, in remembering social concerns for all who needed care and attention.

Remembering My First BCA *Sensei*

This piece is based on a translation from a Japanese interview with the late Rev. Junjo Tsumura, former Buddhist Churches of America (BCA) minister of Sacramento, Watsonville, San Mateo, San Jose and Monterey as well as Hawaii Bishop.

Rev. Sensho Sasaki was my first *sensei* (teacher) during my first BCA church assignment to the Sacramento Buddhist Church (now Betsuin) in 1952. This is now more than half a century ago—unbelievable! During this period Rev. and Mrs. Sensho Sasaki introduced me to my future wife, Terry, and as a young bachelor minister from Japan, I was truly indebted. I still remember how well-liked and appreciated he was by the church members.

It was November 25, 1952, when I sailed from Japan to San Francisco aboard the ship *President Cleveland*. During the voyage, I reflected deeply on my new career as a young and inexperienced minister completely unaware of what was to come during the next 60 years. The anxiety of meeting my first BCA member was quickly erased when LaVerne Senyo, son of Rev. Sasaki, greeted me so cheerfully and warmly by saying: "Welcome to the United States!! It's great to have you come!" This friendly and informal welcome was so different from a formal and traditional Japanese way of greeting a new person. I was truly relieved and felt genuinely welcome in this new country of mine.

I am what I am now because of the kind and generous guidance of Sasaki-*sensei*, my BCA *sensei* during the first four years of my ministry. I learned so much from *Sensei*, who was so untraditionally informal and friendly compared to many formal and "straight" Japanese Buddhist priests. His compassion for life was not limited to human beings. His hobby of caring for *koi* (carp) in his fish tank exemplified his deep feelings for all living beings. He was truly a natural human person who loved foods, cooking, sports, movie-making (16 millimeter film) and even enjoying naps. He loved to cook soba noodles and the Chinese *hamuyu* (steamed pork). His 16 millimeter movies of church activities are archival materials for the BCA.

What stands out most for me, though, was his talent and ability to work with all people—not just church members, but everyone he met. He had the knack for making friends and making people feel at ease. I remember the times when he and I went to see professional wrestling in Sacramento's Civic Auditorium. We saw well-known wrestlers such as the famous Japanese wrestler Rikidozan, as well as Mike Sharpe and Ricky Torres. After the matches, we would meet Rikidozan at a local Japanese restaurant. I can still remember seeing this Japanese strongman gulp down more than 16 bottles of beer. He liked *Sensei* and me so much that he surprised us by showing up at a church service!

Mrs. Sasaki was also an amazing *okusan* (minister's wife). Not only was she totally dedicated to the church, she was like the "other minister" with her talent to remember and welcome anyone, church member or not. She was a "self-made professional counselor" who not only had the ability to listen to people's problems but to help them in a most friendly manner.

It was truly due to the kind guidance of Rev. and Mrs. Sensho Sasaki that I was able to complete my ministry of some 40 years here in BCA and Hawaii Hompa Hongwanji.

March Memorial Service: Reflecting on My Parents

For me, the March *Shotsuki Hoyo* (March memorial service) is a special time of personal reflection each year. Both of my parents passed away in the month of March (also my birthday month). Both died suddenly, my father from a stroke and my mother from a traffic accident.

My memories of their deaths are still vivid. I am grateful I was there when they passed away, and I hope that my presence gave them some comfort in their last moments.

On the day before my father's stroke, my father and I conducted the monthly Mountain View Buddhist Temple memorial service. Was his impending death portended when he mentioned how grateful he was to be living? He even wrote the Japanese word character for "stain" (*sen*) on the blackboard, telling us how our lives are stained by ignorance. I did not erase this word from the blackboard for a long while.

The karma of March 3, 1972, the day of my father's stoke, was strange and remarkable. It was the first Friday I had gone golfing with three minister/golfer friends; we usually golfed on Mondays, our day off. Also unusual was, after we all had bad tee off shots on the 10th fairway (the halfway point of the game), we quit playing and decided to have an early lunch. I returned home around 12:30 p.m., mentioning on the phone to my mother that I was back early. Half an hour later, my mother called me back and told me, "Papa *ga hen*" (something was odd about Dad), so I rushed to my parents' home. My mother told me Dad had been tired, so she let him sleep late while a church member visited. After the church member's visit, she went into Dad's bedroom and discovered him unconscious. If I had not returned home unusually early from golf, it would have been more difficult for my mother to cope with this unexpected turn of events. Dad was in a coma for four days before he died on

March 7 at the age of 68.

My father's death, while shocking, was in some ways not such a surprise. He had been slowing down noticeably. A few weeks earlier, Dad and I had gone to visit a church member at a senior home, and after the visit, since dad walked so slowly, I told him I'd meet him in the parking lot. As I stood by my parked car, I saw my Dad come out, soon followed by one of nurses, who had come running after him, thinking he was one of the nursing home residents. When I told Mom, she laughed, saying, "This is why you shouldn't drag your feet like a nursing home patient!" We laughed, not realizing we would later see a more serious side to the incident.

March 1, 1985, the day of my mother's death at age 74, is also a day I will never forget. It was around 9 a.m. when I was about to have breakfast at my parsonage home on the Mountain View Buddhist Temple grounds. Distracted by sounds coming from the busy street in front of the temple, I heard a few people say there had been an accident. I immediately went out to view the scene. I recognized my mother's shoes on the pavement, then I saw her lying on the ground unconscious. I shouted at her, but she did not respond. She had been struck by a pickup truck's side view mirror, which was found on the ground. The driver did stop and tried to assist. My mother had been walking to the beauty shop in the shopping center across the street. She crossed this street regularly, and we never worried because there was an island in the two-way street. This time, however, she probably tried to outrun the speeding truck to the island, but didn't make it. I accompanied her in the ambulance to the hospital. She died an hour or two after this terrible accident.

Mom was a main cog of the Buddhist Women's Association in Mountain View and Sacramento. After her sudden passing, many visitor/friends and ministers told me how important it is for a child to be present at the time of a parent's death. Friends told us that mother, although unconscious, was able to hear my voice before she died, which probably comforted her and let her die in peace. A minister friend told me that my mother's *arayashiki* (a term used in Buddhist philosophy referring to consciousness deeper than regular human consciousness and subconsciousness) witnessed me, even if her hearing may have been impaired. This Buddhist outlook truly comforted me.

My brothers and I were not able to fully express this love for our parents as many families do through the traditional Japanese expression of *oya ko-ko* (filial piety). I regret that they were never able to enjoy retirement from their lifetime dedication to the teaching and spread of our Buddhist religion. They did, however, show *kodomo ko-ko* (devotion to the children) to us, as we never had to look after them, help with problems or financial burdens or have to worry for long periods about them. I regret that I wasn't able to return all that they did for me. In contrast, my wife's Yokoi family was able to do a lot for her parents after they retired, good deeds that I witnessed with bittersweet feelings.

'Goodbye, Sasaki-*sensei*'

Sumi Uyeda delivered this message at a Sunday School Memorial Service for the late Rev. Sensho Sasaki on March 12, 1972.

Dear Sasaki-*sensei*,

As I look back to all the years I knew you, I see you as a man walking among crowds and crowds of people touching them with your goodness and imparting that goodness to the people so that goodness became part of their lives. I feel that we in this Sunday school are among those fortunate people.

Thank you for your compassion and understanding.
Thank you for your friendship.
Thank you for dedicating your whole life to spreading the words of the Buddha.

Your sermons always had a message for us. We listened and we understood. In your humorous sermons, in your serious sermons, in our sermons in which you performed magic tricks for us—the message of compassion, love, gratitude somehow reached us. For some of us, these words became part of living for us. Isn't this what Buddhism is all about? To live the teachings of the Buddha?

And this is what you did, *Sensei*. You lived Buddhism so your teachings of Buddhism reached us. You had respect for yourself. You had respect for people. You had a genuine feeling for people so you were able to communicate with us. We listened and we understood.

We owe you a debt of gratitude.
Thank you for touching our lives and making our lives brighter and more meaningful.

Goodbye, Sasaki-*sensei*. We shall miss you. But you will remain with us always in our hearts.

— *Namu Amida Butsu.*

A Personal Recollection of Mrs. Kinuko Sasaki
Rev. Richard T. Schellhase, a clergyman in the Evangelical and Reformed Church, and its successor, the United Church of Christ, and a supporter of Buddhism, shared these thoughts about my mother after her passing.

Quick and agile in movement, animated and passionate in conversation, Mrs. Sasaki was one of a kind. Faithful spouse of a priest, devoted mother and loyal friend, she occupies a special place in my memory as a superlative example of one who lived within the compassionate embrace of Amida.

I learned to know her well because she prepared noon meals for members of the Steering Committee of The Campaign for Buddhism in America, which met monthly at the Mountain View Temple and which I attended as director of the campaign.

For two years, and until her tragic and untimely death, we enjoyed hospitality in her home on more than 20 occasions. Each time we were filled not simply with excellent Japanese food, but we were also fed by her joy and exuberance, her zest for life, her direct and hearty laughter and her feisty spirit.

The night before her passing, she attended the kick-off event for the campaign in the Mountain View Temple and greeted everyone personally at the refreshment period following the meeting. Through word and deed, she made clear her personal commitment to the campaign and its vision for the future of the Dharma in this country.

To think of Mrs. Sasaki as silent and still is a contradiction; she was always so alive and vibrant. As a tribute to her life and memory, I have hoped to let her life so affect mine that I may live more gratefully, more joyously and more committed to the values and ideals she exemplified on such a grand scale. The void I have felt personally by her physical absence has been filled by the generosity and compassion her life epitomized for me in direct proportion to how I have let her spirit inspire mine.

For her life and for my memory of her I am immensely and eternally grateful.

2

BEGINNINGS:
STOCKTON, TACOMA, PENRYN,
SACRAMENTO, AND TULE LAKE, 1930–1945

Coming into the World

I was born in Stockton on March 5, 1930, while my father was serving the Stockton Buddhist Temple. Mrs. Haruyo Nishioka, a midwife, brought me, Helen (who later became my wife), and more than 2,000 other babies into this world. Midwife-supervised child birth was common then compared with today's practice of having babies in a hospital. Mrs. Nishioka's birth registry can be found at the Japanese American National Museum.

Our family left Stockton when I was three years old, moving to Tacoma in 1933, where my father served as resident minister for one year, from 1933 to 1934.

My primary Tacoma childhood memories are from the 16 millimeter films taken by my movie-camera-enthusiast father. These films are now in the archival history and shown daily at the Japanese American National Museum in Los Angeles, including footage of my late brother Conrad (known as "Senpo" when we were young) and me walking down a Tacoma sidewalk and talking with some Caucasian neighborhood girls.

While the family was in Tacoma, my father met pioneer Rev. Sunya Pratt, who was a Caucasian woman from England, and welcomed and accepted her into the ministry. At the time, an anti-Caucasian mentality existed in the Japanese community. My father helped Rev. Pratt receive ordination from

Bishop Masuyama in 1936. I remember visiting her and her husband after a Buddhist Churches of America national meeting and being amazed at hearing a Caucasian recite Nembutsu (recitation of gratitude to Amida Buddha) for the first time.

In and Out of Penryn Elementary School

Penryn, the small town just northeast of Sacramento where the old Placer Buddhist Church was located (now relocated to a newer facility near the I-80 Freeway), holds many fond and vivid childhood memories.

I remember playing Samurai warrior with bamboo sticks, acting out the Japanese movies we saw at the Buddhist Church. Our church neighbor Hiroko Kashiwabara was our "big sister" who took care of my brothers, Conrad and Lou, and me. I remember basketball star George Goto[19] (who went on to play basketball for Stanford) paying me two cents to clean each one-gallon *shoyu* (soy sauce) bottle with a water hose at the Goto Fish Market. One of the neighbor ladies, Mrs. Mikami, would sometimes chase us home, where Conrad and I would hide under the bed, while Mrs. Mikami complained to our parents about our childhood antics, such as stealing candy from her store.

Another time, my brother Conrad and I got into our Dad's church car, which was parked on the hilly church parking lot. We released the hand brake, and the car rolled into, as I recall, a water fountain.

Another recollection: walking all the way from Penryn to the Rocklin quarry to fish. One time we visited a church member's chicken farm, where I saw a chicken's head chopped off with an ax. The chicken ran around headless with blood spurting out—I was deeply touched and shocked. Another time, I shot a robin with BB gun—and I could never kill a bird again. We did go rabbit hunting with a friend, though, and brought home a cottontail rabbit; we ate it and it tasted good.

Another time, we got the mumps shortly after "swimming" in a mud pond during non-summer months. I also remember Dad waking me up during my sleep to go see a Placer High School football game, where one of the church members (Kay Kashiwabara) was the star player.

With my two brothers, Conrad and Lou, my mother clothed me in then-fashionable corduroy pants to go to school. She bought them long, and we'd roll the ends several times and suspenders held them up. After several

---

[19] As a living tribute to George Goto's many accomplishments in the community, the City of Roseville has a park named after him.

washings, the pants would shrink and fit my brother, Conrad. By then, the yellowish pants were white.

My elementary school teacher Miss McGuire, who was pretty and nice, would often call on me to draw Peter Rabbit. I was happy and proud to be called on to do this in front of the class. There were quite a few Japanese kids in class. In another class event, a Christmas school play, I was dressed as a Christmas gift with my head sticking out of the box. I was to repeat these words: "Do not open until Christmas…" and I would forget the words to follow. Miss McGuire would whisper the remaining words to me… "or sorry you'll be" from behind the stage curtain.

I have always wished that I could host all my school teachers to a weekend get-together to thank all of them. This will remain only a dream, though, as these teachers are probably all deceased or of a very advanced age.

To remember these events of some 80 years ago is an important way for me to know and understand myself as I am today because of the causes and conditions of life we call karma. The story of the long, long past is so much more important than the "present"; it is the history of the past that makes the present. What, then, is the future? It is the accumulation of the long past, together with the present. My late father constantly emphasized the importance of the past by using the example of a person jumping. He would point out that without bending your knees (knowing the past), you are not able to jump (progress ahead).

Church Kid

Looking back, I think I didn't have the same parental guidance as many of my peers. My parents were so devoted to church that they didn't have a lot of time for us kids.

Not only was my father, Sensho, mostly dedicated to church, there were high expectations for *bomori* (minister's wife whose duties are to look after the temple) and *okusan* (title of respect to minister's wife), as playing an important (unpaid) role behind the scenes. Mother Kinuko still took care of most *okusan* duties. Mom had the longest tenure as a minister's wife—from 1930 to 1985—55 years, close to 60 years as an active minister's wife role. Because I moved to Mountain View Buddhist Temple in 1972 and appreciated

---

[20] The new generation's expectations have changed drastically. Today, many ministers' wives have jobs outside the church and home.

her help, she stayed on in that role.[21]

I do still wonder how the ministers' kids were expected to be role models given that their parents spent most of their time at church.[21]

My father was also very active in Japanese language school as its principal, and my mother was one of the teachers. We went to Japanese school six days a week, Monday through Saturday. On Sunday we went to Sunday school.

While we sometimes missed our parents' attention, the members of my father's church clearly appreciated his service. They gave him a huge send-off when he moved from Penryn to Sacramento. There was such a warm feeling of appreciation/loyalty/devotion. The feelings of church members toward ministers are just not the same today.[22]

Pearl Harbor Day

In 1939, we settled into our lives in Sacramento, where we lived on top of the church,[23] a big *kaikan* (assembly hall) and Japanese school building.

There was no TV at the time, but we had some entertainment. My father was a popular ghost story teller during his sermons. He would scare kids from behind the pulpit and draw them back with tales "to be continued next Sunday."[24] Also on Sunday mornings, we would take advantage of a motion picture projector to watch cartoon movies, including Looney Tunes. The projector was also used to show popular Japanese movies.

On December 7, 1941—Pearl Harbor Day—I was watching a basketball game when I heard about Japanese airplanes attacking Hawaii. As an 11-year-old, I thought it was an exciting change of pace.

The Japanese invasion of the Philippines started the next day. This caused escalating tension between the Filipinos and Japanese in our neighbor-

---

[21] Conrad went to college, but was drafted to Korea and never finished. Maro, born in 1940, attended San Jose State. Rey, born in 1942, didn't finish college. Unfortunately, I lost close contact with my four brothers when I was in Japan for five years (when I was 23–28 years old). My father paid for my education. Back then, I got by with $40/month for rent (which paid for first-class living, including breakfast and dinner every day). With an exchange rate of 360 yen per dollar, haircuts with shampoo were 100 yen and public bathhouses were 10 yen.

[22] The reverence to authority at the time certainly contributed to these feelings. In Japan, when the Abbot took a bath in *ofuro* in temple, the locals would keep the water he bathed in. The expression *sensei* (teacher) is a common term of respect that is extended to ministers.

[23] They used to post donations in Japanese calligraphy with the donor's name and the amount of the donation while services were going on inside the *hondo* (main hall)! To me, it seemed like a distraction, as attendees would be watching the donations rather than listening to the service.

[24] There was also lots of candy given out at Sunday service to encourage kids' attendance.

hood. When we heard a report of shootings of Japanese individuals (such as hotel proprietors) by Filipinos, a gang of us took revenge by positioning ourselves on a rooftop and using slingshots to break windows in a Filipino-owned barbershop.

Our gang leader was tough and good in judo, so we were protected against some of the rough guys. I remember we were concerned a rival Japanese gang would invade our clubhouse. To defend our space, we dug holes around the house and put balloons with air and urine inside, so we could hear if someone was going to make a sneak attack.

We weren't always the most devoted gang members, though. My brother Conrad and I went to a movie instead of attending a gang meeting and then had to sit in a row with two x's on it—for "double-crossers"!

Tule Lake

I could feel the anti-Japanese feeling and discrimination at the time. When Executive Order 9066 was issued on February 19, 1942, the Japanese families started leaving, as required, to report for relocation.

In general, people accepted this unfortunate turn of fate. A few were angry, but most took an attitude of acceptance, as in the Japanese expression *shikataganai* (it can't be helped). The fact that most community leaders were *Issei* (first-generation Japanese) and less educated than the younger generation probably also contributed to this attitude.

We were the last family to leave town and I was the last Japanese American student to leave Lincoln Junior High School. My father had to check with the city regarding what was left behind and who would take care of the church, which became a military facility. We didn't know when we would be back.

Members of the Sacramento Japanese community were assigned to the Walerga Assembly Center (near Sacramento), then most went to Tule Lake, a relocation camp near the California–Oregon border. Many Buddhist Churches of America ministers were assigned to Tule Lake.

My brother, Rey, was born in June 9, 1942, while we were in Walerga Assembly Center.

Tule Lake, which eventually housed some 20,000 people, was organized into seven wards of nine blocks. Each block, which contained 12 to 14 barracks, had a toilet, shower and mess hall. Rooms were assigned based on the size of the family. As a family of seven, we had two rooms (half of a barrack building). The living room was converted to a small chapel, where my father would conduct family memorial services and weddings. On one occasion, my father conducted a huge outdoor funeral service of a Japanese person who had been shot by a century/tower guard.

As kids, though, we didn't have an antagonist relationship with the guards. We would wave to them, then squirm under the barbed wire surrounding the camp to play in the adjacent wild bird refuge, where there were geese and ducks in the thousands.

Tule Lake Camp Schooling

Several Caucasian teachers who had been interested in Japanese people taught in a public high school at Tule Lake, Aquila High School. Looking back, I realized it must have taken some courage and dedication to have chosen to work with us.

Since in those days it was common to have 5 to 10 kids, Sunday school attendance was also high. I started attending Sunday school, which met in the block barracks, as a seventh grader.

Another school at Tule Lake I attended for a short time was an ultra-conservative/patriotic/nationalistic (*Daitowa juku*) private Japanese language school. It was strict, and we had to salute Japan with a deep bow and conduct meditation for the emperor. But the people running the school said that if students went to the American public school, they couldn't attend this one, so we quit and attended a public Japanese language school, which allowed students to also attend the regular American school.

I did well at the public Japanese school. I remember one time I participated in an oratorical contest held in the mess hall on a hot summer day. I was so thirsty, but at the age of 14 or 15, I didn't have the nerve to drink water in front of microphone. (Older students were brave enough to drink water while talking, but you could definitely hear the gurgling.)

Toward the end of the war, I took part in another performance, this time at the American junior high school—a play called *Foreigners Settled America*. My family was scheduled to leave Tule Lake while the play was still on. Since I had a leading role, I stayed in the camp two weeks after my family left, living with another couple, so I could finish the performance.

Out of the Mud Grows the Wisteria

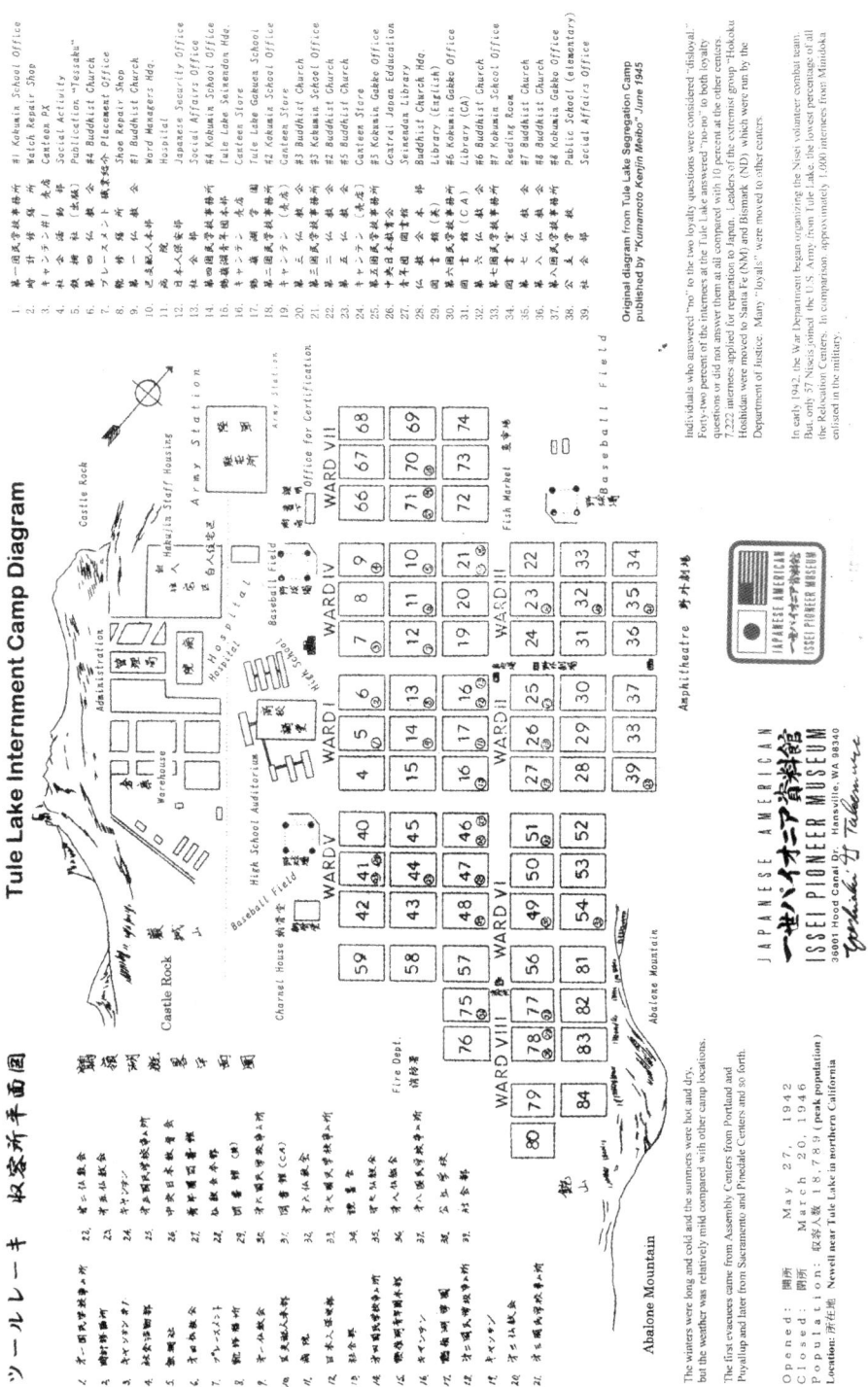

3

COMING OF AGE:
SACRAMENTO, 1945–1953

A YBA Kid

During my time in Sacramento, I had the opportunity to be Sacramento Young Buddhist Association (YBA) president and an athletic chairman for both the Northern California and Western Young Buddhist League. Those were the fun years, with wholesome activities such as hayrides and dance parties (where we would play records).

The Sacramento YBA had a lot of members, maybe 50. Sunday school was also big—families had lots of kids in those days. We also had semiformal dances, where girls wore gowns.

I once chose a girl for the last dance and found out, while walking her home (as was the custom for the girl chosen for the last dance), that she was going home to bake cookies for her kids!! I don't know why she was there. I also found out she was a Christian minister's wife!!! Funny? Not for me at the time! I also once double-dated two sisters with the comedian Pat Morita. I dated the older sister; Pat dated the younger sister. We were two couples in one car.

The statewide YBA conferences sometimes drew about 1,000 attendees. The popular, energetic and creative ones were the Berkeley YBA members, many of whom attended Cal and roomed at the Berkeley Buddhist Church dormitory supervised by Rev. and Mrs. (Jane) Kanmo Imamura, parents of Rev.

Ryo Imamura, a third-generation American Buddhist minister like me. (Other third-generation ministers are Revs. George Shibata of Reedley, Rev. Mark Unno, a University of Oregon professor, and the late Rev. Shousei Hanayama of Watsonville[25]).

It was during the year that I was the Sacramento YBA president that I, representing our YBA, gave a basketball uniform outfit with our team name, "8 Balls," to the visiting sport-minded then-Monshu (Abbot) Kosho Ohtani. It was also during one of those state YBA conferences that actor George Takei of Star Trek fame was one of the oratorical contest speakers.

Did YBA kids know much about Buddhism in those days? In general, since YBA members now are better educated, the interested ones now are more knowledgeable about Buddhism than at that time. But in those days, YBA members were closer to (and more respectful of) their parents and raised with a Buddhist background, with *obutsudan* (home Buddhist shrine). Now parents tend to be more interracial and interfaith and less connected to Buddhism. The difference shouldn't be underestimated.

I remember a time when a custodian at the Stockton church, Mr. Okubo, lived with a friend, a Caucasian person about the same age. People would ask the friend why he was living with Mr. Okubo. He would answer that he wanted to live with a Japanese person, to learn more about Japanese culture. Similarly, it is more important to live and practice in the religious environment than to merely acquire intellectual knowledge about the faith.

In a similar vein, a devout Christian Japanese lady, Mrs. Ishii, was one of the owners of the Eagle Drug Store close to the Buddhist church. I'm not sure how it got started, but she started sending the *Sacramento Bee* Sunday paper to me during my graduate study years in Japan. I looked forward to receiving it, especially the sports section. She would say, "If you're happy, *sensei* [even though I wasn't her teacher or reverend], I'm happy." Now I wish I'd thanked them better, taken them out to dinner. I have the utmost respect for that kind of person, whether he or she is Buddhist or Christian. It is not a matter of following a textbook or labeling oneself with one religion or another. The bottom line is not the religion per se, but the person one becomes from the religion.

---

[25] See Shousei Hanayama's Farewell Message, p. 161

Basketball: Team Players

Our Young Buddhist Association (YBA) basketball team had many exciting, memorable games with the Northern California teams from Florin, Placer, Stockton, Lodi, Walnut Grove, Marysville and others in the Single A League Conference. The games attracted not only parents and friends, like nowadays, but also had good general attendance, thanks to more limited mobility of the population and the fact that TV offered only three or four channels worth of black and white shows (usually with lines from bad reception, even with "rabbit ear" antennae).

The Sacramento church's girls' team, called "the Saints," was really good—good enough to go barnstorming to Seattle to play the teams there. My mother was the chaperone for the trip. Top players included the late Bubbles Keikoan, Lai Fong, Grace Shigaki (the late Grace Ito), Amy Kamikawa, etc. The boys' team was made up of players like my brother Conrad, Joey Ishihara, Fred Shirasago, Gary Muramoto, James Tanihana, etc.

Once, our team was involved in a terrible car accident after a game in Marysville. Our lead car crashed head-on when trying to pass another car. It was a rainy day, and the windshield wipers in those days stopped wiping when you stepped on the gas! I was in the second car, but James Tanihana was so seriously hurt we had to donate blood for his blood transfusion.

At one point we played a Chinese team, and it got really rough—almost to blows. Since we knew where the Chinese guy lived, later we tried to intimidate him by shouting and swinging nunchucks outside his house. I was called to the principal's office the next day. When Conrad jumped in to take revenge, he got into a fight on the floor and also had to report to the principal's office. Our parents were so busy with church work, they took it in stride and we weren't reprimanded.

In addition to playing for our YBA, my brother Conrad and I were water boys during our younger years for the older varsity "Wakaba" church team. They were a good team with stars like Blackie Rodney Imai and Yosh Matsubara; other big-name stars of Sacramento in that period were Hitoshi and Larry Ota, Kint Nishimura and Tosh Matsuura. It was popular then to have a little refreshment cart with sliced oranges and towels, and it was our job to roll it onto the court during time outs.

Learning on Summer and Part-Time Jobs

It was a common among us fellows to have summer and part-time jobs. Sacramento offered various kinds of farming and State of California office work. We chose the physical farm work over junior clerk office jobs, figuring farm work would make us physically stronger and healthier.

The Sacramento Buddhist Church was a place where job ads were common, especially with the many kinds of agricultural help needed by the numerous Japanese farmers in the Sacramento, Clarksburg, Placer and Marysville areas. Eighty cents an hour was the usual pay, working 8 to 10 hours a day. We picked various fruits and vegetables like plums, peaches, tomatoes, ball onions, etc. We also sometimes worked in the canneries in Sacramento, forking empty cans from a freight car into the cannery via a chute; that job is probably mechanized now. I even did housework on Saturdays, cleaning floors and mowing lawns.

I can still vividly remember working with the late Rev. Shig Terakawa—a friend since my teenage years[26] —moving water sprinklers on an onion field from 4 a.m. to 7 p.m. Wearing an old pair of shoes and swim pants, we advanced the sprinkler pipes in the muddy, wet field every hour and a half. While the sprinklers were watering the onion field, one of us kept an eye on the sprinkler pipes, which sometimes separated and flooded the field. It was not straight physical work, because one of us was able to cat nap under the truck. Another onion field-related job was different, but also challenging in its own way. The sacks of picked onions left on the field were being stolen at night, so the foreman asked me to stay up in a pickup truck with a kerosene lamp and act as a watchman. I was a little frightened to do this. What if these robbers really did show up? What was I to do? Fortunately, the onion robbers never showed up.

Another job was just a job, washing muddied celery on a conveyor belt during Thanksgiving vacation, but included a memorable experience for a young lad of 19 or 20 years of age. As we workers slept in an empty freight car, "night women" came in with flashlights to solicit business… Never having been confronted with such a situation, I just hid, burying myself under the blanket.

Yes, all of these summer and part-time jobs were valuable experiences. We learned the value of work, money and physical health, reached some

---

[26] Rev. Shig Terakawa, son of Rev. Chonen Terakawa. Shig passed away on the second day of his BCA Seattle Betsuin assignment.

understanding and appreciation of manual labor and even helped our parents financially. It was an experience I could only have had when I was young.

The Greatest Weightlifter Tommy Kono and *Karate Kid* Pat Morita

Among our teenage friends, two of them became especially famous—one as an athlete and the other as an actor. This was quite remarkable from a small group of Sacramento kids.

Tommy Kono's story as a weightlifter began at Tule Lake Relocation Center during World War II. We were in the same ward and block—Block 27 in Ward 2. The profits from a camp bazaar funded the purchase of a weightlifting set. A group of us 13- or 14-year-olds started practicing. Believe it or not, Tommy was not a healthy kid. He had asthma problems. But that did not stop him from joining us in "fooling around" with weightlifting. Later, in high school in Sacramento, we rode around in cars, while Tommy continued to work faithfully on the sport, carrying weights in a bag.

His dedication paid off when he advanced to three different Summer Olympics, competing in the lightweight (149 pounds) to middleweight (160 pounds) divisions, changing his weight according to the stronger Russian competition. Tommy won gold medals in both the 1952 (Helsinki, Finland) and 1956 (Melbourne, Australia) Olympic games and a silver medal in 1960 (Rome, Italy). Considered "pound for pound" the best weightlifter in weightlifting history, he was inducted into the International Weightlifting Federation Hall of Fame in 1993. As a dedicated body builder, he was named the International Weightlifting Federation's Mr. Universe in 1954, 1955, 1957 and 1961.

When I was a graduate student in Tokyo in 1953 or 1954 and Tommy was between gold medals, he called me to be his interpreter for an interview with a leading sports magazine in Tokyo. Since it was wintertime, we both wore overcoats. The Japanese spokesman thought I was Tommy, the Olympic champion!! That was an unforgettable moment. Tommy lived in Honolulu at the end of his life, and we had the chance to renew our friendship before he passed away. I conducted his funeral in Honolulu on May 23, 2016.

The second "one of us guys" from Sacramento who made it big was Pat Morita. Pat was a natural performer from the beginning. His father owned a small Japanese restaurant about a block away from the old Sacramento Buddhist Church on 418 O Street. Pat would be the jovial master of ceremonies and entertainer at parties in his father's restaurant.

Remarkably, Pat spent some nine years, from the age of two, hospitalized with spinal tuberculosis. He only started walking at age nine or ten. From his determination to excel, by the time he was in high school he even played basketball with our Sacramento Young Buddhist Association team, although he was just a bench warmer.

After high school, his talent and drive led him to the nightclubs in San Francisco, where he started his career as comedian/entertainer. He became very popular as Mr. Miyagi in the *Karate Kid* movie series and won the Oscar as best supporting actor in 1984.

Although Pat or Noriyuki (his Japanese name) did not come from a Buddhist home background, I was happy that he became Buddhist in his later years. Pat once called me to "bless" his small Buddhist home shrine, a gift from his wife, Evelyn, and I conducted a service for Pat and his family in his home in Las Vegas.

Pat passed away in November 2005. I was honored that Evelyn asked me to conduct his funeral service. As Pat was a celebrity, the funeral service was featured on the front page of a Las Vegas newspaper.

Sacramento Church Hosts Japanese Celebrities

During my father's ministry in Sacramento Buddhist Church (now Betsuin) in the late 1940s and 1950s, the church welcomed and hosted many celebrities from Japan. I think it was like a vacation to them, soon after the devastation of WWII. Their visits were made possible by communities like ours of Buddhist churches, which welcomed and hosted them in times when hate toward Japan still existed in some areas.

The Sacramento Church hosted celebrities from many fields, especially entertainment and sports. Visitors included the whole team of Tokyo Giants, popular Hall of Fame actors such as Kinuyo Tanaka, Fujiko Yamamoto (then Miss Nippon) and Sessue Hayakawa, as well as music greats such as Misora Hibari. I remember going back stage of the church *kaikan* (gymnasium/auditorium) to see this soon-to-be musical icon. She was then a young teenager and was startled to see this teenage Japanese American "stranger" greeting her.

I was also the interpreter for Miss Nippon (later a famous actress in Japanese Samurai films), Miss Osaka and Miss Hokkaido.[27]

---

[27] We visited California Governor Earl Warren in the Sacramento State Capital building. Governor Warren later became Chief Justice of the United States Supreme Court.

How times are now different… The cost of sponsoring these celebrities today would be astronomical, but then celebrities visited the United States (and our events) *pro bono*—no charge. It did not cost anything to the church then, except for sponsoring meals and banquets!

Transitions

After the war, the anti-Japanese sentiment lingered. There were several anti-Japanese-American killings. On my return to Sacramento from Tule Lake Relocation Center in the middle of the night, I was scared because I had to walk from 3rd and I Street to 4th and O Street—I stayed right in the middle of the street the whole way.

During this time, my father would answer the door in overalls. He was busy serving people who had lost their homes—several hundred stayed in the church hostel on cot beds. We helped many *Issei* (first-generation Japanese) bachelors, especially with translation and visits to doctors.

After high school, I attended a two-year program at the local community college, Sacramento City College, as a social science major, thinking possibly of going into medicine. At Sacramento City College, I was president of the Nisei Club for second-generation Japanese students. The club advisor was Albert Rodda, who later became a State senator. He was very good to Japanese American students. Mr. Rodda was probably one of the state senators to recommend Rev. Shoko Masunaga (then minister at the Sacramento Buddhist Temple) to become the first State of California Buddhist chaplain in 1975.

I was also president of the International Discussion Group at Sacramento State College. On one occasion, the club went to a mock United Nations assembly at the University of Southern California in Los Angeles. Our team represented Israel. When the anti-Israeli countries declared war against us, we didn't know how to respond.

After graduating from Sacramento State College in 1952, I worked in odd jobs for about half a year before leaving for Japan.[28]

Decisions

My decision to become a minister was a gradual one. At first, working in the church was mostly a matter of helping my father out. I felt sorry for him

---

[28] While other decisions were on hold, I did decide that my formal name would be "LaVerne Senyo Sasaki." A lawyer friend told me if I use the name officially from high school on, it becomes legal. So rather than filling out paperwork, I began to use that name on all formal or legal documents. As part of this process, I dropped the "W" from "Senyow" to prevent mispronunciation.

during Sunday services, when he struggled with the English language. The first talk I helped interpret (during my late high school years) was a sermon, "*Shi On*" (four gratitudes mentioned earlier: to parents, people, country/world, and the Buddha).

As I translated, I became interested in the Buddhist religion and ministry. I did not feel groomed to be a minister, but I was encouraged by my father and other reverends. Also, the tradition was for the eldest son to follow in the father's occupational footsteps.[29]

With others' encouragement, I decided I would continue my studies in Japan and was accepted to graduate school at Tokyo University. At that time, I was already leaning toward ministry-type interests, although I was also considering a social science major. Before I left for Japan, I did have a *tokudo* (ordination to enter the ministry) in San Francisco.[30]

At Tokyo University, I met many Buddhist teachers, colleagues and friends. This gave me the opportunity to see them as role models and to observe how contented/fulfilled their lives were. I was also in a Buddhist environment, where I could experience many aspects of ministry, including counseling sessions on marital and family issues. These interactions entered heavily into my decision to become a minister.

Of course, as I was growing up my parents also set an example of a life dedicated to the church. I saw many positive aspects of their lives, but some negatives, too. When visitors would come visit our home above the church, they would keep talking through dinnertime at 6 to 7 p.m. That left no food and five hungry boys. Mom would give us money for food and we would go out and buy hot tamales and party pack soda water (although I was happy when she did that). Other negative aspects of life as a minister's kid was the limited family time. Unlike today, family vacations and days off for the minister were not common. On the other hand, as a minister's kid I was also able to see and experience the importance of serving others to make for a better world.

---

[29] In America, most of the current generation of generational Buddhist priests have not continued in the ministry; my own father would have accepted it if I decided I didn't want to become a Buddhist priest. In contrast, in Japan there are many generational ministers. The oldest son assumes the temple, and later sons work for the regional or national office doing publicity work. In the Sasaki family, my father was supposed to be the priest in Japan, but he was in the United States and died here. There was a gap that had to be filled. In this kind of case, families adopt a person who will drop his family name and assume the family name of the temple. The current priest of Kozenji was selected by my father's cousin because there was no successor. In the 26 past generations of Sasaki ministers, I don't know if they're all blood related. The records are kept in the temple—one day I would like to see them.

[30] Later, in 1958, I received a full ordination (*kyoshi*) as a minister at our mother temple in Kyoto, Japan.

4

AN EDUCATION: TOKYO, 1953–1958

Bon Voyage

In February 1953, Bishop Shigefuji, my family and others came to the San Francisco dock to send me off to Japan on an American President Lines ship. We left to band music and tape throwing. The tape ripped and we said goodbye. Because we traveled from San Francisco to L.A. to Honolulu, we were sent off three times. In Honolulu, they threw money and coin divers went down to get it. It was very heartwarming. Now you don't even see the plane leaving. Leaving for another country was more personal and emotional then.

It took two weeks to get to Japan. During the trip, I helped out a *Nisei* purser (the person on a ship responsible for the passengers), who had been a basketball star from the San Francisco team. We became friends. I became active on American President Lines as a volunteer officiant of a Sunday Buddhist service, chairman of deck sports tournaments and coordinator of a talent show dance for passengers. I also helped Japanese-speaking *Issei* fill out forms.

When I arrived in Japan, many relatives came to pick me up, but I did not recognize or know them.

Settling In

I lived with Uncle Terashi Hokyo (my mother's older brother) in central Tokyo (near Shimbashi Station) for a year and a half.

Uncle Terashi had good connections. He was a prominent businessman, who also became Japan's judo federation advisor of Kodokan Institute (headquarters of the worldwide judo community). Uncle Terashi also ran as an unsuccessful candidate for the Japanese Government House of Representatives (for Fukui Prefecture). One of his campaign managers was Kyuzo Mifune, regarded as "Mr. Judo of Japan." I remember seeing Uncle Terashi invest all his money in the campaign and being left with nothing after losing the election.

I was spoiled with Uncle Terashi, so I moved because I wanted to live with the everyday Japanese—*tannin no meshi o taberu*, literally to eat what everyday people eat—and be exposed to Japanese people I didn't know.

I moved into a family-style boarding house, where I had my own room and shared the house with three other students. The house was run by a devout Nembutsu (Pure Land Buddhism) woman. We talked religion a lot. We had a maid who would cook breakfast and dinner; she had to take a bath last, after we had washed.

At home in the United States I was known for my voracious appetite—my mother would make a sandwich for me with six slices of bread (the equivalent of three sandwiches), but it wasn't enough, so I would then go out and buy a hot plate for a dollar. At the Japanese boarding house, I once kept asking for more *gohan* (rice). Even though I was on my third serving, the house lady said there was plenty. I ate more, then looked over and felt bad, because I realized I had eaten her share.

That was part of Japanese culture. The Japanese forget themselves. They forget the "I"—literally they often leave that pronoun out of a sentence. I would wonder "who?" and then realize they meant themselves. That impressed me.

Tokyo University Students

Early on, in 1953 or 1954, foreign students from the United States were required to attend a physical exam on the campus. We stripped from the waist up. I was skinny, but I looked like Mr. Universe compared to the Japanese students, who still showed the effects of the difficult war years. The

Japanese students resembled TB patients; the Americans were so well fed in comparison.

I would regularly eat out at restaurants in front of the university. In general, things were very inexpensive then for Americans, as the exchange rate was 360 yen to a dollar. I would go to a restaurant and order curry rice for 150 yen (40 cents), a bowl of udon (noodles) for 35 yen (10 cents), a piece of tofu for 6 yen (2 cents) or *korokke* (a deep-fried dish originally related to the French croquette) for 15 to 50 yen (4 to 14 cents). I was spending less on food than in Sacramento, where I used to spend one dollar for a hot dish (together with sandwiches from home), so I thought I was saving money.

I did not see any college students eating at these restaurants—only older adults and people who looked like professors. So at one point I decided to visit the Tokyo University cafeteria... The price of food there was shockingly inexpensive: miso soup for seven yen; rice for five yen; entrees for 15 or 20 yen. And I was spending something like 150 yen for lunch at the restaurants. I felt terribly arrogant and wasteful when I realized fellow human beings were spending such meager amounts for their meals.

Of course, many of the students could not afford to even go to the college cafeteria and ate only a small bento box container with rice, a small fish and pickled *tsukemono* vegetables. My good friend and classmate Shoyu Hanayama boasted he could finish eating his bento meal in something like 20 seconds!! It was no wonder he was skinny and frail.

Back then, some Japanese graduate students would occasionally even sell blood to buy books, which could cost 3,000 yen per month (less than $10).

Even for a well-fed American, the department's lecture rooms felt very cold in the wintertime because many of the steam radiators did not work. We often listened to the lectures in our overcoats, scarves and gloves. In order to be able to turn the pages in their books, my fellow students would cut the fingertips off their gloves. The American students were warned not to use Japanese *hibachi* (charcoal brazier) because the smoke and fumes were unhealthy, so I purchased an electric foot warmer with my study desk to keep warm. I was kindly scolded by my family dormitory lady, who said I would have to pay extra for the electric bill.

One time a classmate in my house was talking to a housemate who was an instructor at the Japanese medical college and mentioned he had never seen a cadaver. "How about arranging it?" he asked. We went to the anatomy room together, along with my classmates Bando and Hanayama.

It was truly a Buddhist experience to witness 30 to 40 bodies so carved up that they looked like leftover Thanksgiving turkey. We couldn't even tell if the bodies were male or female. The experience gave me a better understanding of life in seeing what our bodies will eventually become. It was a lesson on impermanence, dramatically different from a mere classroom explanation.

My Visit to Japan Medical College

I subsequently gave this mini-sermon inspired by the experience of seeing the cadavers at the medical college.

Fellow Buddhists and Friends,

Like any of you, if I reflect on my life, I recall a variety of experiences and many emotional or psychological reactions. For instance, when things or events pleased my desires, I was happy. When they were contrary to my liking, I was displeased. When harm or obstruction came my way, I was angry. When those other than myself were bestowed with better things and privileges, I was jealous. And when some disaster or sorrow struck those I did not know, I was indifferent. Among these reactions, it is interesting to elaborate on indifference.

It was only last Tuesday when, through my acquaintance with a medical doctor, I was able to truly experience a new chapter in my life. For some of you present this morning, the experience may not be a rarity, but for me it was certainly new. Together with a friend of mine, we visited the *Nihon Ikadaigaku* or Japan Medical College in Hongo, where my medical doctor friend happened to be an assistant in the Department of *Kaibogaku* or Anatomy. Rather than a mere visit to the department, we took a first-hand look at the section where medical students were training to conduct post-mortem examinations with real human corpses.

To be frank, my only emotional reaction to first seeing approximately 30 to 40 corpses lined up in the room was a simple blank. I merely stood and had no words to express my speechless awe. I have seen dead people in coffins and had come across many who had just passed away before me, but seeing these canvas-covered corpses neatly lined up elicited a strange, new feeling. Snapping me out of my almost hypnotic trance, the assistant guided us through the rows of dead bodies and permitted us to examine these objects of medical research.

The wrinkled skins of these bodies were removed and reattached with a string. With a closer look, I could see the exposed internal organs—the muscles, veins, arteries, etc.—which were partly dissected. The room's unpleasant odor did not brighten the entire gloomy atmosphere. In fact, the nauseating smell of the special chemical that had preserved the bodies for several months was an ordeal for a layman such as I.

As I stood watching the medical students, some of them coeds, dissecting the bodies with their scalpels, many questions naturally followed. I wondered to myself: "Whose bodies do they belong to? What are these medical students thinking when dissecting these corpses?" I answered one of these questions by thinking that these bodies are probably there for only one reason—to be studied. However, as I thought about whose bodies they were, I came to realize the question was meant only in the third person and not in the first person.

Then I asked myself: "Could this really happen to me—my warm body turning cold, my skin becoming wrinkled and turning pale yellow, my conscious being no more..." When my parents, friends and priests speak of death, I had usually heard it as if they were referring only to those advanced in years or in poor health. I would hardly associate death with myself—a young, healthy lad of vitality and energy. But in personal retrospection, death cannot help but become a penetrating personal problem of painful reality.

The unbiased picture of our lives, as painted from the eyes of the Enlightened Buddha, is only birth, old age, sickness and death, which the Buddha knows as the leading forms of sorrow and suffering of earthly existence. Among the three, death is undoubtedly the hardest to face by humankind. As for birth, we tend to think in terms opposite from the Buddha and regard birth not as sorrow, but, to the contrary, a felicitous event. When a baby is born, we think not impermanence and suffering, but of continuity with a hopeful future. The Buddha constantly refers to this kind of clinging to life as the ignorance of humankind. However, the Buddha does not mean that we must therefore commit mass suicide or practice birth control, but rather that we truly see, to use the popular expression, "the chips on the table." This clear perception of truth is called "*kanbo*" in Japanese technical Buddhist terms.

Actually, according to Buddhist interpretation, seeing the truth is necessary before one can truly feel and appreciate the workings of the wisdom and compassion of the Buddha. The basic Buddhist theme of suffering can be seen historically, beginning from the first Noble Truth—that life is suffering—in early Buddhism, to the Jodo or Pure Land Buddhism advocation of "despising and leaving this impure world" (*enriedo* in Japanese). Many have misinterpreted this heart of Buddhism as mere pessimism. While Buddhist truth appears pessimistic, in truth it is rather a painful reality for many of us who remain in the bed of dreamy fancy.

Then, the inevitable questions: Is there no deliverance for us? Is there an absolute world? Is there an absolute birth of no birth and death? For answers to these questions, let me conclude by reading the *Scripture on the White Ashes* by Rennyo Shonin, eighth abbot of Shinshu Buddhism and highly revered as the venerable who revived and popularized the teachings of Shinran Shonin:

> *"As we deeply observe the transient form of man's life, we realize that in this world from the beginning to end, what is momentary and passing is the illusory course of human life.*
>
> *Thus, we have not heard of anyone, receiving human form that lasts for 10,000 years. The course of life ebbs very rapidly. Can a person preserve his body for 100 years at the present time? Not knowing whether it will come today or tomorrow, those who depart before us are as countless as the drops of dew.*
>
> *Therefore, in the morning we may have radiant health; in the evening, we may be white ashes. When the winds of uncertainty strike, our eyes are closed forever; when the last breath leaves our body, the healthy color of the face is transformed, and we lose the appearance of radiant life; our loved ones may gather around and lament, but to no avail. When such an event occurs, the body is sent into an open field and cremated, leaving only the white ashes. What a sad plight!*
>
> *Thus, we see that what man cannot control is the passing away of the young or old alike. Therefore, we should all look to our future life and with faith in Amida Buddha, repeat his sacred name."*

A Different Kind of New Year's Eve

As a young ministerial student of Buddhism from Sacramento, my first New Year's Eve in Japan in 1953 was strikingly different than I was used to.

When we were young kids in Sacramento, I remember going to Sacramento's famous downtown K Street to celebrate our New Year's Eves. They were noisy evenings of celebrating the New Year by drinking, shouting and hugging each other, whether the person was friend or stranger.

On my first December 31 in Japan, I started that evening by leaving my uncle's home near Shinbashi and going to the not-distant Tsukiji Honganji Temple, the largest Nishi Honganji Buddhist Temple in Tokyo, for a New Year's Eve *"Joya-e"* service sponsored by our International Buddhist Association (see photo in this book). It was a quiet Buddhist service with my *Nisei* and Tokyo Buddhist friends with the ringing of the temple bell at the end of the service.

Following the service, I walked over to the nearby famous Ginza area to find out how the Japanese people were about to celebrate the coming of the New Year. To my surprise, not a soul was there. Stores were closed, and it was as quiet as a ghost town. I could not believe this scene! The Japanese were spending a quiet time at home with their families to listen to the "Joya bell ringing" of some nearby Buddhist temple or, as is now popular, viewing a TV broadcast of the bell-ringing ceremony of a famous Buddhist temple in Japan.

Even to this day, the Japanese stay home on New Year's Eve, listening to the bell and eating *toshi koshi soba*—connecting from old to the new like a strand of noodle.

While this quiet custom of reflection rather than celebration is not commonly known outside Japan, it is certainly something to think about. In the Buddhist view, the coming of a new year is like another ordinary day, as in a popular Buddhist saying, "Every day is a new year; each moment, a new day."

Life is changing all the time. Every moment is new. Every day is another challenge or experience awaiting us. We could wish each other Happy New Year every day!

Japanese Expressions Are So Interesting and Funny

Many English words have become part of the Japanese language—so much so that I doubt my late *obasans* and *ojisans* (aunts and uncles) would ever comprehend a contemporary Japanese news broadcast.

When I first heard the expression "Obon U-Turn" from a Japanese newscaster, I did not know what it meant. It turns out this newscaster was describing the traffic congestion caused by the thousands of Japanese road travelers returning home after visiting their family cemeteries during the Obon season. Obon is the tradition where the Japanese go back to their home towns to pay respect to their ancestors. "Obon U-Turn" was describing all the cars coming back into a city such as Tokyo after Obon cemetery visitation!

As another example, a popular term for residences in Japan is "mansion"—although they are mere condominiums and apartments!

I still remember ordering *gohan* (cooked rice) at a Tokyo restaurant and the waitress asking me, "Do you want 'rice'?"

The Japanese are Westernizing their language in a crazy way. They want to sound contemporary by using English instead of old-fashioned words, but it comes out mumbo jumbo—clever, erratic and crazy all at the same time.

The Hanayama Family

My Tokyo University classmate Shoyu Hanayama and I became very good friends. Every week after Friday class sessions were over, we rode the train for an hour to his family's residence on the outskirts of the city for dinner, study and an overnight stay. The Hanayama family became one of my primary Buddhist influences, providing me with Buddhist teachings, role models and close friends until the present day. It was my "family" for more than five years (1953–1958).

Of all the people in this family, Dr. Shinsho Hanayama, Shoyu's father and my Buddhist teacher/professor/former Buddhist Churches of America bishop, probably had the most influence on me. Dr. Hanayama was a former Tokyo University professor who became famous in postwar Japan as the Buddhist chaplain at Sugamo Prison in Tokyo, which was the prison/execution site for the leading Japanese World War II "criminals," including the top Japanese military leader Hideki Tojo. Dr. Hanayama's book on this experience became a bestseller entitled *Heiwa no Hakken,* translated into English as *The Way of Deliverance: Three Years with the Condemned Japanese War Criminals.* Dr. Hanayama is also considered the leading scholar on Prince Regent Shotoku Taishi, a sixth-century figure regarded as the father of Japanese Buddhism and culture whose commentaries on three Mahayana Buddhist sutras set the doctrinal direction of Japanese Buddhism (emphasizing the equal importance of laity as compared to the priesthood, the equality of women and men for attaining enlightenment, and the one vehicle from the three vehicles to enlightenment).[31]

When I returned to the USA after my studies, Dr. Hanayama gave me a huge personally calligraphed scroll with the famous words of Shotoku Taishi, *Wa o motte to-toshi to nasu* (Sacred treasure the true peace through Buddha's teaching).[32] Later, when Dr. Hanayama was elected as a Buddhist Churches of America bishop, I called him long-distance and asked him not to accept the office because I did not want him to suffer and get frustrated in a foreign organization with which he had no experience—he was a dedicated Buddhist scholar/teacher and not an administrator/politician/troubleshooter. He accepted anyway.

I have many warm memories of the rest of the Hanayama family, too, which included four sons. Mrs. Hanayama was like a second mother, calling me "*raban-san*" and sharing her calligraphy, motherly advice and weekly dinner. Once, one of the girls I dated, a former *odori* dancer and airline stewardess, came all the way to rural Tokyo by herself and looked me up at the Hanayama home. Dr. Hanayama was so impressed with her beauty, grace and bilingual ability that only a few minutes after her arrival he rushed to his library to get her his best-selling book, signed it and gave it to her; Mrs. Hanayama always laughingly talked about that evening, saying, "Never has my husband acted like that."

I became best friends with Katsutomo (known formally as Shoyu). We reviewed Buddhist lecture notes, and I would give him English conversation lessons. We studied from midnight to 3 a.m., even though his father would wake us up early for Buddhist service.

Katsuoto, another brother (the third son), wanted to be either a Zen priest or to go into the self-defense forces to teach about Buddhism and infuse spiritual content into military leadership. He was very different from Shodo, Katsunori and Katsutomo. Many years later, when I was in Kyoto, I called Katsuoto and a military chauffeur picked me up and brought me to see him.

My classmate Katsutomo Hanayama and I stayed friends over many years. I visited him many times in Japan, and he became a prolific author of popular books on Jodo Shinshu and Buddhism. His community outreach ex-

---

[31] Shotoku Taishi accepted Buddhism from Korea and some scholars even think he was Korean, not Japanese. I find it strange that some modern Japanese discriminate against Koreans due to recent politics when Japan is highly indebted to Korea for the introduction of Buddhism and Buddhist cultural influences in the arts, architecture, etc. Shotoku wrote the first Japanese constitution, called the "17 article constitution"; one of the main articles states the importance of "true peace" (*wa*) via Buddhism for Japan. He was also an early veterinary pioneer and started a veterinary hospital for animals, since in Buddhist thought even animals could become the Buddha.

[32] See photo of calligraphy included in this book.

tended to conducting "spiritual conversation sessions" at popular coffee shops. Together with Shojun Bando, we co-authored a book in Japanese entitled *Indo Busseki Junpai Kiko-ki*[33] (pilgrimage of Buddhist sites in India). Shoyu later came to the US to become a minister at Seabrook and taught at Seton Hall University and University of Wisconsin.

Shoyu passed away in 1995, and his son, Shousei Hanayama, who became a minister in Watsonville, passed away in 2016 (as discussed in the "White Bones... So REAL" chapter of this book).

Reflections
By Mrs. Takaye Hanayama, wife of the late Dr. Shoyu (Katsutomo) Hanayama

It was August 28, 1951, when the late Dr. Shinsho Hanayama, a Tokyo University professor/scholar and well-known Buddhist chaplain for top World War II military and political leaders such as Premier Hideki Tojo, came to lecture at my home temple Hoonji in Yamaguchi Prefecture.

We were happy to have such a distinguished speaker, but I was more impressed with his lively, straight-forward and sincere son wearing a Tokyo University cap.

It was on this visit that the son, Katsutomo (later called Shoyu when he became an ordained priest), proposed marriage to me. I was totally stunned but with real personal joy! Nervously and awkwardly, I served tea to our special guests. During our conversation, Katsutomo's father invited me to come and visit the Hanayama family in Tokyo after my graduation. I joyously accepted the invitation, but told them it would be after my study and training to become a wife as was the traditional Japanese custom. They agreed and noted that Tokyo was not far from Kyoto where I was studying so I should come as often as possible. I did take advantage of this kind invitation and visited the Hanayama family often and became acquainted with my future husband.

After my graduation, the Hanayama parents taught me many important subjects, including calligraphy, tea ceremony traditions, cooking and music. Therefore, I came to know the family well. I also met many scholars, teachers and priests while living with the Hanayama family. It was during this

---

[33] The topic was our participation at the Third World Buddhist Conference in Rangoon, Burma, and following pilgrimage to India, Nepal and Ceylon (now called Sri Lanka).

period I was introduced to LaVerne Sasaki from California. He enrolled at Tokyo University graduate school majoring in Japanese Buddhism under Dr. Hanayama and became a classmate of Katsutomo. They became such good friends that he was invited to come to our home every Friday night for some five years. LaVerne—called *"Raban-san"* (as it was difficult to pronounce LaVerne)—came to the house so often he became a part of the family. He studied with Katsutomo—whom he nicknamed "Kats"—and stayed overnight with him in the same study house.

As he was from affluent America, we were concerned about whether he had enough to eat to his satisfaction. We were not sure whether he would be satisfied with common Japanese meals, such as curry rice, udon noodles and other common Japanese food.

It was during these years that *"Raban-san"* would take us out to restaurants; at that time in post-war Japan, eating out was not common as the country was still recovering from the devastating war. It was also during this time in 1954 that LaVerne suggested attending the World Buddhist Conference in Burma. With LaVerne's plan and help (financially, also from his parents), they (with another classmate Shojun Bando) were able to make this wonderful and fortunate decision. Foreign travel during this period was unheard of, especially for young college students.

Together with father Hanayama, Shojun's mother and Katsutomo's oldest brother, Shodo, and his wife, we went to see them off from Kobe port. We did not know they had negotiated the cheapest fare to go to Burma with a British shipping company. As they were dressed in suits and ties, they were first directed to go up to the first-class section of the ship… but such was not the case. They booked the sea trip as "fourth-class passengers." We were shocked they were led to the bottom of the ship. Under such conditions and visiting unknown foreign countries, we were very concerned about their general health and safety.

However, they came back safely from a three-month-plus trip to Burma, India, Nepal and Ceylon (now called Sri Lanka). I was so relieved to see them back. From the film and slides, I saw what a great trip it had been. They also had port stops in Vietnam, the Philippines and Malaysia. Katsutomo, however, was ill for a while but not so for *Raban-san* and Shojun. Both Katsutomo and Shojun were most appreciative to LaVerne for his planning of this great experience.

After some four years and seven months living with the Hanayama family, the Hanayama parents suggested that Katsutomo and I get married. With Dr. Hajime Nakamura of Tokyo University as our marital honorary advisor, we were formally married in the Tsukiji Hongwanji Temple in downtown Tokyo on March 29, 1955. The wedding reception was different from a traditional formal wedding reception. It was informal, but more socially enjoyable. The special Ceylonese tea brought back from Katsutomo and LaVerne's trip to South East Asia was different and enjoyed as a special treat.

Following my marriage, I continued to dedicate myself to being economical, respectable and helpful to my husband in becoming a true, respectable scholar.

As for becoming a mother, I was concerned because I was not physically strong. My husband, however, was understanding and supportive of my physical health. His loving assurance was most encouraging. On January 2, 1956, I gave birth to our first child, a daughter named Uiko. Katsutomo was a very loving father. LaVerne became very fond of her, so much so that he was called "*Raban Oji-chan*" (Uncle LaVerne) by Uiko.

It was November 11, 1957, when our second child, a daughter Fujiko, was born. Katsutomo now became a loving father of two daughters. LaVerne also enjoyed them both while continuing studies together with Katsutomo. They not only studied but also had fun together, even going to see the Tokyo Giants play baseball.

Katsutomo continued his studies and qualified to enter the doctoral program at Tokyo University.

The sad day of bidding farewell to our beloved LaVerne came in June 1958. Katsutomo's mood changed when he realized he must separate from his best friend and classmate. Together with our family, including young Uiko and Fujiko, we went to Yokohama to see LaVerne return home after five years. Katsutomo shouted, "Bye, *Raban*! Bye, *Raban*!" and LaVerne threw the tape from ship and shouted, "Bye, Kats! Bye, Kats!"

This lasting friendship between Katsutomo and LaVerne is unforgettable.

After LaVerne's departure, Katsutomo was listless and down-hearted for a long time.

In time, Katsutomo became himself again and fully understood that life is one of constant change and separation. He truly understood that all of us

Vancouver Buddhist Temple with Rev. Senju Sasaki, son Sensho identified with arrow, ca. 1905

Dad (Sensho Sasaki) with his mother Tomie and sisters Chiyoko and Masako, 1924

Grandfather Rev. Senju Sasaki at Kozenji Temple, Fukui, 1927

Senju Sasaki with Lady Takeko Kujo (six months before her passing) in Hokkaido, Aug 21, 1927

Mother, Kinuko Hokyo, Ajimi, Fukui, ca. 1928

Parents Sensho Sasaki and Kinuko Hokyo marriage ceremony. All five Sasaki family couples at Kozenji, May 20, 1929

Grandfather Senju Sasaki, Principal at Nishi Hongwanji Futaba Women's College, August 31, 1932, Otaru, Hokkaido

Senju Sasaki visiting Shiraoi Ainu Tribe (Hokkaido, Japan) with Futaba High School teachers from Otaru, Hokkaido, June 14, 1931

Stockton Buddhist Church, 1933

Cowboy Senyo (me), 1933

Tacoma Buddhist Church with BCA Bishop Masuyama, Rev. Sunya Pratt, and Rev. Robert Clifton, 1934

Living room of Kozenji Temple, Fukui, Rev. Senju Sasaki third in back, 1935

Penryn Elementary School (Miss McGuire), Senyo second row, third from left, 1935

Senyo (me) and Senpo (Conrad) with Parents, 1932

Dad (Sensho) as college student, ca. 1923

Penryn (Placer) Buddhist Church, Japanese Language School Graduation, June 5, 1937

Penryn School, Miss Williams, 3rd-4th grade class,
Senpo (middle row, second from left) and Senyo (sixth from left), 1939

Sasaki Family, ca. 1938 with Senyo, Senryu (Louis), Senpo

Helen (middle) with sisters Florence and Margaret Yokoi at Rohwer incarceration camp, ca. 1943

Tule Lake Nippon Baseball Team, ca. 1943
Front: Mits Domen, Keizo Komura, Senpo Sasaki, Ricky Yamashita, Hideo Takemoto, Yosh Negi.

BCA Ministers at Tule Lake Relocation Center, CA, Sept 18, 1945

Tule Lake internment camp, ward 2, Sunday School. Front row: seventh, Rev. Onoyama, eighth, Rev. Sensho Sasaki, ninth (child), Senrey, tenth (child), Senmaro. Back row: first, Senpo, third, me

Mom and Dad with Louis, Conrad, Senrey, Senmaro, and me, ca. 1947

With Abbot Kosho Ohtani, Sacramento, 1950

Uncle Mitsuru Hokyo (seated far right), wife Aunt Kayoko (standing third from right) and her Nakasu family, Tokyo, 1950

Sacramento Buddhist Church Obon, ca. 1950

BCA Leadership Training Class with Dr. D.T. Suzuki, San Francisco, 1950

With Miss Nippon Fujiko Yamamoto, mother Kinuko, Amy Kamikawa (Wong), Bill Matsumoto, old Sacramento Buddhist Church, ca. 1950

Abbot and Lady Kosho Ohtani, Sacramento Mayor Bert Geisreiter, 1950

Old Sacramento Buddhist Church (Betsuin) welcome Abbot Kosho and Lady Ohtani, with BCA Bishop E. Shigefuji, Rev. K. Kumata, 1950

Sasaki Family Portrait, with Senrey, Louis, LaVerne, Conrad, Senmaro. Sacramento, 1950

Father Sensho with Japanese actor Sesshu Hayakawa

1950-51 season: Joey Ishihara, LaVerne, Toko Fujii coach, Harry Keikoan, Joe Ikami, Gilbert Matsumoto, Aki Honda, Conrad, James Tanihana

Bodhi Leaf, Buddhagaya India, 1953

LaVerne at Mother's former home, with Grandmother Hokyo and Uncle Hachireimon Hokyo, ca. 1953

Kozenji Temple with Uncle Rev. Raion Sasaki

"Hip LaVerne" on *SS President Cleveland*, Feb. 1953

My first Tokyo family: Uncle Terashi, Aunt Hisako, Tsugio, Hiroko

On way to India, 1954

With Shoyu Hanayama and Shojun Bando, World Buddhist Conference, Rangoon, Burma, Dec. 1954.
Back row includes Ven. Amitananda and Richard Gard.

Helping with Interview of Weightlifter Tommy Kono in Tokyo, ca. 1954

World Buddhist Conference in Rangoon, Burma, LaVerne in 4th row middle behind BCA ministers Revs. Kumata, Hojo, and Terakawa, Dec 1954

Tokyo University Professors and students, ca. 1955

Tokyo University social event, with Prof. Jack Brinkley, ca. 1955

Mother Kinuko Hokyo's siblings, ca 1955.
Front: Misao Senshu, Susumu, Shoten, Mitsuru, Kosho.
Back: Hachireimon, Yachiyo Mayekawa, Terashi

With Rev. Gyodo Haguri, Kyoto, ca. 1955

Higashi Hongwanji Abbot and Lady Ohtani at Sacramento Church with Rev. Tsumura, Rev. Odate (Berkeley Otani), ca. 1955

With Hanayama family, ca. 1955

With Aunt Chiyoko (dad's sister and Kozenji's last Sasaki priest) and Yoko Sakow Kozenji Temple, Fukui, ca. 1955

must pursue our individual paths of life.

Life's karma finally changed for the better for us. As my father-in-law was elected to become a bishop for the Buddhist Churches of America, Katsutomo was able to rejoin LaVerne as a fellow minister in America.

LaVerne always told us that he would get married and have many children. He certainly did accomplish his goal by marrying Helen. They are now blessed with five wonderful children and many grandchildren. Whenever I receive their family photos, I am so, so happy and envious of their good fortune. If only Katsutomo were living, he would feel the same way and continue their great friendship.

Writing in behalf of my late husband, I am happy and honored to remember our long friendship with LaVerne and [grateful] to Helen, whom I believe is most responsible for their good happy family. To me, they are the happiest family in the world.

Many Excellent Teachers

My years as a graduate student provided the opportunity for me to meet many excellent academic Buddhist teachers, whose influence on my life cannot be understated.[34]

As a result of the excellent education in the program at Tokyo University, many of my then-classmates are now top Buddhist scholars. One of my five *Nisei* (second-generation Japanese American) classmates was Dr. Kenneth Inada* of Hawaii, who became the first *Nisei* to get a PhD in Buddhist studies and went on to be a professor at the State University of New York, Buffalo.[35]

One of my teachers was Professor Reimon Yuki, who was the leading scholar in the "mind only" philosophy, which posits that what we perceive as truth is only a creation of the mind.

---

[34] Buddhist studies fell under the "Indian Philosophy" department, whereas Christian studies were under the "Department of Religion." We would see the emperor's brother (prince) occasionally—he was studying Christianity. Also lecturing at the university once was world-famous historian Arnold Toynbee. While I don't remember the lecture, Toynbee is significant to me; I believe he prophesized a future conflict between Christianity and Mahayana Buddhism and believed in the historical impact of Buddhism entering the West as the greatest achievement of the 20th century.

* Note "In Memoriam" page 149

[35] My other *Nisei* classmates were the late Rev. Taitetsu Unno, PhD (a popular BCA lecturer/author), Minoru Kiyota (who went on to be a professor in Buddhist studies at University of Wisconsin); Shojo Oi (who became a Seattle Betsuin Rinban and Buddhist Church of San Francisco minister); and Akira Hata (who became a BCA minister at the Fresno and Placer Buddhist temples).

In addition to Dr. Shinsho Hanayama, Professor Rev. Gido Undo,[36] a good friend of my Uncle Terashi's and later a private tutor of Abbot Kosho Ohtani was my private tutor. I remember I once looked at a piece of calligraphy and asked, "What does that mean?"—not realizing the answer was being covered during his talk. I got hell for not paying attention to what he was emphasizing.

Despite missteps like this, I was learning a lot. At one point, I even spent four weeks visiting a controversial minister, Rev. Gyodo Haguri,[37] who some in BCA consider a heretic because of his unorthodox understanding of Shinran. And I spent a week in Northeastern Japan (Miyagi Prefecture) living with a Zen master (see below).

An Animal Memorial Service, Not a Pet Memorial Service

The idea for an animal memorial service came to me when we were students in Japan invited to our professor's home for dinner. Dr. Shoson Miyamoto was regarded as one of the leading Buddhist scholars in the field of Mahayana (Madhyamika) philosophy. We had a pre-dinner Buddhist service at his *obutsudan* (home altar).

It was then that I noticed a photo of a cat in the *obutsudan*! I had never seen a photo of a non-human being in an *obutsudan* so, naive me, I simply asked the professor, "Why is a cat photo in your *obutsudan*?" He responded, "You're not listening to the Buddhist lectures carefully… Have I not mentioned many times the Buddhist idea that all living (sentient) beings possess Buddha nature?"

It was from this unforgettable day that the idea for an animal memorial service remained with me to honor and say "thank you" to animals. I introduced this practice to all of the temples I served, in Stockton, Mountain View and San Francisco. My intent for this annual service was for all living beings, but it was popularly practiced by the lay church members as a "pet memorial service." Buddhist teaching is not limited to pets, but lay members brought photos and even cremated remains of their pets to this service.

In Christian history, the love for animals became popular via St. Francis of Assisi, I believe—relatively recently compared with the veterinary hos-

---

[36] Later, in America, I took Rev. Undo to the hot springs. After he passed away, Helen and I went to his home temple, where we met his wife. I still correspond with Mrs. Undo at New Year's.

[37] BCA minister, 1908-1922

pital established by Shotoku Taishi in fifth century CE, 1,500 years prior to St. Francis of Assisi.

Yes, compared to Christianity, Buddhism is not a human-centered religion, but a religion for all living beings. I can still remember the Buddhist wording on a table in the Mountain View Temple altar—in Japanese, it reads, "*Issai shujo shitsu wu bussho*" (all living beings, without exception, possess Buddha nature).

In Buddhism, respect is not limited to animals but also includes plants and vegetables... *Ikebana* (flower arranging) organizations have conducted "flower memorial services" as part of their major activities. Respect goes beyond living things. In Japan, although I have never witnessed it, a memorial service for broken needles is sometimes held by those who make clothes.

It is not for humor that I would suggest Buddhist temples, especially those in the Buddhist Churches of America, conduct annual chicken memorial services for the thousands of chickens we have killed for fundraising! As I sometimes mentioned in my sermons, I once had a dream that humans lived in a chicken world, where chickens ate barbequed humans, naked with teriyaki sauce all over their bodies. It was a cruel reversal.

In Buddhism, not only people and animals, but also plants, such as rice and wheat, have Buddha nature.

When I was growing up, my father had a dinnertime sermon about rice. Frequently, one of us boys would eat hurriedly and drop rice on the floor. Whenever this happened, "Papa" would scold us and say, "It's *mottainai* (wasteful) to drop rice on the floor."

To this, one of would talk back and say, "*Mottainai*? Why *mottainai*? It's just *gohan* (rice)."

Papa would reply, "In each rice kernel there are three Buddhas. That's why it's *mottainai*."

Then we would ask, "How can three Buddhas be in one little rice grain?"

Papa would then respond, "*Hotoke sama* or Buddha is not one of physical size. *Hotoke sama* is one of spirit and energy found in everything, both animal and plant."

Zen Training

The week I spent living with Zen master Watanabe-*gazan roshi*, was a high privilege and only possible because of a personal connection (in this case the recommendation of my friend's younger brother, Katsuoto Hanayama). Usually, it's a teacher with a group, but I was able to study with him one-on-one.

Before I started, I wrote to my parents to ask if it was all right as a Jodo Shinshu to explore Zen. Luckily my parents, who were broad-minded, fully supported the visit.

Part of the training was to hand-scrub the hallway at 3 a.m. with cold water, clean the Japanese toilet (which was smelly), and make a simple meal with mainly rice, *misoshiru* (soup) and tofu. One time the *misoshiru* and tofu were getting low, and I told the priest we needed to go get more. All he said was, "No, just add hot water," and we ate the diluted *misoshiru* and rice for a meal. Another time at the meal, he reminded me not to ever leave the few drops of soy sauce on the dish. I asked, "What do I do with it?" He replied, "Add tea and drink it."

There was no TV or radio. We were out in the countryside and the focus was on training. We meditated five times a day.

Even though when I was meditating I was not supposed to look at the Zen master, I couldn't help but take a peek and it was fascinating to see how relaxed he was. When he sat in the lotus position his forehead practically hit the floor as he was swaying back and forth. He reminded me of the traditional Japanese round, red Daruma dolls—modeled after Bodhidharma, the founder of the Zen Buddhism—that wobble from side to side but always return upright.

At one point, during a Buddhist discussion, I was brave enough to ask the Zen priest bluntly if he had achieved *satori* (enlightenment), and he responded, "I'm aboard the train destined for enlightenment." I found this similar to Jodo Shinshu in that *shinjin* (Jodo Shinshu faith) is an assurance for enlightenment.

Another time he said, "I'm going to town; prepare the bath." I had to gather twigs to put under the bath, light a fire and keep touching the water to make sure it warmed to the perfect temperature. He came back and said, "Sit down." I said, "The bath is ready," but he responded, "Just sit down and we'll talk Dharma." My attention was not on Dharma but on the bath water that I had made perfect. After the discussion, the teacher said, "All right, I'll take a bath now." By then it was too hot and he said, "What's this? I'm not a crab." I said, "It was perfect before." Zen priests will scold you even when they're wrong, to test your patience.

The experience was invaluable. I think a broad, rather than narrow, path provides a better appreciation of Buddhism—and other religions, too. I once spoke to a Catholic nun who told me about her experience at a Zen nunnery. She was beautiful, but more importantly internally beautiful, and said the stay helped her become a better Catholic. She recommended Zen training for all nuns to deepen their Christian faith.

Wise Advice on My Graduate Thesis Selection

When I was about to complete my regular courses for my major in Japanese Buddhism, I started looking for possible thesis topics. At first I was interested in doing a thesis on the "Yuima-kyo Gisho," a commentary by Shotoku Taishi on the *Vimalakirti Nirdesa Sutra*. This was a fascinating study of a great lay Buddhist named Vimalakirti (or Yuima in Japanese), who denounces the formality and falsehood of a deceiving Theravada Buddhist priest who hides behind the Buddhist robe. In contrast, Vimalakirti emphasized the laity and said a lay person can be just as good a Buddhist as a priest. This philosophy had a strong impact on Japanese Buddhism, especially on our Jodo Shinshu teaching.

But one of my Buddhist teachers, Dr. Reimon Yuki, suggested I study Genshin (942–1017 CE), who was the most influential of a number of Tendai (a school of Mahayana Buddhism) scholars active during the tenth and eleventh centuries and one of the teachers revered by Shinran (1173–1262 CE), an exponent of Pure Land Buddhism. Specifically, Dr. Yuki suggested I do research on a book called *Ojo Yoshu* (Genshin's collection of essential passages on Pure Land birth). It was wise advice, essential to giving me broader and deeper understanding of aspects of Jodo Shinshu Buddhism as an American Jodo Shinshu minister.

When Shinran studied on Mount Hiei for 20 years, he was immersed in Tendai teaching, and he felt spiritually unfulfilled because he was not able to be a good monk or achieve enlightenment. When he finally met Honen, a religious reformer and founder of the first independent branch of Japanese Pure Land Buddhism, Shinran began to understand the Nembutsu (the recitation of the name of the Amitabha Buddha) in a new way.

According to Shinran's interpretation, the meditation aspect of the Nembutsu is a practice that he came to see as more of a quiet reflection, awareness of self, and repentance of one's imperfections; the recitation of *"Namu Amida Butsu"* became an outcome of personal faith called *"shinjin."*

This study prepared me to more fully understand and appreciate the spiritual struggle and ultimate joy of discovering the Nembutsu, both academically and historically. These insights are valuable to me, even now. Such an approach to Jodo Shinshu Buddhism — the historical perspective of why Shinran came to *shinjin* (faith)—is more relevant to the 21st century Buddhist educational way than the traditional sectarian study of Jodo Shinshu Buddhism, which emphasizes only the spiritual conclusion and appreciation of Shinran.

Lady Kujo, Asoka Hospital and Sumo Grand Champion Chiyonoyama

Good Buddhist karma has blessed me many times in my life.

Some of the best karma was the privilege of studying Buddhism, meeting many Buddhist teachers and having many good Buddhist friends. One of the most enjoyable times I was blessed with good karma, though, was the rare privilege of having lunch next to the reigning 41st Yokozuna Grand Champion, Chiyonoyama (1926-1977), at his Dewanoumi practice stable (private training center) in Tokyo.

For most sumo fans, the best they can do is to attend a sumo tournament. Only the most important sponsors and well-known people are invited to a stable and have lunch with a sumo champion.

Why was I there? The answer involved the devout Jodo Shinshu Lady Takeko Kujo (1887-1928), daughter of 21st Abbot Myonyo. Lady Takeko was best known as founder of the Japanese Buddhist Women's Association, which assisted the poor and victims of the 1923 Tokyo Earthquake and thus laid the foundation of modern social welfare and, more specifically, Asoka Hospital in Tokyo. In the spirit of social welfare exemplified by Lady Kujo, Asoka Hospital reached out to the many sumo wrestlers who could not afford hospital care.

In the 1950s, the superintendent of Asoka Hospital was Madam Moto Tanaka, who was highly respected as someone who looked after many wrestlers' hospital care. As she had visited the Buddhist Churches of America during that period and had met my father in Sacramento, she called and invited me to both the sumo tournament and a visit to the sumo stable.

It was for this good Buddhist karma that I was invited to visit the Dewanoumi stable.

As a sports fan, what a thrill it was to see the grand champion Chiyonoyama practice by striking the wooden house pillar. The house shook like the pounding of an earthquake.

After this practice, the much-perspiring grand champion sat next to me and greeted me. It was like a baseball fan shaking hands with Babe Ruth! The first thing he did was to drink two big bottles of water, followed by two more bottles of beer without taking a breath. As I was a guest, he said "*Dozo* (please) have the *chanko nabe*." I heard so much of this popular sumo dish, it was a real culinary treat to have this protein-rich simmering stew of chicken, fish, meat, tofu and daikon radish (a combination created to add weight to the wrestler). As a food lover and a sports fan, it was one of the most unforgettable dinners of my life.

I thank Buddha, Shinran and Lady Kujo for allowing me to enjoy this occasion in Tokyo.

Traveling Fourth-Class on a Ship to Rangoon, Burma

When I was a graduate student at Tokyo University, I heard that the World Buddhist Conference was planned for December 1954 in Rangoon, Burma. This was only the third time such a global conference had ever been held (the first was in Colombo, Ceylon, in 1946, and the second in Tokyo, Japan, in 1950) and it was to bring together many different Buddhist schools, sects and even small independent organizations.

As future ministers/priests/scholars of Buddhism, my classmates Shoyu Hanayama and Shojun Bando (now both deceased) and I were most curious and anxious to go to the conference and meet the many kinds of Buddhists from around the world.

Naturally, because we were financially restricted students, we looked for the cheapest way to get to Rangoon. We found it was via a British shipping company in Tokyo. Initially, however, I was told that as an American passport holder and citizen, I could not travel with less than a first- or second-class ticket! After persuading the travel agent that, based on my looks, I could pass as a non-American passenger, we were all able to purchase the cheapest fare as fourth-class passengers. I believe the 15- to 20-day trip, including port calls, cost $75 a person, including meals!!

We boarded the British ship, named *Sirdhana*, from Kobe, Japan. As we were dressed in suits and my friend Bando, who happened to be the first of us to board, mispronounced "fourth-class," the welcoming officer initially led us upwards to the first-class area. I had to correct our status by pronouncing "fourth" correctly. Then, we were led downwards to the fourth-class section. We were shocked to see our "accommodations," literally located in the bottom of the ship. It was like a huge basketball gym with no rooms as such and no toilet or shower facilities in the area—only an open wooden platform hung from the wall. That was our "bedroom." We thought we were prepared for anything, but this was a real letdown.

We tried to make do, though. Before we set sail, we bought pesticide and sprayed the wooden platform, then covered it with a *"goza* mat." After the ship sailed, we were brought food that appeared to be Chinese food—but looked dirty. We negotiated a better and cleaner-looking dish by paying $20 or $25 more per person. After this added payment, the food looked better and more edible. The day-to-day experience also included taking our showers between the crew's showers; this was allowed only after arranging this "privilege" with the crew chief. Still, upon entering each port, the ceiling opened up to bring cargo into our "gym room"!

As we three were the only passengers in the so-called fourth-class section, we ventured to the first-class section on the top floor of the ship. I still remember peeking into the first-class dining room and feeling like we were beggars from fourth-class. We became friends with some of the first-class passengers by playing ping-pong with them. We were better players than these first-class passengers, so it was funny they had to wait for their turn to play us. The ship officers figured us out and told us practically daily to get back to our fourth-class section. We did go back, reluctantly, but always returned to the first-class sections without chagrin. It was like this until we reached Hong Kong.

Then we of the fourth-class section were swarmed with additional fourth-class passengers. Hundreds of Chinese workers, many of whom lived/worked on boats or performed manual labor, boarded with their families. Suddenly there were little children riding tricycles, people burning incense and the constant noise of hundreds of people living together! Our immediate "roommates" were elderly and sick-looking Indian persons. They were using their toilet pots every time we ate, so I had to ask them to be more considerate because it smelled.

When we reached Singapore, the Hong Kong laborers left our ship and we cheered their departure. But as soon as they left, hundreds of Singapore laborers became our new roommates destined for Penang!

This type of travel was most unforgettable. However, now that I look back, I do not regret it. It was a once-in-a-lifetime, learning experience.

Another unique episode took place while aboard this British ship. Some third-class passengers were Nepalese soldiers returning home from the Korean War or related conflict. When one of these soldiers committed suicide by jumping into the ocean, we were told it was the moral obligation of the captain to return the boat to the suspected area of ocean where the soldier jumped even if there was no chance of rescue. Our three-week trip to Rangoon was again delayed as the ship reversed its course to avoid an approaching typhoon.

We, however, did arrive in Rangoon some 10 days or so before the other delegates. The official Japanese Buddhist delegation reached Rangoon aboard a Japan Airlines plane!

After the conference, we took the opportunity to travel within Burma, India, Nepal and Ceylon (now called Sri Lanka). At one point, we joined the Japanese Buddhist delegation on a ship cruise of the famous Mississippi-like Irrawady River, where hundreds of Japanese soldiers were shot to death by the British army during WWII. A memorial service was conducted to commemorate the event and these Japanese soldiers. Later, the Japanese movie *The Burmese Harp* (1956) made me remember these soldiers, who may have been distant relatives or friends of my relatives in Japan. I highly recommend this movie, especially for anyone Japanese or Japanese American.

The return trip back to Japan from Ceylon—traveling with regular economy-fare tickets on a French liner named *Cambodge*—was totally different from the outgoing trip and much less memorable.

I do remember the ship dance, though. Since it required formal attire, we were at first hesitant about attending, as we had gotten rid of our formal clothes at some point during our travels. However, we decided to attend the ship dance wearing the Nepalese clothes we had purchased in Kathmandu. We were happily greeted by the ship captain and were grateful our Nepalese clothes helped make the trip special.

The World Buddhist Conference

We were among only a few young Buddhist student delegates at the 1954 World Buddhist Conference in Rangoon, Burma. The majority were VIPs—well-known priests, scholars and leaders. Prominent Burmese political leaders, including the prime minister (president?), were also well represented. One of the conference's garden receptions was held in the foreign minister's official residence.

We were assigned roommates by the conference committee. My first and most memorable roommate was the well-known American Buddhist scholar Dr. Richard Gard. It was a privilege and honor to room with him, even though it was only for a couple days. Dr. Gard had a prophetic vision of widespread access to the Buddhist books and materials of the world without having to physically go to libraries or temples. In retrospect, it seems like he was describing Internet access to Buddhist sources.

One of the first things that struck me about the conference itself was the seating arrangement of the delegates during the formal Buddhist services and events. The Theravada monks were seated in a higher location than the Japanese (Mahayana) Buddhist delegates, who were probably not recognized as priests according to the strict precept[38]-observing Theravada tradition; they were on the lower main floor with other "lay delegates." Another clash of traditions was apparent in the conference policy of stopping the Japanese delegates from using a kind of mosquito-killing incense in their bedrooms, as this practice was against the Theravada interpretation of non-killing of all living beings, including insects.

The speaker with the most impressive name to me was a famous Indian Buddhist leader Dr. Bhimrao Ramji Ambedkar (1891–1956), principal architect of the constitution of India who brought millions of his discriminated class (untouchables) to be accepted into the Indian Buddhist Sangha. When I traveled to India in 2008, memories of the 1954 conference came back to me when I saw many statues of Dr. Ambedkar in poor Indian villages.

Outside of the conference in the city of Rangoon, I was struck by how lay people expressed their respect with prostration and/or hands joined together in a Buddhist greeting (*gassho*) at the very sight of a person with an orange-colored robe, be it a priest, adult or child. After getting to know a Theravada priest personally, I had the nerve to share my impression that it seemed

---

[38] The five Buddhist precepts are commitments to abstain from harming living beings, stealing, sexual misconduct, lying and intoxication.

arrogant for a priest to be bowed at without the priest returning a Buddhist greeting. He replied, "I am not the one being respected. It is the Buddha that they are bowing to, not me, so why should I return the greeting?"!! I was astonished and very impressed.

During our chartered streamliner train trip from Rangoon to Mandalay via Pegu, the sight of Burmese farmers dropping their farm tools and prostrating on the ground when they saw the orange-clothed priest riding on the same train was unforgettable and inspiring. The Burmese Buddhists told me there are more Buddhist temples and *stupas* (other places of worship and meditation) than people in Burma. While at first I thought they were exaggerating, I started to believe they were right when we saw literally thousands of white temples and *stupas* throughout the countryside.

Sights and Insights from India, Nepal and Ceylon

Here are a few select excerpts and adaptations from the lengthy travelogue describing Katsutomo Hanayama, Shojun Bando and my trip to India, Nepal and Ceylon (now called Sri Lanka), which was printed in Young East: Japanese Buddhist Quarterly and published as a book, Indo Busseki Junpai Kiko-ki. For us young Buddhist students, the trip was both grounding and inspirational.

First Impressions of India (December 17–21, 1954)

We drove for the Maha Bodhi Society through the teeming city of Calcutta. While cruising through our first streets of India, our eyes were only fixed to the new and strange sights. The great number of sacred cows roaming lazily over the street and even the sidewalk, handsome Sikhs with their famous turbans tooting the rubber horn of their taxis, beautiful Indian ladies garbed in their gorgeous saris shopping in Calcutta's Ginza paying the least of attention to the many beggars, business signs done in Hindi, etc....

On arrival to Patna, we were recommended to purchase bedding cover and mattress, for these things were considered travel necessities in India because many of the towns and railway stations are without bed facilities. Therefore, with only bedding equipment, reading materials and cameras, we started out the first journey to our first historical Buddhist site.

Our first trip was to Rajagriha, known as having been one of the favorite places of abode for the Shakamuni Buddha during his preaching of the

Dharma in India. We rode on a bus from Patna for six hours through flatland vegetated with tall Palm and Banyan trees and small huts displaying clay potteries for sale... Finally, at around eight p.m., we arrived in New Rajagriha, where the Burmese Buddhist temple was located and at which we were to stay for the night.

We laid out the bedding on the marble-like floor in the sanctuary where enshrined was a garish image of a Buddha ornately decorated in typical Burmese fashion. Aside from our group, there also were Tibetan pilgrims already preparing to stay overnight at the temple. Although the language barrier prevented us from conversing with the Tibetans, I did feel a sense of a Sangha when we, without racial or class distinction, bowed in reverence before the image of the Buddha.

The Holiest of Holy Sites (December 23–24, 1954)

We left Patna at 10:50 a.m. by train and headed for Buddhagaya, our first sacred site of the Buddha among the four great sacred sites of Shakamuni Buddha.[39]

Of course, the most sacred spot in Buddhagaya is the Vajrasana or the Diamond Throne where the Shakamuni became the Buddha. It is referred as the Diamond Throne to symbolize the firm determination of Shakamuni. He seated himself at this very spot and resolved the following: "Indeed, let only skin, veins and bones remain; let the flesh and blood of this body dry up; never will I abandon this seat without obtaining the state of Supreme Enlightenment."

Upon nearing the city, we were driving parallel to the Naranjara river with the rocky Urvela mountain in the background, and suddenly on the horizon appeared the towering summit of the Maha Bodhi Vihara. On arrival at Buddhagaya, we were literally swarmed by souvenir-selling peddlers who quarreled among themselves in trying to sell their strands of beads, postcards and fake historical curios. However, even in this commotion, the noble Maha Bodhi Vihara did not lose any of its dignified grandeur. It reached up into the sky, as if trying to tell us that Truth of the Dharma cannot be shaken by the mere uproar and turbulence of man...

However, one of the unpleasant impressions of the Vihara was when I entered the main altar room where many Buddhist and Hindu pilgrims were

---

[39] The four holy sites are witness to important events the Buddha's life: Lumbini, where he was born; Bodhgaya, where he attained enlightenment; Sarnath, where he delivered his first sermon; and Kushinara, where he died.

worshipping the image of the Buddha. The inside of this sanctuary appeared not like a Buddhist altar ought to be, but one belonging to a primitive religion. I say this because the floor was filthy and the entire room had an unpleasant odor of uncleanliness. Although one cannot judge a religion by standard of sanitation, I believe that the devotees should possess some sense of cleanliness and tidiness if reverence is to be offered. Uncleanliness may have been encouraged by the Hindu custom of smearing paint-like material on the image of their gods and on themselves as sort of a religious ritual.

Readers may be surprised when I mention both Buddhists and Hindus worshipping the Buddha. We learned in India that the Hindus regard the Buddhists as fellow Hindus because they consider Buddhism as only a part of Hinduism. Good evidence for this is the sign I saw at the Shree Buddhagaya stupa near the main Vihara. Its inscriptions read: "Shree Buddhagaya stupa 1944 A.D.–2001 B.S. This stupa was built through the charity of Shreeman Raja Seth Beldev Bass Birla of Pilani, Jaipur, in memory of Lord Buddha, the ninth incarnation of Vishnu and is maintained by Arya (Hindu) Deva Sangh." In addition, all over the stone slabs were inscribed verses from the Dhammapada!

The Buddhist in charge of the management of Buddhagaya was discouraged. He explained to us that the management of Buddhagaya was formerly solely controlled by Hindus and only recently by a board of Buddhists and Hindus. He sincerely believed that the management of Buddhagaya, the holiest of the holy sites for the Buddhists, should be administered by Buddhists.

The Great Ganges (December 26, 1954)

In Bernares, considered the religious capital and one of the seven sacred cities of the Hindus, we did not miss the opportunity to see the world-famous Ganges river. Hiring a boat, we rowed along the famed river and witnessed sights that can only be seen in India.

Thousands of Hindus and Brahmins were performing their sacred bathing in the river while facing the morning sunrise. Many were chanting hymns and dipping themselves into the water, some were doing their laundering, some gargling and brushing their teeth with the river water, while others were swimming next to a dead sheep floating on the river. There were still other sights which added to this commotion. Cows on the same bank were basking under the morning sunshine, while human corpses with their feet showing were being burned.

Japanese Homage to the Buddha (December 25, 1954)

After a typical Indian breakfast of chapti (like Spanish tortillas) and cauliflower and potato curry, we started on our tour of Sarnath, where Buddha's first sermon was delivered. Of the four great sacred sites of the Buddha, Sarnath had the most number of historical objects and places of interest, including the Choukhandhi stupa, said to mark the actual spot where Buddha met his five disciples who had deserted him when he abandoned the practice of self-asceticism; the excavated area with the remains of the Asoka pillar, said to mark the location where the Buddha delivered his first sermon to his five disciples; and the Dhamek Stupa, thought to mark the site where the Buddha prophesized the coming of the future Buddha Maitreya.

The place that attracted the greatest attention for the Japanese Buddhist was the Mulagandhakuti Vihara, for it was here that the Japanese Buddhists had offered their contribution. As a visitor approaches the Vihara, he/she will easily notice the large gold-filled bell at the entrance. It is said to be the gift from the Buddhist Society of Japan, donated in 1931. Upon entering the temple, the visitor will also notice the fine fresco work on the walls that portrays the life story of the Buddha. This Ajanta-style fresco painting was artistically drawn by the distinguished Japanese artist, Mr. Kosetsu Nosu.

Birthplace and Final Location of the Buddha (December 27–28, 1954)

It was difficult to believe that Lumbini was once a booming capital, a beautiful flower garden and the birthplace of the Buddha. Without the traces of hundreds of red bricks and the mighty Asoka pillar and its deciphered Brahmi script, any visitor would probably think that the place is some uncultivated farmland... The entire area is indeed prosaic and disappointing if one is to think that this was once the glorious birthplace of Buddha.

However, of the four great sacred sites of the Buddha, I was most disappointed with the Angara Chaitya, which at present is not really a *chaitya* [Buddhist shrine or prayer hall with a stupa at one end], but a jungle-like forest with a little pit in the center, and this is the place of cremation.

Although being displeased with this sad situation, I was a little encouraged by the fact that here in this almost "no man's land" lives a Chinese monk who built a hut atop a tree, planted a vegetable garden and for the past 20 years has been devoting his life to maintaining the final location of the Buddha in this world.

Notes from Nepal (December 31, 1954–January 2, 1955)

To enter Kathmandu, we flew over heavily vegetated forest, mountain ranges and the great Himalayas appearing to be right before our nose. Our plane started to dip down into the great valley of Kathmandu in approximately one hour. Upon landing, we were really shocked at the primitive facilities of the airport. Customs inspection was done right on the ground, the "office" was crudely constructed in bamboo, grass and mud, and the "toilet" was only a piece of ground sheltered by a canvas tent…

On our way to the Bhikkhu Amritananda's temple, I gathered some first impressions of the country by eagerly watching the people, buildings and dress. While Nepalese had varied features—some looked like Indians, some like Europeans and others similar to the Japanese—their national dress was truly Nepalese, a costume that can be described from the bottom to top as a riding pants or a Japanese *mompe*, an old-fashioned night gown with a Chinese collar and a "Gandhi cap"…

While in Kathmandu, we had the opportunity to visit several Hindu temples. One of them was the Pashupatinath temple. I had some doubts at first whether this was a temple or not because at the entrance were two soldiers armed with a bayonet-rifle guarding the compound. Leather goods of any sort were prohibited, so we had to leave our shoes and the camera (because of the leather case and strap) outside. As soon as we entered the temple, there was a huge golden statue of the sacred cow. We found cows and monkeys inside the temple compound as if they were just another pilgrim. In the central sanctuary was enshrined the four-faced god Siva with water being poured over its head from a golden bowl. Under the image of Siva were seated the Hindu faithfuls who were feverishly chanting the Veda, while going through a strange gesture of hands. Especially catching my eye were the hundreds of one rupee coins (approximately 22 cents or 75 yen) embedded neatly in the marble floor…

Our experience was further widened when we had the honor of meeting the prime minister (and then later the crown prince) at his private residence. The funny thing about this appointment was that we, being 15 minutes late, delayed the cabinet meeting for a whole 15 minutes because Amritanda was a highly respected Nepalese Buddhist priest (and later appointed as Nepalese Ambassador to Soviet Russia). The head of state warmly welcomed us with the "*gassho* style" greeting and introduced us to the ministers present. Our request to the prime minister was a request for better facilities and a paved road from northern India to Lumbini so that more Buddhists could conduct a religious pilgrimage to the sacred site. The prime minister, although a Hindu by birth, had a sincere interest in Buddhism and acknowledged our request, stating the Nepalese government would do its utmost, especially because the next world Buddhist conference was to be held in Tokyo.

Ceylon: A Buddhist Country (January 23–30, 1955)

After bidding a dear farewell to India (where we had returned), we landed at Jaffna, Ceylon, at 12:55 p.m. for customs inspection. It was during this inspection that we found out how much of a Buddhist country Ceylon is. When the inspector asked the reason for entering the country, we answered saying that we were entering Ceylon as Buddhist pilgrims for the purposes of conducting a religious pilgrimage of the historical Buddhist sites. The inspector smiled and calmly stated that our group would not be inspected because it was comprised of Buddhists!

Life in Columbo was a royal one compared to the traveling we had done to that point—sleeping on concrete floors and station waiting rooms, practically always the same Indian curry for lunch, continuous worry over the baggage, train reservations, etc. Being guests of the most famous lay Buddhist leader and wealthiest rubber plantation owner, everything was just perfect—nice clean rooms, delicious Ceylonese delicacies for dinner and a chauffeur-driven automobile at our disposal. We were not outstanding scholars, state guests, relatives of the families or possessors of a letter of introduction from some distinguished person—we were recipients of this unexpected Ceylonese hospitality simply because we were young Buddhists who met them at the Rangoon World Buddhist Conference. This warm hospitality continued as we traveled across the country.

Parting Thoughts (February 1, 1955)

In reflecting back on our extensive travels, Hanayama, Bando and I wish to express our heartfelt gratitude for everything that made our trip possible. Thank you from the bottom of our hearts to the many fortunate causes and conditions that came with us during the entire journey.

We also hope that our travel has been a kind of goodwill mission. That is, we hope that, however small it may have been, we have contributed to a better mutual understanding between the southern Buddhist countries and Japan and only wish that the continued relation of warm understanding and mutual assistance prevail among the many Buddhist countries in the world.

Lecture Tour of Japan

In 1955, the editor of the *Bukkyo Times* (a Japanese all-Buddhist sect newspaper) invited my Tokyo University classmates, Shoyu Hanayama and Shojun Bando, and me to conduct a lecture tour across Japan, speaking about our experiences at the 1954 World Buddhist Conference in Rangoon and pilgrimage to India, Nepal and Ceylon.

The editor made all the travel arrangements. The itinerary consisted of 40 consecutive days of travel during the summer of 1955. We went as far north as Iwate Prefecture and as far west/south as Yamaguchi Prefecture. Every host organization took care of our travel, lodging and meal expenses, and we were given a monetary gift of 1,000 yen for the three of us, 333 yen a piece (a typical lunch cost 100 to 150 yen).

We traveled third class on the train, carrying all the equipment necessary to show our movie (16 millimeter) and slide show, including the slide screen, movie projector and slide projector. Hauling all that equipment made it difficult to find a seat when the train came in, competing with the hundreds of other "seat-searching" passengers. There is no polite Japanese etiquette when it comes to finding a train seat during a hot, humid Japanese summer.

We conducted presentations in Buddhist temples of various denominations and public school buildings. Whenever it was a Nishi Honganji-affiliated Buddhist temple, Shoyu would be the first person to enter because his father was a Nishi Honganji priest and well-known Buddhist scholar/sensei. Whenever it was a Higashi Honganji-related temple, it was Shojun who would knock the temple door, because one of his ancestors directly received the original version of the famous Jodo Shinshu book, known as the Bando version of *Kyogyoshinsho* (Shinran's work, *Teaching, Practice, Faith and Enlightenment*).

When our lectures took place during the day, we needed to close the *amado* (weather door) to darken the hall for the slide and movie presentation.

That usually made the room uncomfortably hot and humid. Despite this, we usually drew an audience of 30 to 50 people and were typically well received. As the only young delegates to the World Buddhist Conference and pilgrimage, we were able to present fresh interpretations and perspectives.

We sometimes conducted three presentations in one day—morning, afternoon and evening. We were only able to do this because we were 24 and 25 years old. Shoyu, however, had to drop out after about half of the tour because he was not able to physically endure this hectic schedule.

For us as young graduate students of Buddhism, it was most educational to visit temples of various Buddhist sects. One memorable experience was conducting a pre-lecture service of chanting with the lay members of one temple, where each attendee chanted while holding and ringing a Buddhist bell. We also had the privilege of visiting temples prominent due to their priest or history.

We also enjoyed meals at interesting restaurants, such as one with *wanko* soba (soba noodles served in small lacquered wooden *owan* bowls), where the waitresses would drop more soba noodles into our bowls immediately after we would finish a serving. In one town in Miyagi Prefecture, I must have had 40 or 50 small bowls of soba noodles! They were delicious with different toppings, dipped into sauce, *zaru* style.

All in all, the lecture tour was a special experience—a unique opportunity outside the realm of most students of Buddhism.

5

LAUNCHING FAMILY AND MINISTRY: STOCKTON, 1959–1971

A New Life

While I was still in Japan, the Stockton Buddhist Temple contacted me to see if I would become a minister there. The temple was supposed to make these types of arrangements through the bishop, but Rev. Hojo, the senior minister there, knew how to pull strings... I think it helped that both my grandfather (Senju Sasaki) and father (Sensho Sasaki) had served the same Stockton church, making it the only Buddhist Churches of America (BCA) institution to have had three generations of ministers from the same family.

When I returned from my studies in Japan in the summer of 1958, I stayed at my father's church in Sacramento for half a year. I was not officially assigned there, despite the erroneous listing by the BCA.

In January 1959, I did officially become a minister assigned to the Stockton church, which was on 148 West Washington Street (where it was located before its current site on Shimizu Drive), in the old downtown area. I was welcomed as the first English-speaking minister.[40]

My assignment in Stockton was to last 12 years, until 1971. These were fruitful years, both professionally and personally.

---

[40] Unfortunately, some of my first duties were funerals due to tragedies. In one family, the father committed suicide and the daughter was murdered at a Japanese American Citizens League (JACL) conference in Chicago, when someone broke into the hotel. (The roommate, an activist in her younger years, is now a prominent lawyer.) Another "difficult to speak and comfort" funeral was for an 8-year-old girl who drowned in a public pool. Another was for a boy who was killed at an intersection riding a bike. It was challenging for a rookie minister to comfort these families.

My Two BCA *Senseis*

As in the common Japanese saying *okagesama* (gratitude to many seen and unseen conditions), I am what I am due to the guidance of many *senseis* (teachers). Many minister/spiritual teachers helped me on my path, including *Issei* (first-generation American) and *Nisei* (second-generation American) Buddhist ministers, and many others not mentioned here.

In particular, I extend my humble and deepest gratitude to two ministers I served with at the Stockton Buddhist Temple.

I served with the late Rev. Ejitsu Hojo for about two years. As a young 29-year-old bachelor minister, fresh from my college studies in Tokyo, Hojo-*sensei* (to use the term of respect for a senior minister in Japanese) was a most resourceful and intelligent minister with a most helpful and talented bilingual wife, Mrs. Yumi Hojo. They patiently guided me into the real world of Buddhist ministry—very different from the academic classroom atmosphere of Buddhist study from whence I came.

My mother used to advise me to conduct myself like Rev. Hojo, that is, to think carefully before I spoke. And that is exactly how Rev. Hojo conducted himself in various settings, be it meetings, conferences or just meeting people. She probably saw and heard me speak without carefully weighing what I was about to say and thought he set a good example for me.

It was also through Rev. Hojo's vision that the church financed and provided time for my graduate education at the University of the Pacific in Stockton while I conducted my ministerial duties. Rev. Hojo recognized that future ministers needed to be continually educated. Because of his foresight, many Stockton ministers became leaders; these include Rev. David Matsumoto and Rev. Seigen Yamaoka,[41] who both went on to earn a PhD in education.

The lighter side of Hojo-*sensei* was the fact he was a real sports fan—especially of College of the Pacific (now University of Pacific) football, which was quite a powerhouse then. He would never schedule any regular church activity on the Saturday nights when the College of the Pacific Tigers played home games, which he liked to attend.

As for Mrs. Hojo, I can still remember the time I had to ask for her help when I, a bachelor minister then, was confronted with an angry mother who needed advice about her unmarried daughter, who was living with a non-Japanese man. I called Mrs. Hojo and she came over. I would not have been able to survive that evening without her!

---

[41] Rev. Yamaoka also went on to become a Buddhist Churches of America bishop.

The second[42] minister I served with who had a great influence on my life is the late Rev. Tesshin Shibata, the father of Rev. George Shibata (another third-generation BCA minister) and grandfather of Rev. Candice Shibata of Berkeley Buddhist Temple (the first and only BCA fourth-generation minister). I served the Stockton church with Shibata-*sensei* for some 10 years. I can still remember the day he and his family arrived in Stockton from Ontario, Oregon. His family of 10 children (minus George, who was then a college student) literally "marched" into the new Stockton parsonage home at the "command" of their father. They were very disciplined.

It is no wonder that all of his 10 children became good, responsible and unselfish adults. The "old-fashioned" way, as compared to the more liberal/contemporary approach, can sometimes work. With that many children, you can't discuss everything. You just have to command, and the kids were obedient.

Shibata-*sensei's* wife was the traditional hardworking, uncomplaining and patient minister's wife and mother, who raised 10 good kids. With their nine kids and my five, the Dharma school increased by 14 students.

The lighter side of Shibata-*sensei* was that he was a good golfer despite his small stature. When playing with him, I would tell myself, "How can I lose to this smaller person?" But I did. His hits were not long, but accurate—especially the short shots, say 100 yards away. Shibata-*sensei* and the then longtime church office secretary, Yoshie, and I also enjoyed talking about the joys and disappointments of Nevada casino entertainment in the church office.

Rev. Shibata gave his services in Japanese. While I was technically the English-speaking minister, I wanted to do Japanese, too, so we took turns so I could get to know Japanese-speaking temple members.

University of the Pacific Studies

Thanks to the vision of Rev. Hojo and the church board, I was offered the opportunity for further study at University of the Pacific (UOP), while serving as the Stockton temple's first English-speaking minister.

The Stockton temple paid the tuition and all other costs. The church was also good enough to allow me to do my church work according to my class schedule. If the classes were in the morning, I would be an afternoon and evening minister. If my classes were in the afternoon, I would be a morning and evening minister.

---

[42] I also served briefly with Rev. Fujikado in between Rev. Hojo and Rev. Shibata; however, he only remained in Stockton for about a year due to disagreements with the board.

My post-graduate studies at UOP's graduate school in the Department of Religious Education (1960–1965) meant I could become a more relevant minister in changing times.

Another reason for further study was that the Buddhist studies in Japan for us ministerial aspirants were not really connected to the ministry—it was directed more at teaching us how to be Buddhist scholars than Buddhist ministers. This was like the difference between teaching theoretical physics to future scientists and applied science to laypeople with more practical interests, such as how physics affects their TV or computer. Buddhism can impact our everyday lives by making its profound doctrine into practical guidance for lay people.

For this reason, I believed studying religious education, basically Christian education, was more relevant than just studying philosophy, as Christianity had been made more accessible to the layperson. I studied what they were doing and tried to relate it to Buddhism, picking topics relevant to Buddhism to focus on. At one point, I attended a national Christian education conference in St Louis with my head advisor/professor, Dr. Frank Lindhorst. They never tried to convert me—I probably had more influence on them than vice versa.

My graduate thesis was on educational curriculum—developing a Buddhist curriculum for high school seniors, as Buddhist education at that time was mostly directed to children in the lower grades. I also applied my graduate work by leading a group called the High School Senior Pioneers, seeking to make Buddhism relevant to them. Nowadays, Buddhist youth education is more accessible, so Dharma school is not just curriculum such as teaching the Four Noble Truths[43]—we need to teach living examples of how we can reach these profound doctrinal goals.

Later, around 1969–70, a Chinese American UOP professor, Edwin Ding, asked if I could teach an Oriental philosophy class—starting the following week. This would be my first teaching experience. I accepted. I woke up at 4 a.m. every day for three hours of preparation for the one-hour lecture. The experience gave me the confidence to later teach at San Joaquin Delta College. I was able to introduce the first Oriental philosophy class offered at Delta College. I taught it for four semesters. The first semester, 25 students enrolled, but

---

[43] The Four Noble Truths are: 1) life is suffering (*dukkha*); 2) the cause of suffering is thirst/craving (*samudaya*); 3) the end of suffering can be brought about by a deliberate cessation of craving (*nirhodha*); 4) following the correct path (the Eightfold Path of Right View, Right Intention, Right Speech, Right Action, Right Livelihood, Right Effort, Right Mindfulness and Right Concentration) frees us from suffering (*magga*).

the class became popular and they had to stop enrollment at 50 students.

As a student at UOP, I made good friends with many of my classmates, who went on to become ministers and directors of Christian education. This background led me to become very active in interfaith friendship/dialog in the communities I served. Without community outreach, we can be unaware of the community and its resources.

Marriage

I married Helen Toshiko Yokoi on July 1, 1962.[44]

The courtship was a mix of Japanese and American ways. My father suggested I meet her, as she came from a good Buddhist family in Sacramento. There were also go-betweens from each of our families, as is the custom in Japan.[45] But it was our choice whether or not to get married. Either one of us could have called it off at any time. But we didn't.

Instead, impressed by her intelligence and poise, on our sixth date I proposed. And she said "yes."

We had a formal wedding, officiated by Rev. Shibata and BCA Bishop Shinsho Hanayama from Japan, whom I had gotten to know during my student days in Tokyo. The wedding was a real community affair. The Stockton church members cooked chicken teriyaki. Members of my father's church in Mountain View (then a partially agricultural area) sent flowers grown by congregants. There were so many people to invite, we had to limit attendance to one person per family! The wedding was reported in the Stockton newspaper.

After our honeymoon in Lake Tahoe (interrupted briefly when we returned home to meet a visiting abbot from Japan), we settled into an apartment above the church. Helen, who had been a high school science teacher in Sacramento before we met, found a job as a math teacher close by at Edison High School. While most of the traditional duties of the minister's wife were handled by the wife of the senior minister, in this case, Mrs. Shibata, Helen volunteered to teach Sunday school (now called Dharma school) and would sometimes play organ during services.

Helen and I have been married more than 50 years now—with five kids and 13 grandchildren—and I don't regret it one bit.

---

[44] I was 32; she was 24.

[45] Traditionally, these go-betweens stay involved, and help troubleshoot any difficulties in the marriage.

Many Trips to the Maternity Ward

Our five kids—Brian, Sharon, Stanton, Ellen and Rina—arrived close together in the years from 1964 to 1970.

This involved many trips to the maternity ward. I wasn't allowed in the labor room, but could hear the moaning and groaning of women in labor, and I could peek through the door from a hard metal chair in the hallway to see my wife, Helen, going through the pain we men never have to endure.

The family ended up moving to a house nearby the church and Helen was able to quit her teaching job to devote herself to our children. When my schedule permitted, I went home for lunch and helped with the children's baths.

A lot of the kids' activities took place at the church, which limited the need to drive[46] and provided a welcoming community. Because there were so many of them and they were all good kids, our children had a positive impact on church youth activities at my ministry in Stockton, and later in Mountain View and San Francisco.

The circumstances in those years were more compatible with family life than when I was growing up. Back then, my parents were faced with helping many dislocated people in the Japanese American community during the aftermath of WWII,[47] and my brothers and I were often left to feed ourselves. Our children grew up in more favorable times.

City Redevelopment and Fundraising

The City of Stockton began a redevelopment project to build a new downtown freeway, right through the church's 148 W. Washington Street site, so we needed to relocate.

This was a momentous project that required massive fundraising beyond the redevelopment financing the church received. To rise to the challenge, Rev. Shibata and I organized two teams to solicit donations from some 150 to 200 families each.

Rev. Shibata's team included Paul Matsumoto, Frank Kosugi and Jack Matsumoto. My team included Art Hisaka and Frank Inamasu.

The fundraising solicitation was initiated with the understanding and support of the church membership, except the fact that the church members did

---

[46] These were the days before minivans and seatbelts. When we had to drive together, the five kids would all pile into the back seat. Once, we went around a corner and Sharon fell out of the car. Luckily, she wasn't hurt!

[47] At one point, the church was turned into a hostel and my parents slept in the office.

not know when they were to be solicited. It was therefore, somewhat amusing for the soliciting team (and probably not the church members) to see the rustling of curtains in the members' homes whenever a church car parked in front.

The cooperation and participation of the church members with this much-needed fundraising campaign was remarkable. In only a few cases, the light was turned off at night when we parked the car and started to approach the home.

My team was effective and successful because both Art and Frank were well-respected and popular. Although Art was a self-assured leader with intelligence and a friendly personality, he was reluctant to ring the house bell, so I rang the bell and Frank was the outgoing fellow who greeted the church member who opened the door, abruptly asking, "Where's the beer?"

We visited church members of all ages. It was most interesting to get to know their common response to the subject of donation.

A 20+-year-old couple would respond, "We can donate better in 10 years, but as we currently just got married, it is difficult to do more."

A 30+-year-old couple or family would respond, "We can donate more, but as we are starting to raise our children, it is difficult to do as much as we can. Maybe in 10 more years?"

A 40+-year-old household member would tell us they could do better in 10 years, because they were restrained by cost of the children's college education.

A 50+-year-old family member would tell us that they could do much better if it were not for the high cost of living; things would probably be better in 10 years.

A 60+-year-old family member would tell us that work as gardeners had been curtailed because of their own injuries and hospitalization. "When I retire soon, I can do much more."

A 70+-year-old family member would tell us that it is difficult to do more, because they are now retired and need to look after their aging parents.

The stories are all true, but such is the changing situation of life. There is never a good time?

Impermanence of the Human Body

As we Buddhist ministers conduct many funeral services, our religion is often labeled as "*Soshiki Bukkyo*" (Funeral Buddhism). This is especially true of Buddhist practice in Japan. In many ways, it is unfortunate, because Buddhism is truly for the living, not for the dead.

In another way, possibly the more important way, what human event is more important than death?

Our American culture heavily emphasizes the living, as we look to birthdays, weddings, reunions, anniversaries and just having a "good time." This is fine, except when we are confronted with sickness, death and dying: the "realities of human living." They are the realities that are not planned, as are the happier events of a family, but realities that affect all living things, not just human beings, but also animals and plants.

We ministers are in continual touch with morticians, funeral directors and funeral homes. As funeral homes are not homes in an ordinary sense and not commonly attended like schools, restaurants and movie theatres, they are viewed negatively and as totally foreign to the younger generation. It was for Buddhist education that I often brought youth groups to funeral parlors, to confront the realities of life.

As a minister, I was curious as to how a mortician would prepare a deceased body before it was presented in a coffin. I therefore contacted my funeral director friend and he readily agreed to have me visit him to show me.

As I entered the funeral home, the secretary told me that he was expecting me, so I was led to a room on the second floor. I knocked on the door and was told to enter. Upon opening the door, the odor of formaldehyde overpowered me, and, a second later, I saw my mortician friend with his arms inside a man's open chest, washing the interior. The odor, the sight and the mortician's casual greeting of "Hi Reverend, come in!"—these were an instant lesson in life.

How could he greet me so casually and so insensitively? The deceased man's body was literally "in his hands." Was the body just a professional object to him? Or, was he "enlightened" to human life and the frailty of the human body?

The answers did not matter. It is wisdom when one views life as in the popular expression, "It is what it is."

As I steadied myself, he led me to another body. He poked the veins of this body until he remarked, "Beautiful, the blood is flowing out." Again, I was overwhelmed by his remark.

This experience was similar to the time when I observed a man at a crematorium placing cremated remains into a container while listening to radio music!

These visible lessons in human impermanence certainly are different according to a person's occupation and philosophy of life. Is it ignorance or enlightenment?

It is not for me to judge. But is it not important to have the "Right View" of life, as taught in the first of the Eightfold Path of Buddhism?

Community Service

As a Buddhist minister, my membership in the Rotary Club was important. It could have been the Lions, Toastmasters, Kiwanis or any of the community service organizations—the important thing was the service to community and helping others less fortunate in the spirit of *dana* (selfless giving). It was the Bodhisattva way idealized in Buddhism, especially emphasized in Mahayana Buddhism.

I was originally sponsored for membership to the Rotary, the oldest of the service clubs, by a Catholic priest, who was broadminded enough to invite a Buddhist minister. I am indebted to him, as I became very involved with the club's community and became friends with leaders in the community—businessmen, lawyers, the mayor, University of the Pacific professors, etc. My badge had a notation "religion: Buddhist," which reinforced my feeling I was representing Buddhism to the community. I would like more ministers to get involved in the Rotary/Lions/Kiwanis Clubs for that reason. In the American community, the Buddhist Churches of America (BCA) is not well known, especially compared to the Tibetan Buddhism of the Dalai Lama, Zen Buddhism popularized by D.T. Suzuki and Vietnamese Buddhism of Thich Nhat Hanh.[48] The Rotarian motto is "service above self"—you can't get more Buddhist than that.

When I was assigned to be minister at Mountain View, I persuaded Hiroji Kariya, an active BCA leader, to join the Rotary Club. Because of Hiroji's continued participation, the Rotary Club there has close ties with the Mountain View Buddhist Temple, and many Rotarians participate in the Sasaki Memorial Golf Tournament, which has raised $50,000 in college scholarships for tem-

---

[48] At Stockton, I also took part in other efforts to reach out to the community at large. To introduce Buddhism to the public, we once held a "Japanese Night Obon Festival," not at the church, but at the civic auditorium. The community program chairperson Art Hisaka and I thought we should get a celebrity to help draw people. We succeeded in recruiting Miiko Taka, an actress of *Sayonara* fame with Marlon Brando. We were concerned about people showing up—but people came in droves.

ple youth over some 30 years. An annual Rotary Club crab dinner fundraiser is also held at the Mountain View Temple Sangha Hall.

The Rotary Club also has an international presence. In Japan, my uncle Susumu Hokyo, a Rotarian in Fukui, asked me to speak at the Fukui Rotary Club. I spoke at one or two other Rotary Clubs in Japan, too. In Japan, most members are presidents of big companies; Rotarians there tend to be more prominent than in the United States, so the group's impact must be even bigger.

U.S.-Japan Sister City Activities

My belief that Buddhism was a viable way to promote a more peaceful and wiser world and better U.S.-Japanese relations led me to participate in a number of sister city programs. President Dwight Eisenhower launched the initiative, called Sister City International, in 1956 to improve international relations through what he called person-to-person "citizen diplomacy," outside the realm of professional politicians.

I was involved in my first sister city as one of the charter members of Stockton's program with the city of Shimizu, Shizuoka Prefecture, Japan. Former Stockton mayors Dean De Carli and Roger Huckins and University of the Pacific Professor Harold Jacoby were some of the prominent people who helped initiate this sister city program. I was grateful that the Stockton Buddhist Church board and members supported it, too.

Through the sister city program, I was able to get to know various Shimizu city leaders, mayors, business leaders and educators. The church sponsored many welcome dinners whenever the representatives from Shimizu visited Stockton. It was through this type of support that the street in front of the new church was renamed Shimizu Drive.

Another legacy of the program was the church's Japanese stone lantern. The decision to receive this wonderful commemorative gift was a "10-minute transaction" due to the power of a mayor from Shimizu who came to a welcome dinner at the Buddhist church with other prominent delegates. Following the dinner with much "Japanese-style drinking," the Japanese representatives were in a happy mood. As we were walking to the church parking lot, the well-known former Japan Diet member and then-current Mayor Torajiro Sato asked me, "Would you like to have a Japanese stone lantern for your church garden?" I asked the Stockton mayor, "What do you think?" He said, "Great!" Then, the mayor walked into the garden and asked, "How tall a stone lantern would you like? As tall as my height?" I simply said, "A tall one would be nice." Then, a minute later, he asked one of his Shimizu delegates, "Doesn't your relative make those stone lanterns? Have him make one for the church." I was amazed how quickly this decision was made. The mayor then asked another Shimizu delegate, a shipping line executive, "How about one of your ships transports it to the port of Stockton?" Our Stockton representatives responded, "Wow, that's great!"

Following my assignment to the Mountain View Buddhist Temple in 1971, I worked with city leaders to charter a sister city program with another Shizuoka prefecture city, Iwata. The mayor at the time was Mayor Yamauchi. Again, the program was enthusiastically supported by leaders in Mountain View, including the prominent former mayor and local businessman Andy Anderson. We launched an active student and city employee exchange program with Iwata and personally hosted some students. Together with the Buddhist Churches of America youth exchange program, the sister city initiative created a valuable opportunity for involvement for our then-high school-age children. Our children were exposed to Japan and its culture for the first time and established a vital link to and friendship with our Japanese relatives.

The third sister program I was invited to join was between San Francisco and Osaka. My expected level of participation, however, did not become a reality due to health problems. Through my involvement in San Francisco community affairs, I did go to Osaka as one of the hundred delegates from San Francisco in one of its sister city anniversary programs. Together, the San Francisco clergy representatives tried to communicate how a city like San Francisco worked with churches to address various social issues such as emergencies and homelessness. Unfortunately, City of Osaka representatives didn't seem to understand how to work with the religious community and preferred a clear separation of church and city.

My fourth sister city involvement—with the airport city of Narita near Tokyo—was when I was a resident of San Bruno following my retirement. I had the honor of being "mayor of Narita for the day" and took the opportunity to provide an update on the Narita-San Bruno sister city relationship. Since I was retired, I volunteered to help in San Bruno, translating English speeches into Japanese, letting people know what to expect when they went to Japan and occasionally assisting with delegations of five to ten kids.

6

CARRYING THE TORCH: MOUNTAIN VIEW, 1971–1990

A Fortunate Move

For many years, I would drive from Stockton to Mountain View once a month to conduct a study class in English at my father's church, which served not only the town of Mountain View but also the surrounding area of Sunnyvale, Los Altos, Cupertino and other parts of Santa Clara County.

By 1971, my father's health was deteriorating and I asked the Board if I could join him fulltime at the church in Mountain View. Fortunately, they agreed.

My father graciously offered to be assistant minister when I arrived, but I proposed we be co-ministers, and that's what we did.

The timing for the move turned out to be good. The children were still young—our oldest, Brian, was only in first grade—so they integrated easily into their new life. And the move provided precious time with my father, who passed away a year later.[49]

After my father's death, I became the minister at the Mountain View facility.[50] This was again fortunate for the family. My mother, who was a real go-getter and who had had years of experience serving the church, was able

---

[49] See earlier chapters for more information on my father and his passing.

[50] The Mountain View Buddhist Temple, situated in a centrally located area in California and blessed with dedicated temple members and excellent facilities, is chronologically listed number 58 among the 65 temples in the country, older than only seven others (Southern Alameda County, Orange County, Seabrook (New Jersey), Marin County, Fowler, Honeyville (Utah) and Vista (near San Diego)).

to continue her traditional duties as the minister's wife (*okusan*), with only a minor change of title to "minister's mother." This arrangement lasted 13 years.

Over the course of her lifetime, my mother greeted and hosted so many people that she seemed to know everyone in the Buddhist community. When she died in 1985, more than 50 ministers attended her funeral. Her tenure as active minister's wife for more than 55 years will probably never be challenged.

The Taste of a Japanese Rice Cracker Described by a Prison Inmate

In about 1980, when I was a minister in Mountain View, a Catholic prison chaplain invited us Coast District BCA ministers to conduct a service in Soledad Prison, located near Salinas, California.

My first visit was a strange and intimidating experience. Led by the chaplain, I walked through the prison yard. The inmates just stared at me and it was quite uncomfortable. We went through many locked doors before we finally entered the prison chapel.

A Christian cross was there, so I hesitatingly asked the chaplain if I could do something about it for the Buddhist service... He casually responded, "Just move it aside. Do whatever you wish." While arranging the portable Buddhist altar, one of the inmates came and very politely asked, "May I help you, Reverend?" I was touched by this simple gesture.

As some 15 other inmates, also courteous, entered the chapel area, I thought to myself, "Am I in the confines of a prison or not?" I do not usually experience this kind of courtesy, even inside a Buddhist temple.

I conducted a typical Buddhist service of chanting, meditation and talk. Following the service, I had the participants form a circle for an informal discussion. I asked if I could tape-record the discussion so my church members could get to know their thoughts and feelings for educational and spiritual reasons. They said "fine," even to my inquiry of the type of crime that caused their imprisonment (which included drug charges, theft and assault (no murder)). I was quite amazed by their openness.

I had brought Japanese green tea and *arare* rice crackers as an ice-breaker for the discussion session. I was struck by one inmate's description of the rice crackers I served. I asked, "Do you like it?" He responded, "The taste of this rice cracker explodes in my taste buds!" I told him I had never heard a Japanese person describing the enjoyment of a rice cracker in such a way... Most of us hardly look at it. We simply grab it and put it into our mouth like any other common snack. I was stunned and impressed by his description and inspired by his appreciation.

I came out of the prison with the attitude that some of these inmates are no different than us. In fact, some of them are perhaps more courteous, intelligent and caring. The prison experience may have sparked positive changes... Buddhism describes this as *gyaku-en* (reverse karma), entrance to the path to enlightenment by initially opposing it, as compared to *jun-en* (regular or common karma), entering the path via reading, meditation, services, lecture/discussion, etc.

What Big Things After a Glass of Wine!!

I believe it is vital for a minister to be involved not only in his or her own church, but also in the larger religious community. This can introduce the church and Buddhism to the community, as well as learning from other churches and leveraging community resources for the church's good.

One example—a big example—of this from the early 1980s was the way our BCA's Institute of Buddhist Studies (IBS) became an academic institution affiliated with the Graduate Theological Union (GTU) in Berkeley.

As a board member of National Conference of Christians and Jews (NCCJ),[51] I attended a lecture one evening at the home of the San Jose NCCJ executive director. During the post-lecture social hour, I was conversing with the various community members with a glass of wine. I met a friendly gentleman and started a casual conversation, mentioning that I was a Buddhist minister and that our national organization had a small academic institution in Berkeley looking to become accredited.

This gentleman, who was a San Francisco attorney, simply stated, "My name is Gordon Weber. I am the board chairman of Graduate Theological Union in Berkeley. Perhaps your Buddhist organization would be interested in joining us." I was quite astounded and responded, "Thank you. Let me look into this."

I contacted then-Bishop Yamaoka and we got the organizational process started, leading to the BCA Board's final approval and acceptance of the relationship.

While unfortunately Gordon Weber died suddenly in 1983 during a

---

[51] The National Conference of Christians and Jews (NCCJ) was started by Jews to help ease some of the conflict with Christians. I was surprised to hear about the conflict, given that Judaism gave birth to Christianity. Since the Hindu religion was the mother of Buddhism, Hindus look at Buddhists and say, "Great, you're a fellow Hindu!" and we have the same respect and friendship with them. The NCCJ came to include Muslims and Buddhists, and the name has since changed to the International Fellowship of Christians and Jews.

visit to Japan, his wife, Martha Weber of Palo Alto, recently wrote this letter to our national Buddhist organization:

Dear Friends:
I am glad you asked about the early beginnings of the IBS/GTU connection. Several years ago a friend asked us to attend a meeting of the Santa Clara County chapter of the National Conference of Christians and Jews. A remarkable Buddhist priest named Reverend LaVerne Sasaki was also in attendance.

He and Gordon had a stimulating conversation, and some weeks later he introduced Gordon to Bishop Yamaoka. From that chance meeting the interest between the IBS and the GTU grew and blossomed, and I am pleased to know that it has at last borne fruit with the recently announced affiliation.

Gordon spoke Japanese. In fact, we met in Colorado where he was learning the language after his graduation from Harvard Law School. He was so committed to interreligious dialogue and understanding that I am sure he would want me to express every hope that this new relationship will prosper and grow and that the mutual respect of each for the other, and for their respective religions, may be a sign to all humanity that harmony and peace can come through understanding and acceptance of each other's religious experiences and expressions.

The late Arnold Toynbee, one of the finest historians in this century, was a respected friend of ours. Please permit me to quote one of his passages, which reveals how he felt about the importance of the Buddhist/Christian dialogue. He wrote:

"A future historian, writing 1000 years hence about the 20th Century, might take a greater interest in the first mutual penetration of Christianity and Buddhism than in the disagreements between democracy and communist ideologies."

You have my heartiest congratulations as you move into the future.
Sincerely,
Martha Q. Weber

My Sports-Related Buddhist Karma:
The Los Angeles Summer Olympics

Buddhist karma is regularly described in Japanese Buddhist expressions as "*fushigi*" (beyond thought) and "*fukasetsu*" (beyond speech).

This happened again and again, but for me, as a real sports fan, it was "lucky me" again. I was able to go to the Los Angeles Summer Olympics in 1984! It was that "good old Buddhist karma."

I was blessed with this good Buddhist karma when I attended a national Dharma School (Buddhist Sunday School) teacher's conference in San Mateo. I "happened" to be at a small group discussion session with a Caucasian American Buddhist volunteer teacher, Mr. John Kehoe from the Pasadena Buddhist Temple Dharma School. During the time of self-introduction, he invited anyone in the group to come and volunteer at the following year's Los Angeles Summer Olympics.

I had always wanted to attend the Olympics (not counting the 1932 Los Angeles Summer Olympics, which I attended as a two-year-old; I still remember watching the movie my Dad had made of the impressive Japanese swimmers at that event).

I contacted Mr. Kehoe, who was one of the officials for the L.A. Olympics. I guess he gave me special consideration and respect as a minister because he allowed me to bring along my wife and daughter Sharon to the event of our choosing... the track and field competition.

Since we wanted to actually see the action, we volunteered as ushers and not as interpreters. He even allowed us to be at the same area as the competition.

We stayed at the home of my wife's sister, Florence, in Fountain Valley, and hundreds of volunteers were transported on buses from a huge parking lot.

I think now it would be physically impossible for me (a minister who sits most of the time in offices, altar chair, meetings, etc.) to volunteer at my age, since we "worked" from about 9 a.m. to 9 p.m. (two separate times in one day), standing in the aisles, mainly instructing ticket holders to their seats, pointing to the restrooms, interpreting for Japanese tourists, etc.

Mr. Kehoe came to inquire on how we were doing daily. After a few days of poor performance by Japan's track team, I asked Mr. Kehoe if we could see a sport where Japanese athletes were doing better. We decided to see the top-flight Japanese team in the judo competition held at Los Angeles State University, where Mr. Kehoe would drive us. We ushered for three days and witnessed "Mr. Judo Yamashita" win the gold medal. He did this even after injuring one of his legs in the first match.

We returned to the coliseum to see the spectacular closing ceremony.

It was most memorable to see the Olympics for some 7 or 8 days… for free!

We even accidentally met some big names in the stands, such as the then-famous Redskins quarterback Joe Theismann and actor Jack Nicholson.

We were even given a hat, Olympic volunteer uniform, and shoes.

Our twice-a-day cold cut sandwiches (practically the same type of sandwich daily), cookies and fruit were a little too "ordinary and boring," so we sometimes attempted to trade these "same old sandwiches" with some other kind of food. On our way home every night, we would stop to have hot Chinese noodles.

Yet, all in all, it was our good Buddhist friend (the good Buddhist karma) that allowed us the rare opportunity to see and experience the popular Summer Olympics.

My Visit to Israel

In 1988, during my time as a minister for the Mountain View church and member of the National Conference of Christians and Jews, I was selected and sponsored by a National Jewish Organization to go to Israel with some 20 Christian and Jewish ministers to better understand the Israeli situation and the problems there. I was the only minister who wasn't either Christian or Jewish. I paid only $300 for the whole trip, including air travel, hotel stays, meals, daily seminars and sightseeing.

The 10-day trip was like a half-year course, as it included not just visits to the historical/religious sites of Christianity, Judaism and Islam, but daily seminars and field trips. We heard from top government officials and prominent religious leaders, including the co-leader of the Palestine Liberation Organization.

At one luncheon with some Israeli Tank Corps officers, who seemed friendly, I told them that I was a Buddhist minister and asked, "Do you think it would be possible to have a Buddhist chaplain in the Israeli army?" They said, "Why not?"—a response so liberal I was amazed.

Another meal I remember was a dinner with an African Muslim family under a tent with an unlit desert sky outside. It was a nice meal. We ate with our hands—a whole pot of chicken over rice with lots of gravy. I asked, "What do I do with the bones?" I was told to just throw them behind me. When I did, I would hear hungry cats running after them.

I was amazed by many things on this trip, including the ingenuity of the Israeli people. Surrounded by unfriendly countries, Israeli men and women soldiers carried weapons everywhere; the country was highly militarized and fortified against attack. Even in the face of this threat, the Israeli people had converted a dry desert into productive agricultural land.

Mini-Sermon: Make Room for What Is Important

I delivered this invocation at the Rotary District Conference on April 22, 1989, reminding the audience of the importance of spirituality and service.

The business of earning a wage has become primary, and spiritual thinking is crowded out of the individual's sphere of awareness. Because the time and effort needed to do business are so demanding, we are left mentally numb and emotionally tense. A life of dedication and service has no authentic meaning for persons of such lifestyle.

To such people, the illusion of progress has given them the notion that the men of the past were primitive and uncivilized. But the basic difference between primitive and modern man has not really changed appreciably throughout the ages—the former was honest with his instincts, whereas, the latter has learned to rationalize them.

There is still greed, hostility and fear. The same ultimate questions still face us: Why are we living? What is the meaning of life? Why must we die? Where do we go from here? These eternal questions seem to be forgotten. It seems that there are other immediate and necessary things to worry about.

Is this all pessimism? Yes, and yet there is a way out of this incompleteness of life as the Buddhist saying goes, "Out of the mud grows the lotus."

Let us think and act upon this ideal and be honest with ourselves. Let us discover the spiritual potential within us so that we may, as Rotarians, serve above self and put life into our lives. As Rotarians with the goal of service above self, let us reflect upon this goal and challenge.

Mini-Sermon: Nembutsu in a Nutshell

What is the essence of Nembutsu faith? Nembutsu, to me, is a personal experience and awareness that enables me to:

1. See my shortcomings, faults and ignorance
2. Realize that my personal problems are rooted within myself
3. Slow me down so that I can have a better hold of my life
4. Become less critical of others and more critical of myself
5. Meditate or reflect upon matters that require deliberate and thoughtful concentration
6. Learn to better accept change, whether for worse or better
7. Cast a light of wisdom on a variety of human experiences that I cannot comprehend with worldly knowledge
8. Accept death and dying when it comes as a natural and harmonious course of the life cycle
9. Feel gratitude in many things that I take for granted and am unable to see due to my ego-centeredness
10. Respect humility as a deep human experience that grows from true understanding of the interdependence of all life
11. See my true undisguised self in the quiet of personal reflection
12. Appreciate the Dharma and Nembutsu as my most reliable sources of wisdom and comfort because this experience will never leave me
13. Practice compassion to anyone, regardless of his/her background
14. Motivate me positively when I am disheartened, frustrated, disillusioned or lonely
15. Learn to respect all life as having the potential for Buddhahood
16. Become more open-minded to many changes and new situations
17. Learn to respect a true religious experience, whether it agrees with my preconceptions or not
18. Learn to accept each person, whether or not he/she reflects my values

Etc., etc., etc...

Haruko Muranaka—a Life of Inspiration and Challenge

It is sad but true that we often do not know the full worth of a person until he or she is no longer with us. I have found this to be the case as I contemplate the 57-year life of Haruko Muranaka (1932–1990), who passed away in New York on March 20, 1990. Her funeral service was conducted in her beloved hometown of Los Altos, California.

I had met Haruko several times during her visits from New York for her family members' funeral services. I knew that she was a teacher possessing personal charm and warmth, but I didn't learn the extent of her teaching excellence until I was informed that she had been selected as the 1989 Teacher of the Year for the State of New York!

A close friend/teacher noted this honor was well deserved, remarking, "She was an excellent teacher. There was one pupil, for example, who was thought to be mentally retarded, but Haruko did not believe it. She worked with him extensively, in class and in tutoring sessions after school. Today, this 'mentally retarded student' is working toward his doctorate degree."

The late Helen Keller's teacher was called "the miracle worker." Similarly, I believe we can term Haruko's contributions as "like a Bodhisattva." Another Hawaiian *Nisei* educator interpreted the Nembutsu way of life as "a life dedicated to returning to the world what the world has given her." Haruko's life challenges all of us to do just that.

Some time ago, the Buddhist Churches of America theme for the year was "*dana* [the practice of cultivating generosity] is joy." As a teacher of students who had learning difficulties, Haruko undoubtedly had this spirit. Personally, I regret that I did not have the opportunity to know her better, for I believe that my life as a Buddhist minister would have been enriched by her acquaintance.

Lessons from Lady Eshinni's Life

I gave this talk in 1990 at the Ninth World Buddhist Women's Convention in Vancouver, Canada, addressing President Lady Noriko Ohtani, Monshu Emeritus Kosho Ohtani, President Emeritus Lady Yoshiko Ohtani, Hongwanji Bishop Fujioto, Host Bishop Murakami, ministers, convention members of the Buddhist Churches of Canada, Fujinkai members of the convention and other guests.

As we assemble for this Lady Eshinni and Convention Memorial Service, I feel only humility and gratitude as I stand before you as your speaker. I certainly do not deserve nor qualify for this great honor.

The reason that I am here is for no other reason than that I am the grandson of the late Rev. Senju Sasaki, first minister of Vancouver Buddhist Church and the Buddhist Churches of Canada. He was here in Vancouver exactly 85 years ago—from 1905 to 1912. How fortunate I am to have inherited and received this wonderful Buddhist karma!

The late Rev. Shinjo Ikuta, father of Rev. Kyojo Ikuta of Calgary, has described my late grandfather in his Japanese-language book, *Enkakushi (History of the Buddhist Churches of Canada)*, regarding his arrival as follows:

> *"On October 26, 1905, only 14 days following his family's arrival in Vancouver from Japan, with hardly any time to get settled, Rev. Senju Sasaki delivered a talk on the Buddha at Vancouver City Hall. The Dharma talk, heard for the first time in Canada, thundered like the Lion's Roar to the ears of some 500 persons in the audience. The audience was enthralled by the wisdom of the Buddha. Rev. Gendo Nakai of Seattle Buddhist Temple was also in the audience to give moral support..."*

Speaking of support, the behind-the-scenes support for my grandfather was in the person of Grandmother Sasaki. She, indeed, was an *okusan* (person in the rear), *naishitsu* (person within the room) and *bomori* (protector of the temple). My aunt has told me that the duties of the minister and his wife were diversified at the time. The wife was involved in teaching the many Japanese immigrants various skills such as sewing, homemaking and etiquette. She also provided room and board care to bachelor men.

It is appropriate that I speak of *okusan, naishitsu* and *bomori* during this Lady Eshinni service. The subject leads us to the dedicated and spiritual support and faith of Lady Eshinni, wife of Shinran Shonin. I am convinced that it was her presence in his life that allowed Shinran Shonin to lead his life of Nembutsu.

Prince Regent Shotoku Taishi selected three important Mahayana Buddhist sutras that established the doctrinal direction of Japanese Buddhism. *The Sutra on Queen Srimala (Shomangyo)* in Japanese) describes a devout Buddhist practitioner who eventually attained enlightenment. This example of an ideal Buddhist woman, together with the noble One Vehicle salvation teaching for all beings as stressed in the *Lotus Sutra*, along with a depiction of an ideal lay Buddhist as dramatized in the Sutra on *Vimalakirti (Yuimakyo* in Japanese), firmly rooted Buddhism in Japan some 1,400 years ago.

Such was the Buddhist background of Japan into which was born the lady we remember today, known to us now as Lady Eshinni. She was a remarkable, inspirational wife and mother, a person we can emulate as an ideal Buddhist woman.

In preparing for this Dharma talk, I read both the Japanese original and the English translation of the book *Eshinni-sama*, authored by our president emeritus, Lady Yoshiko Ohtani. I was personally very much moved by the dedication of our Zenurakata in bringing to us the relatively unknown message and spirit of Lady Eshinni.

In reading about the life of Lady Eshinni, one cannot help but be awed and amazed by the reverence in which she held her husband, Shinran Shonin. Her famous dream of seeing Shinran Shonin as the Bodhisattva (Kannon Bosatsu), would only come from a person of profound faith. Lady Eshinni's letter to her trusted daughter, Kakushinni, reads: "Although I never told your father about the dream in which I saw him as an incarnation of Kannon Bosatsu, since then, I never regarded him as just an ordinary person and continued to serve him. I hope that you, too, will appreciate him the same way."

Not only was Lady Eshinni a woman of profound faith, but she has impressed me as a most caring mother. There are many instances of this in her letters; for example:

> *"Especially since you are my youngest offspring, I think of you fondly. I shall probably never have the opportunity of seeing you again, but it is unbearable that I do not hear from you as to how you are getting along... and I often think of your children and would like to hear the most recent news about them. I would really like to know about your oldest child. Oh, will there ever be a chance for me to visit you, or for you to come to see me once more while I am alive? Most likely not..."*

Furthermore, I believe that Lady Eshinni became a complete, total person though enduring hardships of life she encountered in Echigo Province. In letter Number 4, she wrote these words, following the passing of Shinran:

> *"This year I have turned 82 years old. From the 11th month of the year before last to the fifth month of last year, my illness was so severe that every day I expected to die at any moment, but somehow I am still living. But I may die of starvation because of this year's famine. I am saddened that, in spite of this good opportunity to send you something, I am unable to send you anything since your father's death, but there is nothing I can do. Please relay to Masukata the gist of this letter. Since it is an effort for me to write, I will not be writing to Masukata."*

Lady Eshinni's life points out two aspects of Buddhism/Jodo-Shinshu: *Nyushin no Jun-en* (the way of faith by the regular, direct approach, such as reading, reflecting and learning from teachers) and *Gyakuen* (the reverse, indirect approach to entering the Nembutsu or way of Dharma). I would say that *Jun-en* was the Nembutsu life given to Lady Eshinni in her devotion to her husband-teacher. *Gyakuen* was the Nembutsu life deepened by her life of hardship. This all-encompassing approach, by which an imperfect human being can be transformed and lead a life of the highest good, has universal appeal to us who are about to enter the 21st century.

Living Amida's Light: A Life of Reflection

This article, which was published as a BCA Theme, offers some thoughts on the Buddhist values of self-reflection and awareness.

"Enlightenment," "non-attachment," "faith," "other shore," "oneness," "harmony" and "Pure Land" are all familiar Buddhist terms. Although we use these terms freely in Buddhist conversation, they are difficult concepts to truly understand for various reasons.

One of the ways we might look at these ideals is by contrasting each of them with their opposites. The opposite of enlightenment is ignorance and illusion; the antonym for non-attachment is attachment or grasping; faith, when translated as true mind, is contradicted by false mind; other shore is different from this shore; oneness, from division and many-ness; harmony, from conflict/contradiction; and finally, Pure Land's opposite is this imperfect, suffering world. These very opposite and contradicting ideas actually describe our daily lives. They are also the very reason why the Buddha Dharma came to be.

This should not be hard to comprehend upon self-reflection. However, non-reflection seems to be the rule rather than the exception in the way we conduct our lives. How can we learn to be more aware of our true selves?

There are numerous Buddhist symbols and parables that point out the human predicament caused by non-reflection. Buddhist symbols such as the Wheel of Life (dharmacakra) and parables, such as the ones of the burning house or the white path and raging river, illustrate vividly the truth of our ignorance of ourselves and the workings of Amida.

The familiar Buddhist wheel is more than just a symbol of Buddhism and Buddhist temples. A real story of the Indian design with its profound meaning should stir us out of our daily doldrums of mental stagnation, boredom and constant repetition of acts of arrogance and foolishness. The wheel basically represents the six imperfect worlds of karma (hell, hunger, constant fighting, beasts, human beings and heaven). According to Buddhist thinking, the wheel is vigorously turned or rotated by the three poisons of ignorance, greed and hate.

The *Lotus Sutra,* a Mahayana sutra, is best known for its parable of children playing in a burning house. The story describes how a father (symbolizing Buddha) leads his children (living beings) from afar, out of their burning house (life of karma sufferings) by use of various *upaya* (wise means). The *upaya,* furthermore, was applied individually to the differing needs (symbolizing the various capacities and paths of seekers) of each child. The parable concludes by pointing out that there really was but one Great Path in the final analysis.

The burning house parable is a favorite of Buddhist scholars because of its simplicity as well as its generalities. Students of Buddhism are fascinated by this quality that leaves room for many interpretations. When we read it, we come to see that we are no different from the children in the story. The children are totally engrossed in the pursuit of pleasure in their playing and are unaware of the burning of the house or the fervent calling of the father.

Another parable, that of the raging river and white path, is one of Pure Land Buddhism. In the climax of the drama, a lone traveler is forced to make a choice, as he is pursued to a raging water, between two hazardous conditions. If he retreats, he might be killed by his pursuers; if he attempts to cross a narrow white path over the raging river, he might fall in. Can he trust in the call of Amida Buddha on the other side of the river that he will not fall? This parable illustrates the way of Nembutsu in a most dramatic, poignant way. It points out our hazardous life situation that we must acknowledge. At the same time that this deep realization is attained, the urgency, need and importance of a personal decision to follow the path of truth or faith is revealed.

And yet, we seem to keep repeating the same mistakes in "turning the wheel of life." The speed of this rotation is further accelerated by what Buddhism teaches are other minor poisons (in addition to the aforementioned three major ones): laziness, unbelief, shamelessness, arrogance, concealment, etc. The list numbers 108!

Our problem is that we continue to sleep right through this turbulence by not opening our eyes or not acknowledging our true state. According to the Dharma, this is similar to an inebriated person claiming that he is unaffected by or strong enough to overcome the drunkenness caused by the liquor he has consumed. The Japanese word for an alarm clock (*mezamashi dokei*) is derived from the Buddhist idea of awakening *(mezame)*. The goal of Buddhism is simple and clear like the ringing of an alarm clock for a sleeping person submerged in a world of dreams and nightmares... it tells him to wake up to reality!

A life of reflection based upon Amida's light makes this awakening possible. It is like looking at ourselves in front of a mirror. Without both a mirror and light, there is no way we can see ourselves. Amida's light is one that penetrates beneath and beyond the surface of the skin. Let us look at ourselves in the mirror with this light, which can change the person who has hitherto been a mystery, even to himself, into a self of awareness, joy and gratitude.

The Mountain View Buddhist Temple:
My Cultural, Social and Spiritual Home

Dr. Kenneth K. Tanaka, professor of Buddhist Studies at Musashino University in Tokyo, recorded these recollections of his experiences at the Mountain View Buddhist Temple.

Starting Out

As I look back to 1960, the year when I started attending the "church" (that's how we used to refer to it), what I see is the Sangha Hall and the Reverend's house. The Mountain View Buddhist Temple was nowhere near the large complex that it is today. The church was surrounded by open fields in all four directions, with only a few buildings and houses standing here and there.

I had just quit going to the Seventh Adventist Church in town, which I had attended for about a year and a half. I had found it no longer satisfying, and the move to a new house on the other side of El Camino Real opened up a chance to attend the Buddhist Church. Mrs. Murakami, our new next door neighbor, insisted we go to the Buddhist Church, and Mrs. Hamada, our neighbor, was kind enough to drive my brothers and me to the church.

Initially, I hesitated going to the Buddhist church since my family knew hardly anyone, having arrived in the U.S. a few years earlier. We were FOBs ("fresh off the boat") in the community. In fact, that was what I was called, half-jokingly, by one of my Sunday school classmates. It didn't take long for my hesitation at the new church to dissipate, as I felt comfortable with the church environment. In particular, I enjoyed the Sunday service and the Sunday school classes. There were so many kids our age; there must have been at least 35 students in the Sunday school eighth-grade class taught by Mrs. May Shimoguchi.

Minister

The minister at the time was Rev. Sensho Sasaki, the father of Rev. LaVerne Sasaki. His sermons were in "broken" English, but the students listened attentively, even though we didn't understand the details. The services, too, were well attended with least 250 students (kindergarten to high school seniors) every Sunday morning, and extra chairs had to be set up to accommodate the overflow of students on the stage located on the opposite end of the hall from the altar.

At the end of the service, we would go up to do the offering of incense and then line up in a single file to greet and shake hands with Rev. Sasaki near the exit door. What I still recall vividly is the warmth and the softness of *Sensei's* hand and his warm smile. It symbolized for me the sense of welcome that I felt at the church and the positive image of Buddhism. The warm hands and the smile were certainly expressions of Sasaki-*sensei's* personality and his innate ability to make you feel at home.

In those days, the temple had an "at home" or a "mom and pop" atmosphere. I saw many of the old-time members visiting Sensei's parsonage at any time of the day. It must have been hard on Mrs. Sasaki, who served tea and often invited them to stay for meals, members who dropped by their house without any advance notice. Yes, I realize that in those days that's how ministers and their wives served the membership, but, nevertheless, it too must have been difficult on the wives and the children, who could not have the same kind of privacy as ordinary families. I am sure as we look back, there were the positives and the negatives for everyone involved, but the one certain thing was that the temple was not only a spiritual, but a social and cultural "home."

Dedicated Church People

Within this "at home" environment, I witnessed the presence of many members who were deeply spiritual, living the life of Nembutsu and quietly demonstrating their devotion and commitment to Buddhism by being selflessly involved in the many programs at the church. The vibrant Sunday school program that I talked about earlier is one good example. Another program was the YBA (Young Buddhist Association), which grew large as we baby boomers reached high school age. So at one point, we had 100 members, whose number today would be unthinkable.

Speaking of dedicated people, I cannot go without mentioning the wonderful YBA advisors we were privileged to have, particularly Mr. and Mrs. Hiro Sugimoto and Mr. and Mrs. Kay Ikeuye. They spent untold hours attending the numerous meetings and taking us places, whether on ski trips, to YBA conferences or to district meetings. Without their dedication and the support of the church, I would not have been able to participate in the YBA, where I made lifelong friends, particularly, Sterling Makishima, Ken Nakano and Dennis Tsukagawa. Also, YBA is where I was able to meet people beyond the hometown and be given opportunities to develop my leadership skills, which helped me eventually to serve as WYBL (Western Young Buddhist League) President, NYBA (National Young Buddhist Association) President and RAB (Relevant American Buddhist) co-founder and national coordinator.

Another of the dedicated people was Mr. Yas Shimoguchi, who like Mr. Sugimoto and Mr. Ikeuye, have passed on to the Pure Land, but knowing them, they are now continuing to serve others as Bodhisattvas. As a temple leader, Mr. Shimoguchi cared deeply about the youths and would listen to what we had to say. He heard our wish for a gymnasium and helped to get it approved by the board. The result is the magnificent gymnasium that is the pride of the temple today.

Influences on My Life and Profession

All of these causes and conditions led me to eventually become a minister and scholar of Buddhism, allowing me to make a living by doing things that I enjoy, that is, learning about Buddhism and sharing it with others through teaching and writing. As I write this essay, I am currently a professor of Buddhism and the director of the Institute of Buddhist Culture at Musashino University, a Jodo Shinshu-based college in Tokyo of about 6,000 students. I am also an active member of several academic associations, including the International Association of Shin Buddhist Studies, of which I currently serve as president, and the Japanese Association of Buddhism and Psychology, which I co-founded three years ago. Before moving to Japan in 1998, I taught at the Institute of Buddhist Studies for 11 provocative years from 1984 to 1995 and served as the resident minister at the Southern Alameda County Buddhist Church for three enjoyable years from 1995 to 1998.

This meaningful life as scholar and minister of Buddhism would not have been possible without the spiritual environment of the Mountain View Church as expressed through Rev. Sensho Sasaki and the many deeply religious people and the activities that they promoted.

The other important factor was my being able to attend the monthly Buddhist study classes conducted by Rev. LaVerne Sasaki during my high school days. *Sensei* came once a month from Stockton to conduct the classes in English. This was a delight for those yearning to study Buddhism more seriously in English. I was one of them, for I had begun to have existential questions about life and death, impermanence and of the proverbial "meaning of life."

Around age 13, I began to think about many such existential questions, but the Christian church that I first attended could not fulfill my needs. I could not understand why an omnipotent and all-loving God could have created a world filled with so much suffering, stemming from wars, interpersonal discord and family conflicts. So, by the early high school years, I was looking for a place that would address these questions. And they began to be addressed at Rev. LaVerne's English study classes. *Sensei* was so good at systematically presenting the teachings from basic Buddhism to Mahayana Buddhism and to Jodo Shinshu teachings. The classes were extremely interesting, and I believe that I did not miss a single class for the three years that I attended during those high school years.

Rev. Sasaki's classes helped me to take greater interest in studying, which was not the case during my early years of high school. However, by my senior year, I began to study harder and managed to do better academically. This interest in my studies picked up during my first year at San Jose State College. The growing confidence in my academic ability was strengthened by my involvement in the YBA, including my participation in the oratorical contests held in the years 1967 and 1968. And when I decided to apply to Stanford as a sophomore transfer, all these activities certainly helped, as did the recommendation letter that Rev. Sasaki kindly wrote on my behalf. My acceptance to Stanford University in the spring of 1968 changed my life, for it opened many doors, including the conditions for meeting my wife, Kimie, of 35 years and the current position at Musashino University in Tokyo.

The Future

So, it is not an understatement to say that I would not be where I am today without the Mountain View Buddhist Temple and all the people there, who helped to nurture my social, academic and spiritual dimensions. And this fact has enabled me to achieve many of the worldly goals in life, as well as to have come to some spiritual understanding through the Dharma, for which I am profoundly grateful.

The Buddhist teaching reminds us that "life is impermanent," which means not only that we grow old, but that change comes much faster than we think or want. I cannot believe that I am now 69 years old, for in my early 20s we used to say those over 30 were "over the hill." Well, I certainly don't feel "over the hill." In fact, I feel that I have reached a "mature" stage in my life, when I can "bring it all home" by drawing from all that I have experienced and learned by producing a few more books and getting my students at Musashino to appreciate the Dharma for making their lives more meaningful and worth living.

I am certain that my aspirations will be fulfilled, for I have been nurtured by the compassionate workings of Amida, which symbolizes for me the immeasurable life and light that have protected and encouraged me throughout my life. And I would not have felt this way had I not in 1962 met up with the two senseis and the many devout and dedicated members at the Mountain View Buddhist Church, my cultural, social and spiritual home.

Namo Amida Butsu.

Rev. Sensho and Mrs. Kinuko Sasaki
I am grateful to Hiroji Kariya for sharing these memories.

When Rev. Sensho Sasaki first came the Mountain View Buddhist Temple (MVBT) as its first resident minister, I was a member of the Palo Alto Buddhist Temple. Rev. Motoyama of PABT [the Palo Alto Buddhist Temple] was to meet him at lunch, and I was invited to join them. That was my first meeting with Rev. Sasaki.

A few months later, my family and I moved to Mountain View from East Palo Alto. One of the first things I did after moving to Mountain View was to go to see Rev. Sasaki to ask to become a member of the Mountain View Buddhist Temple and was welcomed warmly by both Rev. and Mrs. Sasaki. Since that time, I relied on both for guidance and advice and had the privilege of working closely with them on Temple and BCA [Buddhist Churches of America] matters.

MVBT had newly become an independent temple in the Buddhist Churches of America, and Rev. and Mrs. Sasaki guided the temple in establishing itself as a member temple along with all the other longtime temples of the BCA. Among other things, they developed the "personality" or the collective character of the membership, which I think still prevails in our membership.

There is one incident that I would like to relate that tells how open Sensei was and how committed he was for the betterment of the temple. As everyone knew, he was a rabid SF Giants baseball fan. So much so that he would attend meetings with an earphone in his ear, listening to the baseball game. There were many members of the Women's Association who were just as rabid, or more, fans of the Giants. One day the president of the Fujinkai complained to me that Sensei was more interested in the Giants' baseball game than the Fujinkai activities. As I was president of the temple at the time, I felt it my responsibility to talk to Sensei about how the ladies felt.

At the risk of incurring his anger, I talked to him about it. I told him that most of the ladies at the Fujinkai meetings were just as strong fans of the Giants as he, but that they would forego listening to the Giants game to take care of Fujinkai business which they felt were more important. They were taking their responsibilities seriously. Instead of getting angry, Sensei thanked me for telling him, that he was not aware that the ladies relied on him so much for support. He also gave up the Giants' broadcasts during Fujinkai meetings.

Rev. Sasaki was very easy to talk to. He gave good advice and encouraged the temple leaders to make responsible decisions. I relied a lot on Mrs. Sasaki for help. When I was president of the BCA, I had to make a speech in Japanese at a banquet where there would be hundreds of Japanese guests in attendance. It was a daunting responsibility for me. Mrs. Sasaki came to my rescue and wrote my speech for me, and I survived the evening without trouble.

There were many other ways in which Mrs. Sasaki helped me. I will be forever grateful for all Rev. and Mrs. Sasaki gave to the temple and to me.

7

ON THE CUSP OF A NEW CENURY: SAN FRANCISCO, 1990–2000

A Global City

In 1990, Rev. Ken Yamaguchi, the minister of the Buddhist Church of San Francisco, passed away, and the bishop asked me to serve there. After nearly 20 years in Mountain View, my roots were deep in that community, but I accepted the new assignment.

It was an opportunity to serve in a truly global city. During my tenure as minister in San Francisco, I had the opportunity to meet the emperor and empress of Japan, Pope John Paul and the Dalai Lama—occasions that would never have arisen in a small town or the suburbs.

I also became active in the Japanese American Religious Federation, which led to participation in a national interfaith group, the Interfaith Alliance,[52] based in Washington, DC. At the time, I was the only Buddhist representative. Today, the organization has representatives from many faith traditions.

My community outreach activities did not align completely with my Jodo Shinshu superiors' priorities, which reflected more of a focus on the Japanese American community. I am, however, a passionate believer that we must be connected to our larger society—both for the greater good and for the good of the church.[53]

---

[52] According to its mission, the Interfaith Alliance "celebrates religious freedom by championing individual rights, promoting policies that protect both religion and democracy, and uniting diverse voices to challenge extremism."

[53] See other chapters including "Community Service" for more on this topic.

San Francisco itself and the diversity of its constituency encouraged this broader perspective. The current minister, Rev. Ron Kobata, has continued critical community outreach activities, establishing the church's reputation as a welcoming place for the LGBT community.

Young Adults

By this time, our children were young adults, so we did not have to worry about the impact of the change in my church assignment on their lives. Better yet, they took an active role in the San Francisco church's Young Adult Buddhist Association, revitalizing the group.

As the years went on, I had the privilege of officiating at their weddings.

Brian, a graduate of San Jose State who lives in San Diego and works in biotechnology sales, married Lorin Tomiyama in a ceremony I co-officiated at the Buddhist Temple of San Diego. They now have three kids, Hailey, Chad and Jenna.

Sharon, who graduated with a degree in biochemistry from the University of California, Berkeley, and went on to work in biotech marketing in San Diego, married her husband, Robert Yamamoto, in a wedding I conducted in their living room. They have two children, Zoe and Ava.

Stanton, a graduate of San Jose State University who currently works for an HMO, married Lisa Iino in a ceremony I co-officiated in Orange County. Their kids are Jared and Katelyn.

Ellen, a University of California, Davis, graduate, certified as an elementary school teacher, married her husband, Gus Maseba, at the San Francisco church during my tenure as minister. She is currently at home with her four kids, Lindsey, Emily, Molly and Mitchell.

Rina, a University of California, Los Angeles, sociology graduate who went on to work in the financial sector, is the only one of our children to marry someone without Japanese ancestry. I presided at the ceremony in Montreal, where her husband Eric Vignola's family lived (although the marriage wasn't legally recognized until I signed a certificate back in California). Our whole family flew there for the event. Rina takes their children, Odin and Bodhi, to Buddhist church.

In fact, all five of our children remain involved in Jodo Shinshu Buddhism.

Compassion: Heart of the Buddha (*Hotoke No Kokoro, Daijihishin*)

This was the New Year's Dharma message in 1991 from my whole family, setting the theme for the church for the year.

The spirit of Buddha's compassion (*jihi* in Japanese) is not only a common Buddhist expression, but the heart of our Shin Buddhist religion. If wisdom is the Buddha mind, compassion is its outward expression.

Compassion is defined in the dictionary as a "feeling of deep sympathy and sorrow for another who is stricken by suffering or misfortune, accompanied by a strong desire to alleviate the pain or remove its cause."

From the Buddhist point of view, we are all suffering—physically, financially, etc. To some people, their suffering is unbearable; they resort to suicide to remove life's pain.

If such suffering is the truth of life, compassion is the only source to peaceful and meaningful life.

I once attended a town forum in Palo Alto on the "drug crisis in America," which supported the broad use of compassion. A clinical psychologist said that 90 percent of the drug addicts that he counsels do not need medication. All most of them need is the human contact of expression of love and care.

Compassion is the truest form of communication between human beings. The power of compassion can bring together the temple, community, family and the world.

I like the Japanese Buddhist expression, "*Kokoro to kokoro no fureai*" (the coming together of one person's mind with another's). This interpretation of compassion expresses the necessary link that can unite in harmony to avoid a potential problem, conflict or even violence.

Expression of human compassion is not mere passion and feeling alone. It must be based upon wisdom—that complete understanding that enables one to see life and its situations with all connecting causes and conditions.

We, as Buddhists, are blessed with this potential power by opening our hearts and minds to the Buddha. What greater objective can we have as Buddhists?

May we find within ourselves this spirit of Buddha's compassion. We can then express it within our family and greater community.

In deep retrospection, life is too short, incomplete and unworthy to merely enjoy *personal* pleasures. May we live more complete, joyous lives within Buddha's and Shinran's teachings. Only then, can the new year be a truly HAPPY new year. May joy be with you and your family in the Dharma and Nembutsu. May we become a San Francisco Buddhist Church of true Sangha through the understanding and appreciation of Buddha's compassion.

The Growing Popularity of Buddhism
This article in the Buddhist Church of San Francisco's newsletter, Geppo, appeared in March 1991.

Although Buddhism is regarded as an Asian religion, the growth of interest in Buddhism in the nations of the world will soon make it a true world religion.

I once attended a lecture at San Jose State University. It was not a class on Buddhism, but a course, Religion: Death and Dying, with a strong emphasis on Buddhism (as well as other Asian views) as related to this vital human subject. It was attended by some 150 to 200 students!

The growing popularity of Buddhism (Zen, Tibetan, Chinese and Theravada) among Americans is evidenced by various activities and well-known persons publicly declaring their Buddhist faith.

Rev. Shoko Masunaga, a retired Walnut Grove minister, was the first Buddhist chaplain at the California State Assembly in Sacramento. Rev. Hiroshi Abiko was appointed as a Buddhist chaplain[58] at the Palo Alto Veterans Administration Hospital; leading universities and colleges are offering postgraduate and undergraduate degrees and courses in Buddhist Studies; well-known persons in the world of entertainment and sports, such as Tina Turner, Orlando Cepeda and Patrick Duffy, are Buddhists; California Governor Jerry Brown practiced meditation at the Santa Cruz and San Francisco Zen centers. I once read in a leading magazine that some 25,000 persons attended a Tibetan Buddhist retreat in Colorado. I am, furthermore, sure that there are many, many other "closet Buddhists" who practice, but do not publicly state their private beliefs.

What does this all mean to us of San Francisco Buddhist Church? I believe that this growing interest in Buddhism will challenge us in different ways. First of all, if we are to be sincere Buddhist temple members, we must

---

[54] At one point, I inquired about being a Buddhist chaplain in the military. I was very interested, but unfortunately you had to be under age 40. A chaplain serves institutions without a church. It is a way of life to help and give peace, comfort and wisdom to help others live this life more peacefully.

study and know our Buddhist teachings as taught to us with Jodo Shinshu Buddhist traditions. Secondly, if we are to communicate well with our neighbors, non-Buddhist relatives (and growing numbers of non-Buddhist in-laws), job peers, non-Buddhist friends and other members of the community, we truly need to practice and know our religion.

I, furthermore, hope that we fully utilize the great Buddhist tradition and legacy given to us by our parents and ancestors.

Senior Citizen!?

These reflections were first printed in the Buddhist Church of San Francisco's Dharma Corner in 1995.

Having achieved an important milestone of my life—age 65—I share with you some of my thoughts...

I am reminded of Buddha's description of human life as consisting of birth, sickness, old age and death. Now that I have experienced 3/4 of them, the last stage is approaching; the subject of death seems not so remote as it was even 10 years ago. The subject of my eventual inevitable death must be dealt with as the most important fact in my future (of this life and beyond). This is relayed to us at funeral services in the epistle titled "White Ashes" by Rennyo Shonin.

Even as a professional minister who officiates at many pillow services [a brief rite conducted upon death in the presence of others at the bedside] and funerals before the deceased persons' bodies, my senior status now forces me to view these events in a more personal way. Actually, I do not have to be labeled by a doctor as a "terminal patient." Our lives will terminate, whether it be a day, a week, a month or years from now. However, realizing that my death is now more imminent, the Dharma and Nembutsu have become more real and, therefore, more appreciated.

Simple daily events and meetings with people have become more precious and meaningful. It seems that we take for granted all the ordinary things and events in our lives until time becomes limited. I can never forget the conversation that I had with a Buddhist friend, who had terminal cancer. He lived in the San Joaquin delta town of Walnut Grove. He told me that he had never noticed the little things that he passed every day during his drive on the levee roads; now he savored the sight of every tree, shrub and curve. During the "prime time" of his life, his thoughts were always about things that pertained to the future. Now he was living in the present, mindful and thankful for everything around him.

The Japanese expression *meinichi* refers to the day of the month that a person died. Literally, however, it means "day of life." The day of death means day of life? This apparent contradiction has a Buddhist message. When we are living, we are not truly living; it is a very temporary life. The Japanese *gatha* [song] *"Nori No Miyama"* (mountain of profound Dharma) states that our human life is temporary and floating, similar to a bubble, ready to burst at any moment; it is like one short night. Even personally, as I look back upon my 65 years, my childhood, teenage years, college years and professional career often seem like parts of a dream, an illusion. The "dreams" are made "real" by memories, photographs, recordings and writings. Our memories become more and more faint as time goes by. What will then remain? Our true life begins when we pass through this life.

What message can we receive from the above observation? What is "true life"? Can we live a life of hope, strength and optimism in spite of the fact that our human life is so fleeting? The message of Shinran Shonin states that Amida Buddha arose from wisdom and compassion to specifically focus on living beings who suffer the consequences of ignorance, anger and greed. His practice and vow assures us of birth in the Pure Land. We need only to open ourselves up by listening, reflecting and accepting. In gratitude, the Nembutsu, *Namo Amida Butsu* comes to our lips. I believe that this gratitude becomes real when we understand the nature of ourselves, that we are surrounded and constantly sustained by other living beings and innumerable favorable conditions. Often, we must undergo great suffering or upheaval in our lives to truly appreciate this fact. Becoming a senior citizen helps!

Senior citizen!? The exclamation point and question mark are not indications of anger or surprise, nor of fear or mystery. To me, they represent my feelings of gratitude for the assurance of hope and joy within the Dharma and Nembutsu.

Personal Memories of Past Bishops
of the BCA and Ministers of the Buddhist Church of San Francisco

This article, which appeared in the June 1996 issue of Dharma Corner, recognizes the many influential figures who devoted themselves to the BCA.

The Japanese language theme of the 75th anniversary of the BCA (1974) was "*Aoide Kansha, Mukaete Yakushin*" (with reverence and gratitude for the past, we progress into the future). I feel this deeply as we look forward to our annual BCA Bishops and BCSF Ministers Memorial Service on June 23rd (guest speaker, Rev. David Matsumoto of IBS). I would like to share with you some personal impressions and memories of my senior *senseis*.

Bishop Kenju Masuyama (1930–1936): Father of the late Rev. Kenyu Masuyama, he was president of both Kyoto Women's University and Ryukoku University. He was known to be a traditional Japanese-style leader whose authority was respected and admired.

Bishop Ryotai Matsukage (1938–1948): I was a teenager when he visited my father in Sacramento in the post-World War II years. His style as bishop was said to be different from his predecessor in that he was more outwardly personable and friendly. I remember that he was fond of sake and soba.

Bishop Enryo Shigefuji (1948–1958): He was the bishop who wished me well in my Buddhist studies in Japan as he saw me off at the San Francisco pier in 1953. His major study in Buddhism was the same as mine, Genshin's *Ojoyoshu (Collection of Essential Passages on the Absolute Birth)*.

Bishop Shinsho Hanayama (1958–1968): Bishop Hanayama was my lead Buddhist teacher during my 1953-1958 period of study at Tokyo University. He was as a father/teacher to me, as he and his family treated me like a family member. Outside of my own family, *sensei* was the most influential in my Buddhist life, as a person and as a minister.

Rev. Senju Sasaki (1922–1925): My grandfather served our Buddhist Church before I was born. My direct recollection of him is limited to when I visited Japan (Kozenji Temple in Fukui) in 1935. I was told that he was quite a storyteller and lover of English and American studies. As the first minister of Canada and Vancouver, he gave a Buddhist talk before the Vancouver City Council. When he lived in Singapore, he reported to the Japanese government about a planned attack of Japan by a Russian naval fleet; the attack never occurred, perhaps due to his reporting.

Rev. Kenshi Iwao (1925–1926): I knew him when he was a minister of San Luis Obispo Buddhist Temple. A good golfer, he was married to the *Nisei* sister of Kats Tokunaga of San Jose Betsuin.

Rev. Shintatsu Sanada (1935–1945, 1946–1954, 1964–1970): Sanada-*sensei* was a kind, sincere, humble and cordial man. He was the father of

Mrs. Michiko (Rev. Kosho) Yukawa. Older BCSF members probably remember him well, for he served our church for some 26 years in different periods.

Rev. Eiyu Terao (1938–1939): *Sensei* passed away in November 1994, as a retired minister of Alameda. Mrs. Joyce Terao (former Tateyama of Stockton) still resides in Alameda. His sermons were given with enthusiastic joy and power.

Rev. Hoshin Fujikado (1945–1946): I was Rev. Fujikado's associate minister in Stockton in 1960. He was a longtime minister of Senshin, Palo Alto and Marysville Buddhist Churches. He was a minister who was dedicated to the sharing of his Nembutsu faith (*shinjin*).

Rev. Chonen Terakawa (1960–1964) (second term with Rev. Yamaguchi): *Sensei* was a minister of many talents and interests, among them: movie-making, writing, Buddhist art and the San Francisco Giants. His wife continues to attend our Sunday afternoon services. It was a great sadness when his son Shigeru passed away on the first day of his church assignment at Seattle Betsuin. Rev. Terakawa passed away in 1986.

Rev. Ken Yamaguchi (1981–1990): Rev. Yamaguchi is well-remembered as a friendly, caring, bilingual minister with a good sense of humor; he was a lover of good food, parties and karaoke. His sudden passing was a great shock to me, as it was to all who knew him in the BCA. I am indebted to Rev. Yamaguchi for his dedicated leadership and hope to bring to fruition some of his dreams for the church.

How important it is that we remember these *senseis* and others who dedicated their lives to the perpetuation of our Nembutsu teachings and the prosperity of our church, the BCA and the greater Sangha!

The Universal Buddhist Way of Life
Is Not Confined Within the Walls of a Church

The November 1996 edition of Dharma Corner printed these reflections, inspired by my love of sports.

"Doh" *(michi)*, "way" or "path" are terms sometimes used in connection with the way a Buddhist conducts his or her daily life. It is a not a path that most would consider "religious," in that it does not conform to "a faith or belief" that binds to a supreme being. Rather, it is a way in which the person is guided by Dharma truth.

As a sports fan, I am inspired by the Dharma path of Phil Jackson, well-known coach of the Chicago Bulls of NBA championship fame. He describes how Buddhism has influenced him in his book, *Sacred Hoops: Spiritual Lessons of a Hardwood Warrior* (1995). Following are excerpts that I found especially revealing:

> "My brother Joe introduced me to Zen Buddhism. His description of Zen baffled me. How could you have a religion that didn't involve belief in God? What did Zen practitioners do? Joe said that they simply tried to clear their minds and be in the present... To someone raised in a Pentecostal household—where attention was focused more on the hereafter than the here and now—this was a mind-boggling concept...
>
> "My next step was to explore meditation... Then I turned to Zen. It wasn't until the mid-seventies that I started practicing seriously, using Zen Mind, Beginner's Mind, by the late Japanese roshi, Shunryu Suzuki, as my guide... What appealed to me about Zen was its emphasis on clearing the mind...
>
> "What pollutes the mind in the Buddhist view is our desire to get life to conform to our peculiar notion of how things should be, as opposed to how they really are...
>
> "Another aspect of Zen that intrigued me was its emphasis on compassion. The goal of Zen is not just to clear the mind, but to open the heart as well. Awareness is the seed of compassion.
>
> "I learned early that one of the most important qualities of a leader is listening without judgment, or with what Buddhists call bare attention. This sounds easier than it is, especially when the stakes are high and you desperately need your charges to perform. But many of the men I've coached have come from troubled families and need all the support they could get. I find that when I can be truly present with impartial, open awareness, I get a much better feel for the players' concerns than when I try to impose my own agenda."

I've shared these words of Coach Jackson to point out the universality of the Buddhist way. The Sporting News weekly newspaper recently referred to Coach Jackson as "the Basketball Buddha."

The Buddhist Way is not confined within the walls of a church or within religious dogma. The Dharma lives wherever you are and whenever there is awareness. I have no doubt that the way of wisdom and compassion described by Coach Jackson has helped him produce a cohesive basketball team in spite of the difficulties that he must face working with multimillion dollar athletes such as Michael Jordan and Dennis Rodman.

There are many books dealing with Buddhism and sports that support the fact that right mental attitude is critical in achieving high goals. Some titles are: *A Zen Way of Baseball, Zen Running, Zen in the Art of Archery, Communicating with Ki: the Spirit in Japanese Idioms and Sumo* (especially the chapter on *shikiri naoshi*, psychological warfare).

Many Japanese arts are described as paths to peace and harmony in life. They all have Buddhist origins or have been greatly influenced by Buddhism. Included are: *sado* (way of tea), *kado* (way of flower), *kendo* (way of sword), *judo* (way of gentleness), *aikido* (way of spiritual center), *kodo* (way of incense) and *shodo* (way of calligraphy).

Shin Buddhism Is Neither a Religion of Ritual, Nor of Prayer
This article, which ran in the Buddhist Church of San Francisco's Dharma Corner in 1996, reflects on the title of this piece—a statement made by the respected late Dr. Ryukyo Fujimoto of Ryukoku University.

Many Buddhists still cling to the notion that our religion is only a set of beliefs, ritual and even prayer. To these people, our Buddhist way consists of having a home Buddhist shrine (*butsudan*), conducting memorial services, reciting Nembutsu (like a prayer) and stepping into the *hondo* (main shrine room) of churches. These activities, in a true Jodo Shinshu Buddhist sense, are but the product of something more basic and important—personal faith (*shinjin*). Personal faith is to truly hear, feel and accept (receive) the unconditional compassion of Amida Buddha in realization that this compassion is personally directed to my ignorant self, helplessly mired in aimless foolishness, frustration and pain.

A Jodo Shinshu Buddhist Teacher (the late Zuiken Inagaki) expresses this idea as follows: "Without getting rid of foolishness, one is able to attain

Nirvana. Leave them as they are; just as you are, one will be born in the Pure Land."

Shin Buddhism in its true essence is not a ritual. I recall a Zen teacher in a remote rural temple telling me many years ago that Zen priests in famous temples are only "Kabuki actors with gorgeous costumes," referring to their elaborate robes and complex rituals. Ritual, by definition, is only a prescribed procedure, ceremony or formality. Without spiritual awareness or involvement, it is meaningless and superficial. Rituals in themselves are but "pointing fingers" to direct us to the path to discover a personal Buddha.

Shin Buddhism is also not about prayer. Prayer is a petition, request or asking for a favor. Faith (*shinjin*) is not something asked for, but that which is received: a personal awakening or realization of Amida Buddha's great compassionate vow/practice that will allow the person to live a life of joy and peace even amidst life's frustrations and pain.

May we, as followers of Shinran Shonin, walk and live the path of *Namo Amida Butsu*, the life of gratitude.

Religion Should Be a Cause of Unity

It is unfortunate and possibly a testament on the human condition that the title of this section uses the word "should" instead of "is." We Buddhists strive to make religion not a cause of disunity, but the cause of unity of all living beings.

As I noted in a 1997 address at World Religion Day at the Palace of Fine Arts, Buddhism describes our existence as a wheel, consisting of eight spokes and a hub. The wheel—suffering, violence and war—revolves around the hub of three poisons: greed, anger and ignorance.

This is not as pessimistic as it sounds, because the eight spokes of this spinning wheel symbolize the Eightfold Path of Buddhism—cultivation of Right View, Right Thought, Right Speech, Right Conduct, Right Livelihood, Right Speech, Right Mindfulness and Right Meditation. These represent the basic, but difficult, practices that enable one to leave this spinning wheel (karmic world).

When there is freedom from the three poisons, which torment our minds, there is peace of mind that becomes the springboard for uniting those around us. Extended, it spreads to our family, community, nation and the world. In this united world, the world of Oneness as we say, wisdom and compassion prevail over greed, hate and ignorance.

This world of Oneness or Brotherhood (Sangha in Buddhism) follows from these basic Buddhist ideas:

1. All living beings possess Buddha Nature, the potential or seed to become enlightened. The traditional Buddhist greeting when meeting someone is the placing of one's two hands together and bowing; this practice acknowledges that the other is a potential Buddha. Moreover, Buddha Nature is not restricted to human beings, but is in all living beings (animals and plants).

2. An attitude of compassion is founded on the belief that all human beings are basically equal to each other; we only differ because of our individual karma, which is developed by the environment and culture in which we live. We may be born poor or wealthy; become educated or uneducated; be raised in violent circumstances or in a peaceful environment; or encounter conditions that cause us to be wise or ignorant. If the karma was reversed, the violent one might have been the man of peace; the unlearned one, the wise; and the foolish one, a Buddha.

3. The goals of enlightenment, true freedom or peace are said to be possible to all people from the viewpoint of Buddhism. When one finds one's own true path, or the path of wisdom, it would be among the infinite paths (the Buddha described it as 84,000 paths) to enlightenment. Each path is the person's own and therefore to be respected and recognized. Similarly, one cannot be the judge of another person or group's way of life. This is a denial of the others' karma.

4. The Middle Path is another ideal of Buddhism. The Middle Path means the avoidance of all extremes. The Shakyamuni Buddha exemplified the Middle Path when he renounced both the life of leisure and pleasure as a prince and the extreme life of self-torture and self-denial as the way of some spiritual ascetics of India during his day. In practical human terms, one who follows the Middle Path avoids dualism or division. We have a tendency to compare or divide things in two—black and white, good and evil, truth and untruth, love and hate, superiority and inferiority, rich and poor—when their essential nature is one. This division results in much suffering, such as arguments, mistrust, ill feelings, prejudice, wars. The Buddhist way is to transcend these human comparisons so as to understand their basic essence or nature. When we avoid making judgments based on dualism, we live a life of peace, wisdom and compassion.

Gift of Amida Buddha

Here is an insightful story from the article, "Myokonin—Kono ue mo naku subarashii jinsei" (Myokonin—One Who Lives the Greatest of All Lives) by Rev. Joen Amagishi of Saikoji Temple, Osaka, which I translated for Dharma Corner.

A Fujinkai [women's club] lady told me of this happening: "I was with a group of women who were performing cleanup and yard work in the temple compound when we heard some passersby jeering, shouting, 'Look at those holy wonders! What are they trying to prove?' I felt that I was involved in an incident of human foolishness. However, after some pondering, I began to realize that although I was seeing and hearing their actions and words, I did not know their real motive. Was it with good-natured teasing or malicious intent that they expressed themselves? I came to realize the futility of my own mind in judging their words. The Nembutsu way of life teaches me that I, too, am leading a life of foolishness. I am happy when I am praised and angered when criticized. I was too busy to go to the temple when I was young; now I am able to go. As a member of the Fujinkai, I am realizing the wonderful Nembutsu teaching as I participate in temple and yard cleanup. Nembutsu truly gives me peace of mind as Amida Buddha teaches me of my own frailties. I find that even anger can vanish."

I was able to learn an inspirational lesson from a *myokonin* (simple practicing Nembutsu person) living right here in my own town. She was not relating this incident to me as a complaint toward the jeerers. She was telling me that she was learning about herself and was grateful. Amida Buddha functions through me, not when I am without anger and other foolishness, but just as I live each day, aimlessly and foolishly. The way of *Namo Amida Butsu* is the tireless action or working of Amida Buddha showing me a life of peace and joy unexcelled by any good on my part.

Nirvana Day—What Can It Mean for Me?

This article, which appeared in the Dharma Corner newsletter, shares my thoughts on Nirvana Day, the day of the Buddha's physical passing and completion of Nirvana.

On February 15th, we will remember the day of Shakyamuni Buddha's passing. Is there something we might think about in relationship to the peaceful passing he experienced?

A Buddhist minister friend, in his New Year's message referred to the Zen master Takuan, who wrote the character *"yume"* (dream) just before he died. He mentioned this in describing his thoughts about another year's passing, at a "fearsome pace."

His note made me reflect on my own life. The definition of the word dream is a succession of images, thoughts or emotions passing through the mind in sleep. From my early childhood through my years as teenager, student, new minister, husband, father, community representative, etc., up to yesterday, there just remains innumerable passing images, some barely remembered. Do you feel the same?

We then start questioning. What is the purpose and meaning of life? Why do we educate ourselves, raise a family, become so devoted to our occupations, indulge in hobbies and activities?

As we have just stepped into the new year, we might look at practical ways that we can change our attitudes/lifestyles to be in tune with Buddha's Eightfold Path.[55]

1. Try to look at issues from the other person's viewpoint.
2. Try to focus on the better side of the other person.
3. Try to be a good example to others.
4. Try a little harder to do a better job.
5. Be more gentle and thoughtful in what you say.
6. Try to do more for others in and outside the workplace.
7. Try to diligently and faithfully do our tasks.
8. Try to find time to meditate (quiet the mind and reflect).

Obon, Obon, It's Festival Day

The rhythmic song sung during Obon Service (a Japanese Buddhist tradition honoring ancestors) goes: "O, the streets are lined with our lanterns gay, and the wind bells twinkling atop the trees, sway to and fro, to and fro in the breeze. Obon, Obon, it's festival day!"

---

[55] The Eightfold Path is represented by Right Views, Right Thoughts, Right Conduct, Right Effort, Right Speech, Right Livelihood, Right Mindfulness and Right Meditation. This represented part of Shakyamuni Buddha's first sermon.

With Mrs. Moto Tanaka
(Tokyo Asoka Hospital) on right, Jan 5, 1956

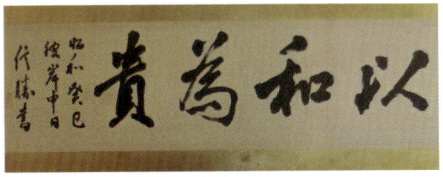

Shotoku Taishi quote, "Wa o motte to-
toshi to nasu" by Dr. Shinsho Hanayama

A little shrimp with the mighty Grand Champion
Chiyonoyama, Dewanoumi-beya, Tokyo, Jan 5, 1956

International Buddhist Association (IBA), with Revs. Taitetsu Unno, Kiyoshi Yamashita and
David Iwamoto, Tsukiji Honganji, Tokyo, 1956

Kyoshi Ministerial Ordination, August 1957 with Rev. Tetsuo Unno, now Mrs. Teruko (Susumu) Ikuta, Rev. Shiro Nishii, Rev. Kiyoshi Matsukuma (Hawaii)

New Sacramento Buddhist Church Ground-breaking ceremony (Riverside and X Street) with Rev. Sensho Sasaki and Mr. Kanichi Kataoka, Minister's Aide, October 1958

With my Zen teacher Rev. Gazan Watanabe, 1958

Arrival of Bishop and Mrs Shinsho Hanayama with Rev. & Mrs. S. Sasaki, Rev. & Mrs. Sakow, Mrs. Fujinaga, Rev. & Mrs. Terakawa, May 9, 1960

Wedding Photo,
July 1, 1962, Stockton, CA

Old Stockton Buddhist Church (148 W. Washington St., now freeway). Bishop Shinsho Hanayama, Rev. Tesshin Shibata, Rev. LaVerne Sasaki, and Northern CA Ministers

Stockton Buddhist Church Ground-breaking Ceremony, Frank Kosugi, Don Yamaoka, Rev. Tesshin Shibata, Ted Oseto, Bishop Kenryu Tsuji, Art Hisaka, Rev. LaVerne

Family Holiday Card, Sharon, Rina, Ellen, Stanton in front, Brian in back, 1970

1972 BCA Ministerial Meeting, Dad's final before his passing.

Dad's funeral, Mtn. View, 1972

Rev. Sensho Sasaki Funeral Casket departure, led by Bishop Kenryu Tsuji, Rev. K. Fujinaga, and Pallbearers, March 13, 1972

Stockton Buddhist Temple Stone Lantern, gift from sister city Shimizu

BCA 75th Anniversary with Abbot Kosho Ohtani, Stanton, Sharon, Kent Sakae, 1974

At Old Mtn. View Buddhist Temple with Dad's final Japanese service word on blackboard *Sen* (stained, tainted by ignorance), 1977

Mtn. View Buddhist Temple Dedication, with Sharon, Stanton, Brian, Ellen, Rina, Helen, me, mother Kinuko, 1979

With Mtn. View Buddhist Women's Association ladies, 1979

With Conrad, Senmaro, Senrey, Conrad's wife, Joyce, Louis, and Helen, Thanksgiving in Sacramento, ca. 1980

Mtn. View Buddhist Temple, with mom Kinuko, Pat Morita, Helen, LaVerne, 1980

Mtn. View Buddhist Temple Cabinet, 1980

Mtn. View Temple Choir, 1979

LaVerne, Helen, Sharon, volunteer ushers at 1984 Summer Olympics, Los Angeles Memorial Coliseum

BCA Ministers Basketball, 1985. Front: Yoshiaki Takemura, Ken Fujimoto, Akio Miyaji, Jay Shinseki, Ken Tanaka, Charles Hasegawa. Back: Newton Ishiura, Ron Nakasone, George Shibata, Gerald Sakamoto, Kanya Okamoto, Ron Kobata, me, Masaaki Yamamoto, Will Masuda, Nobuo Miyaji, Bob Oshita

Bike Ride with Nat-chan Kikuchi, Nagoya, 1985

Rev. & Mrs. Shojun Bando and me, Tokyo

25th Wedding Anniversary Party, June 22, 1987

Mtn. View Rotary Club event, 1987

Frank and Yuki Yokoi, 50th Anniversary, with children Tom, Florence, Helen, Marge, and Steve, 1987

Mtn. View Home, Mrs. Chizu Iwanaga, Mrs. Yumi Hojo, Aunt Masako Sakow

BCSF Welcome Luncheon with Mr. Hiroshi and Mrs. Sadako Kashiwagi, 1990

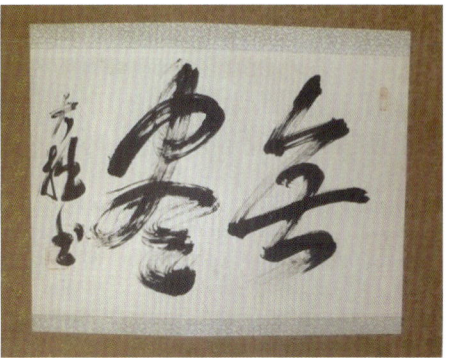

"Mujin" calligraphy scroll by D.T. Suzuki, which was a farewell gift from Rev. Gido Undo

With BCSF Buddhist Women's Association members, 1990

With Helen, Ellen, Hokyo family, Tokyo, 1992

Interfaith Wesak Service, Buddhist Church of San Francisco, 1994

BCSF Young Adult Buddhist Association, 1994

With San Francisco Buddhist Women's Association ladies, 1994

Family at BCSF Stupa containing Buddha's relics (gift from King of Thailand)

Rev. & Mrs. Gido Undo at BCSF with Bishop Seigen Yamaoka, Rev. Seikan Fukuma, and Masako Iwase of BCA, ca. 1995

San Francisco Buddhist Council with Dr. Ken Tanaka and Ven. Seelawimala

Yokoi family reunion, Sacramento, 1997

San Francisco Japanese American Religious Federation, 1998, when I served as President

Templo Budista Ekoji (with Rev. G. Takemura), Mexico City, Dec 13, 2003

With Abbot Koshin Ohtani, Lady Noriko Ohtani, Helen, daughter Sharon and family, Nishi Hongwanji, Kyoto, April 2012

But why is it a festival of joy? Why is there street dancing? Why is it one of the major Buddhist holidays?

The tradition is based on the *Ullambana Sutra*, which tells the story of Maha Maudgalyayana (Mokuren in Japanese), a disciple of the Buddha, who uses his supernatural powers to check on his deceased mother. He was disturbed to find she was suffering in the World of Extreme Hunger.

The disciple asked the Buddha how he could help her and was told to make offerings to Buddhist monks who had just finished their summer retreat. He did, and his mother was released. Appreciating the freedom of his mother, he danced in joy.[56]

As I wrote for the July 1997 issue of *Dharma Corner*, there is a sharp contrast between the word "Obon" and "Ullambana," which in Sanskrit literally means "hanging upside down in extreme suffering."

The traditional interpretation of Obon is a time when food, flowers, money and other material things are offered and sutras chanted in order to sooth the torments of the deceased in the hell of hunger.

Our Jodo Shinshu interpretation differs from this traditional interpretation. We offer food, flowers, money and other material things as only an expression of gratitude to Amida Buddha for embracing the torments of our foolish existence with his wisdom and compassion.

Our extreme suffering is changed into joy with the following personal interpretation of Ullambana (Obon):

> *Utmost joy is that joy which comes from the Nembutsu Dharma*
> *Loving kindness is a Buddhist virtue*
> *Lasting diligence is needed to become true Buddhist*
> *A life of selfishness is the cause of extreme suffering*
> *Metta is happiness to all living beings*
> *Bon is abbreviation for Obon (Urabon-e)*
> *A world of hunger is extreme suffering*
> *Non-attachment to worldly pleasures is so difficult to practice*
> *Amida Buddha possesses all the virtues needed for us to realize true joy.*

Our annual Obon festival dance is a Buddhistically significant observance as an expression of our Buddha of infinite wisdom and compassion.

---

[56] One of the interesting aspects to this story is the idea of merit transference—you can transfer your good deeds to people who are suffering so they can use that good karma to be born in a better world.

Bodhi Day Service: Its Buddhist Meaning

The article ran as a Dharma Corner article in December 1996, on the occasion of three active Buddhist Japanese American Religious Federation (JARF) churches of San Francisco participating in a first-time ever (I believe) joint Bodhi Day Service.

Bodhi Day can be considered the most significant of all Buddhist holidays including our Jodo Shinshu, Zen and Rissho Koseikai (Nichiren lineage) denominations. Without the historical enlightenment of Prince Siddhartha, there would be no Buddhism! We will be celebrating his enlightenment, together as a "Sangha" (Buddhist community).

Why are there many different Buddhist sects? This is a good question to raise and understand as Buddhists of different temples. The historical and doctrinal justification of the rise of Buddhist sects can be summarized as follows

1. The goal of all Buddhists is enlightenment (freedom from suffering, Nirvana)

2. The historical Buddha (Shakyamuni) taught according to the spiritual capacities of his followers. The "founders" of various Buddhist sects such as Shinran, Dogen (Soto Zen) and Nichiren (Rissho Kosekai and others) arose from the needs of the people of the day for a path that could be meaningful to them.

3. The historical Buddha is purported to have declared that there are "84,000 paths to enlightenment." The possibility of reaching the top of a mountain by many different paths is given as a visualization of the idea that each person must find his or her own path to reach the same ultimate goal of enlightenment. This path will be determined by the seeker's ability, intensity of study/practice, determination, faith, etc.

The real challenge is to find the right path for oneself. The Sangha is very important for each of us, for we all need to have some help along the way. May we participate in this year's Bodhi Day Service with this perspective and an attitude of gratitude for being allowed to pursue a life of Buddhist sharing, enrichment and growth.

Okagesamade: Into the 21st Century

This piece, which appeared in Dharma Corner in October 1998, also expressed thanks to the centennial committee headed by Teresa Ono for the undertaking and completion of the excellent 100-year anniversary program for the Buddhist Church of San Francisco.

Okagesamade (with humble gratitude to all known and unknown conditions), we have been able to meaningfully and joyously conclude our 100-year anniversary during the Labor Day weekend. We are now prepared to focus on the expectations and challenges of our next 100 years as well as the 21st century of the modern world calendar.

I consider the following events as highlights of our centennial celebration, which will hopefully propel us energetically and spiritually forward: message from our Monshu Koshin Ohtani; the services; the lecture series; the oral history project; and the photo exhibit.

Upon reflection of the centennial activities, I have come up with the following thoughts:

1. The need for a broader perspective and presentation of Jodo Shinshu and Buddhism to reach the needs of a diverse and changing society and world.

2. Community outreach and involvement is Buddhism, for the very definition or foundation of Sangha brotherhood or the Bodhisattva ideal of Mahayana Buddhism involves sharing the teachings with others.

3. The paradoxes of the present world are challenges to our intellect and feelings; we need to deal with them with wisdom (understanding) and compassion (caring) and personal faith.

4. The world is critically in need of cooperation with all living beings including human beings, animals and plant life (environmental/ecological awareness, caring and follow-through).

5. The Buddhist home, not the church and organizations, is the foundation to start and nurture the Buddhist way of life.

(Personal note: hopefully, this nurturing of the young person would lead to consideration of the ministerial profession.)

6. The pull of religious cults or similar spiritual directions is oftentimes the very human way that a person who is troubled reacts. One who has been brought up with an understanding and appreciation of his own religious tradition usually can discover his/her own personal path.

7. True appreciation of the past might very well give one motivation to act in the future. The photo exhibit was visual testimony to motivate us to carry on. I was particularly moved by the letter of request of the members of the YMBA of San Francisco[57] who (in 1898) expressed "the burning desire to hear the Dharma" to the then-Monshu of Nishi Hongwanji. I hope that this spirit is never forgotten.

The Indescribable Power of Religion
I wrote these reflections for Dharma Corner following a trip to Japan from October 24 to November 3, 1998.

The popular Jodo Shinshu Japanese Buddhist expressions *fukashigi* (beyond thought) and *fukasetsu* (beyond speech) succinctly and squarely describe our recent trip to Japan. Eleven members and students of Asian philosophy joined in the tour arranged by and for the Japanese American Religious Federation (JARF). The main purpose of the tour was to "promote the goal of religious and cultural dialogue and friendship between the Buddhist, Christian and Shinto lineage religions serving the Japanese community in San Francisco and to share these goals with the people of Japan with talks and discussion sessions."

---

[57] The signatories of this historical 1898 petition were (in Irohana Japanese alphabetical order): Shingo Imai, Yoshigoro Izumi, Namihei Imazu, Kanemoto Ishii, Iuemon Idenishi, Toyojiro Ishikawa, Katsugoro Haida, Yasunosuke Hashizume, Shozo Hashimoto, Kamenosuke Hatanaka, Eishichi Hamamoto, Yohei Hashimoto, Chokichi Hashimoto, Kensuke Hayashi, Kantaro Hotta, Uzo Tokunaga, Tsurukichi Okada, Tokumatsu Okuno, Seikitsu Okamoto, Kumaji Oda, Tsunesaburo Kono, Kojiro Yoshida, Yomojiro Yoshida, Asakichi Yoshida, Hidesaburo Yoshida, Mitsuzo Yoshida, Kunosuke Yoshihata, Heikichi Yoshida, Kametaro Yoshida, Tamizo Tanabe, Eikichi Takayama, Yonejiro Sogi, Masajiro Tsumura, Yujiro Tsuda, Ikunosuke Yamanaka, Tatsujiro Nanbu, Rikito Nakano, Fusakichi Kubota, Tokujiro Yamane, Daijiro Yamamoto, Isuke Yamaguchi, Hisakichi Matsushima, Sankichi Maeda, Isamu Matoba, Takichi Maruyama, Kumatoro Funabashi, Toshiki Gotanda, Minekichi Enomoto, Nisaburo Aihara, Tatsuhei Sasaki, Shichiro Saiga, Sataro Kishi, Katsunosuke Kitamura, Tamezo Kishi, Shinkichi Kishi, Chiyokusu Kishi, Masanori Misaki, Tetsunosuke Mizuno, Yasukichi Shimamoto, Chokichi Shimada, Tokujiro Shimada, Nisaburo Hirano, Ihei Kaida, Nizo Hirota, Yasutaro Himeno, Matsutaro Hirano, Iwakichi Hirano, Chokichi Hirano, Ukichi Hirano, Bunemon Hirano, Yonezaburo Suzuki, Takazo Matsubara, Kumaichi Kuramoto and Hirojiro Nakane.

I use the expression "the indescribable power of religion," because I feel that because we were in intimate contact with those who share the aspirations common to all religions, we were treated with special warmth and without any reservation. There were no boundaries or barriers among participants (tour members or people of Japan) despite the fact that we were of different nationalities, religions and sects.

As I would like to limit the length of this article, my comments will be limited to these 10 personal highlights:

1. Day one in Narita gave us a great start as we experienced Soto Zen Buddhist life in rural Japan. We did meditation, Zen chanting, tea ceremony and ate *shojin ryori* (vegetarian meal) and slept in the *hondo* (chapel hall)!

2. In a Buddhist workshop in Inawashiro (Fukushima-ken), we met with about 35 Soto Zen priests and discussed areas of concern and the challenges of propagating religion in our contemporary society. One subject was whether the karma of the donor of an organ would affect the future karma of the recipient!

3. I conducted a Buddhist **service at the replica of the Okei**[58] **grave** (the original headstone is in Placer County) in Aizu Wakamatsu (her birthplace). In Tokyo, we also conducted a service at the cemetery headstone site of the late Archbishop Nitten Ishida (one of the founders of JARF 30 years ago)—this was especially meaningful to tour member Brian Dempster, his grandson.

4. We had the special privilege of witnessing *gagaku* music and dance performed at Meiji Jingu (Imperial Shrine), as well as a special Noh dance performed by the father-in-law of a hosting Nichiren Buddhist Temple priest.

5. I was personally touched when the highly recognized and respected President Nichiko Niwano of Rissho Koseikai (new Nichiren religion) brought out an old family album that included photos of me with his family at the Stockton Buddhist Church on his first visit to the U.S. that was 29 years ago!

---

58 Okei Ito was first Japanese woman known to have died on American soil.

6. The energy and cordial hospitality of the Nichiren Buddhist priest (Rev. Miyoshi) of Myojuji Temple in Tokyo was amazing. He is the cousin of Brian Dempster (mentioned in #3)

7. It was gratifying to have Rev. Gene Sekiya (formerly of Fresno) show us some of the private historical artwork and buildings and gardens of the Nishi Honganji in Kyoto.

8. At Hieizan (Mount Hiei), it was an inspiration to imagine that Shinran Shonin and many other founders of other Buddhist sects had studied, meditated and practiced at this home of Tendai Buddhism where we were privileged to stay.

9. Tenri City (the home of Tenrikyo religion) was truly an amazing place. The vastness of the main worship hall and grounds reminded me of the largest of temple complexes in Beijing, China. I was truly impressed by the dedication of the members who chant in the morning and evening services in unison with hand gestures to the beat of huge drums and bells.

10. At the Konko Church in Osaka, we shared and exchanged thoughts with representatives of various religious groups. Again, we were happy to see that all had the wish and goal of working together to build a more happy and harmonious community and world.

Jinenhoni: The Importance of a Life of Freedom and Naturalness
This article first appeared in Dharma Corner in November 1999.

Jinenhoni is a Jodo Shinshu Buddhist expression that describes a life of freedom (despite one's many imperfections) and naturalness (not restricted by social morality and customs).

Why is the life of *jinenhoni* needed? Because *jinenhoni* is a Buddhist way of life that gives the believing and practicing Buddhist a life of freedom and naturalness without having to purify/control our many defilements.

In examining our own lives honestly, we find that we do not live in freedom and naturalness. It is shamefully and unfortunately characterized by qualities of unnaturalness, disguise, imitation, role-playing, dishonesty, unreality, untruthfulness, uptight feelings, hang ups, popularity- and reputation-consciousness, restrictions, etc.

The life of Nembutsu can change this. It can awaken us to many realizations and make us as free as a soaring eagle! This Nembutsu prompted by Buddha's wisdom can allow us to leap up and dance in joy like Mogallana of the famous Obon story. His display of spontaneous joy of Buddha was not just lip service happiness or happiness created by intellectual understanding.

How, then, do we acquire or cultivate this rare feeling? We must learn to open up, drop many of our shallow values and prejudices and reawaken and readjust to a lifestyle that is within the reach of anyone because Amida Buddha embraces me as I am.

But it begins in the solitude of oneself. A book on poetry explained it beautifully: "In real solitude we are expansive, limitless, free. We do not disguise our feelings from ourselves, but rather we renew contact with ourselves and discover who we are."

This solitude is a solitude of cultivating an awareness and deep gratitude that Buddha (Amida) accepts me as I am with all my 108 imperfections with wisdom and unconditional compassion.

Amida Buddha then changes my imperfections into good, my foolishness into an assurance of enlightenment, and my frustrations into gratitude and joy.

Jinenhoni then becomes my everyday life unbounded by my ignorance, social mores and customs.

I once heard the visiting Rev. Chisho Yanagida from Japan. His Japanese message on "transformation" expresses this *jinenhoni* ideal perfectly. The following piece, translated by Dr. Taitetsu Unno, goes as follows:

TRANSFORMATION

When the soil receives waste material,
The waste material is turned into soil.

One need not change into soil
To become part of the soil.

The soil receives whatever is given it
Without demanding change from it.

Namu Amida Butsu receives
A person as he is.

When the Nembutsu receives a problem,
No matter what it may be,
It is transformed into the Nembutsu,
Adorning and glorifying one's life.

The Nembutsu takes in
Myself as I am
With worries and problems
And transforms everything
Into the highest virtue.

Dharma Appreciation—What? How? When? Why?

I shared this letter from Mrs. Della (Marvin) Bruens of Crystal River, Florida, in the Buddhist Church of San Francisco's Dharma Corner because it expresses how Buddha Dharma and Nembutsu were real and relevant for friends of our church. May each of us, through Amida's wisdom of compassion, truly experience Dharma appreciation.

What is Dharma appreciation? It is the incomprehensible and inexpressible understanding that provides peace of mind to accept any given life situation. For the late Marvin Bruens (a church member of many years ago), it was exhibited in his ability to address and cope with his illness, pain and impending death. Death, to him, was like the passage of the seasons of the year continually repeating themselves: spring warming to summer, summer cooling to fall, fall turning into the cold of winter, with spring's warmth beginning another cycle. This is a reminder for us to live and enjoy each day fully rather than to wonder what is in store in the near or far future. Life and death is described as one big ocean in Buddhism, because the journey is more important than the place of embarkation or the place of destination, which could be anywhere.

How does Dharma appreciation begin? I believe that the seeds are planted or discovered and nurtured. For the Bruens, they may have stumbled upon it in their journey of life. For many of us with a Buddhist family background, it was planted before we were conscious of it. But a seed requires nurturing, sunshine, water, etc. to grow. We, ourselves, need to slow down and reflect upon life's innumerable gifts.

When does Dharma appreciation take place? I believe that it varies according to the person. It may happen when "good karma" becomes apparent. It may not happen when karmic circumstances do not allow the seed to grow well. However, in Jodo Shinshu, Dharma appreciation or *shinjin* (Nembutsu faith) can occur like the gradual sweetening of a bitter persimmon (from bitter inedible to sweet tasty fruit—or person!)

Why is there Dharma appreciation? Dharma appreciation is a human response to something that has happened or is happening to a person. It comes from the discovery of a path of peace and joy while living in an imperfect world of pain, struggle, and limitations.

When Marvin said his eventual death was "no big deal" and that his life was but a memory, this is the same insight as that of a Buddhist priest who described his life just before his death with one Japanese character, *yume* (dream).

Thoughts on *Kazoe Doshi* (Age 70 by Japanese Age-Counting)

This article, which appeared in the April 1999 issue of Dharma Corner, begins with a quote from Colette (1873-1954): "What a wonderful life I've had! I only wish I'd realized it sooner."

The above quote happened to be the "thought for the day" on my (daily) Zen Buddhist calendar on my birthday (March 5th). I was astonished, because those words perfectly described how I felt! I suppose this is a thought that would relate better to older persons than the young. Hopefully they would agree.

The teachings of the Buddha and Shinran emphasize that happiness (or unhappiness) is strictly in the eyes of the beholder (individual). They constantly remind us that despite the frustrations, pains and sufferings of life, there is a path that allows us to feel and express joy, harmony, understanding (wisdom) and gratitude.

As I turned 69 years old (by the Japanese way of counting, 70 years), I reflect on what Jodo Shinshu calls the "four gratitudes" (*shi-on*):

1. My late parents (Rev. and Mrs. Sensho Sasaki) and ancestors personally exemplified and pointed out to me the Buddhist way of life.

2. Innumerable teachers and friends have supplemented and enriched me along life's journey. This includes many non-Buddhist teachers, friends and acquaintances.

3. My country (the United States) and others—Japan, Korea, Thailand, Sri Lanka, Burma, China, India and Israel—have allowed me opportunities for study and growth, academically and spiritually.

4. Gratitude to Buddha: The Three Treasures that we recite states: "Hard is it to be born human. More difficult it is to hear the teachings…" How fortunate I am to have been exposed to the Dharma in this lifetime!

As days, weeks, months and years go by, I realize more and more that each day (moment) is precious and is not to be taken for granted. A Buddhist friend, before he died, told me that it was not until he was declared terminally ill that he began to really notice the trees and turns along the road that he traveled daily. His work and family responsibilities had kept him from seeing the beauty or the total realm of his surroundings. This certainly describes the life that most of us lead.

I have now out-lived my late father and Rev. Ken Yamaguchi, my predecessor San Francisco minister friend, who both passed away at age 68. This thought reminds me of how fleeting and precious life is. This also prompts me to reflect upon the Japanese expression "*arigato*" (thank you), which means "difficult to be." It would be impossible to enumerate the costs to my family to have educated, nourished, clothed, sheltered, transported and entertained me. And this is only in terms of monetary costs! Even more incomprehensible are the contributions mentioned in the others of the four gratitudes. *Arigato*, therefore, perfectly expresses the acknowledgment that my life is only possible because of other sentient beings with whom I share our fragile earth's environment. Yes… very "difficult to be."

8

RETIREMENT: SAN BRUNO, 2000–PRESENT

Retirement

In 2000, I had served the Jodo Shinshu ministry for 43 years. We had celebrated the 100th anniversary of both the San Francisco church and Buddhist Churches of America; I had been minister in that location for 10 years; and I qualified for full retirement benefits. The time seemed right to step down. The transition to retirement was made easier because we had planned ahead. At the time I had been assigned to the San Francisco church, instead of living in the apartment on the premises, we had asked for and received a housing allowance. This enabled Helen and me to buy a home in San Bruno, so we weren't left wondering where to go when the time for retirement came.

While I have stayed active in a variety of ministerial activities, retirement has afforded me the luxury of spending time with family, travel (without needing to get approval) and engaging in simple pleasures like watching sports and the *Charlie Rose* show and exercising (swimming or slow jogging).

We have been able to travel to Japan four times in the last five years, each time bringing different sets of grandchildren. It has been a pleasure to connect the younger generation with their "roots" in that country and the relatives I have the privilege to know there.

Also, when asked by churches (and individual families/couples), I have been guest speaking, conducting weddings, funerals and memorial services.

Caucasian Senior Center Buddhist Services

I have been conducting a Buddhist service at a huge Senior Center facility called Meadows in Los Gatos, near San Jose, twice a year for the last three or four years. The service, which they call the weekly Sunday evening Vesper service, is given by various clergy members of the Santa Clara County area in a handsome chapel. My service is attended by 15 to 20 people, who say they look forward to the Buddhist experience.

These visits started after an elderly Japanese American Christian lady, Mrs. Haru Baba, asked me to conduct a Buddhist service at the center. She was an acquaintance of mine because her grandson, Ken Wong, had dated our daughter, Rina. How strange that a Buddhist service came about by such karmic chance of a social relationship… and that this grandmother had the respect of a religion beyond her own.

Before conducting the Sunday evening service, I usually have dinner with the coordinator. I then set up a Buddhist altar atop the altar shelf by placing a wooden *omyogo* (with *Namu Amida Butsu* written on it), with the usual candle holder, incense bowl and flower bowl. I now do not light the incense stick because a lady once told me it bothered her breathing.

Wearing the *fuho* black robe, I conduct the service in the following order: 1) opening words of welcome; 2) chanting of "Ti-Sarana, Gassho to Amida" (composed by late Bishop Tsuji) or "Juseige"; 3) meditation with a bell and reading of a Buddhist passage by me or the group; 4) Dharma talk; and 5) question and answer time.

From the positive responses I have received, the joy and gratitude of our Buddhist religion can be appreciated by persons without any Buddhist background. I will note, however, that the people in the senior center come from the middle- to upper-class professional backgrounds, and they include some prominent people or parents of prominent people. One of the ladies there, a former acquaintance of mine from various interfaith activities, was the former San Jose director of the National Conference of Christians and Jews.

Through this type of experience,[59] I am confident that our Buddhist way of life and thought can be accepted far beyond our Japanese American community. Buddhism, indeed, is a universal religion.

---

[59] I have also been to high schools and colleges talking about Buddhism.

21 Years Later, a Letter

I received this remarkable letter from Michael (who is Caucasian) in 2001. Performing his marriage seemed like a minor activity to me at the time, but it was very important to the couple—and this Buddhist beginning launched their involvement in Buddhism. I would accept anyone with this kind of spirit—church member or not.

Dear Rev. Sasaki,
Namo Buddhaya, Namo Dhammaya, Namo Sanghaya.

You married me and my Taiwanese wife Shoman in the Buddhist Church of SF on November 13, 1990, I think. A couple of weeks ago I re-entered for the first time since then in the company of my 16-year-old daughter, Pema. I am enclosing a picture of us from that visit. My wife and I are still together and happily married. She is in Taiwan right now.

We always remember your kindness to marry us. Maybe you will remember that we are the two who just showed up at the door one day with no preparation and asked to be married. I remember you said that this was "not Las Vegas." We were rather poor of means and on our own at that time. But after some discussion about Buddhism and what we were thinking, you agreed to marry us on very short notice. In fact, you allowed us to get married in the morning two days hence and use the elaborate and beautiful decorations that a much more well-prepared and well-financed marrying couple had installed at the church and was going to use for their marriage ceremony later in that day.

After our marriage, Shoman and I moved overseas and lived in Taiwan and later China for about eight years. In 1998 we moved back to the USA and have been living in Eugene, Oregon, since that time, raising our daughter here. We have continued involvement in Buddhist activities and have helped create a Buddhist Church and a Buddhist retreat center here in the US. This is in the Tibetan Buddhist tradition. Right now I have been assigned the responsibility of creating a Buddhist retirement center. That is why we were in San Francisco, meeting and doing research—someone had recommended we visit the Kokoro center near the Buddhist Church.

I thought you, as a marrier of couples, might sometimes wonder what happened to those people you married. So I thought to send you this letter to tell you about us and to thank you again for your kindness. In our case, I think, you did a good job. During our ceremony I remember you talked about karma and facing hard times. Of course we have faced several hard times and gone through sadness and suffering. But we have kept our positive connection and effort going I think. I hope you have good health and that your Dharma practice is strong. May the Dharma flourish in this world, in the minds of all beings.

Love,
Michael and family

War: A Sign of *Mappo*

I wrote this article on Mappo (the age of Dharma decline predicted by the Buddha) for the Wheel of Dharma in February 2003, two years after retiring, at a time of war in Iraq. While Mappo is somewhat pessimistic, it brings out the importance of Jodo Shinshu and its emphasis on "other power" instead of "self power."

At the time of this writing, our nation has sent our young men and women to the Middle East and war may have begun. We do not know what the consequences of our aggressive actions will be. Although I am very apprehensive, I harbor the humble hope that the world will be heading toward a more peaceful time.

Together with some 60,000 others, my wife and I participated in the February 16 anti-war peace rally in San Francisco. We felt compelled to express our frustration and powerlessness regarding our country's impending invasion of Iraq. Many leaders from the interfaith community spoke eloquently in Civic Center Plaza to express their opposition to war and their fervent desire to find peaceful solutions. It was my first community protest since I was in Stockton during the civil rights movement in the 1960s.

We are presently living in the age of *Mappo*, the third of three periods of human history prophesized in the Buddha-Dharma. The first 500 years after the Buddha's *parinirvana* (ca. 500 BCE) was the period of the True Dharma (*Sho-bo*), when Dharma teaching prevailed and Dharma practice and enlightenment could be attained. The next 1,000 years, to 1,000 CE, was the period resembling the True Dharma (*Zo-bo*), when the teaching existed and practice was possible, but enlightenment was not possible. We are in the third period, encompassing 10,000 years from 1,000 to 11,000 CE, the period of the decadence or decline of the Dharma (*Mappo*). During this period, only the teaching exists, but neither practice nor enlightenment is possible. Indeed, war is one of the many signs of this period.

In our country we are experiencing much violence, racial injustice and conflicts; materialism; mental and emotional imbalance; and political and economic instability and polarization. Our leaders around the globe seem unable to work out differences harmoniously or peacefully. As we read the newspaper or watch television these days, people appear to be losing hope and optimism. The promotion of and our engagement in another war will again lead to the destruction of human lives, property and the spending of many billions of dollars that could be used for vital services such as better health care, education, housing and other projects.

Our nation and many others have been involved in global war and numerous other conflicts during much of human history. Buddhist history, in contrast, shows that it has existed peacefully with many religions and cultures in Asian nations. There has never been anything resembling a holy crusade against the many religions with which Buddhism has existed peacefully. King Ashoka of India and Prince Regent Shotoku of Japan were Buddhist leaders who lived by the tenets of this religion of peace. King Ashoka (ca. 300 BCE) was converted to Buddhism after experiencing the painful reality of war. He is said to have publicly repented for causing suffering during his previous military expeditions. Prince Regent Shotoku (574–621 CE), regarded as the father of Japanese Buddhism, wrote Japan's first constitution in which one article states: "Sacredly treasure the true peace of the Dharma."

Can we rise to such lofty ideals in this period of the decline of the Dharma? I do find rays of hope among the eloquent columns, letters and statements made by many who wish to pursue peaceful solutions to our present global conflicts, especially those expressed by national political leaders and statesmen. These leaders demonstrate courage, integrity and true dedication, often going against popular opinion and jeopardizing their political careers. On February 12, 2003, U.S. Senator Robert Byrd stated on the Senate floor, "To contemplate war is to think about the most horrible of human experience.... On what is possibly the eve of horrific infliction of death and destruction on the population of the nation of Iraq—a population of which over 50 percent is under age 15—the chamber is silent.... War must always be a last resort, not a first choice." On March 7, 2003, diplomat John Brady Kiesling resigned his posting to Secretary of State Colin Powell because he felt a personal conflict between his own conscience and the current administration. In his letter of resignation, he stated, in part, "The policy we are now asked to advance is not only incompatible with American values but also with American interest.... Our fervent pursuit of war with Iraq is driving us to squander the international legitimacy that has been America's most potent weapon of both offense and defense since the days of Woodrow Wilson.... Our current course will bring instability and danger, not security.... Who will tell the people of the world convincingly that the United States is, as it was, a beacon of liberty, security and justice for the planet?"

Shinran lived in this same *Mappo* period. Because of this imperfect world of the Three Poisons of greed, hatred and ignorance, from which corruption and wrong views and practices arise, a world in which enlightenment is unattainable, we are the subject of Amida's great compassion. Shinran's message is that peace is not necessarily found globally but in the peace that begins with the examination of the self. Perhaps then we can begin to share it with our family, community and society.

Realistically speaking, I am pessimistic about the outcome of a war with Iraq. Human suffering will be high, with many lives lost and broken. Nonetheless, I feel that it is still the Buddhist position and practice to minimize the suffering and elevate the human condition for all. Let us humbly become engaged Buddhists actively working for peace. If we do not, what or where is the *raison d'etre* of Buddhism, Jodo Shinshu, the Hongwanji or the Buddhist Churches of America?

A Wonderful Bishop: Kenryu T. Tsuji

I gave this eulogy for Kenryu T. Tsuji (1919-2004), the first North American-born bishop in the Buddhist Churches of America who was an embodiment of the spirit of Buddhism.

Fellow Buddhists and friends, we are gathered here this evening, not to mourn the passing of a wonderful Buddhist but to celebrate the legacy left us by our dear *sensei*.

Our BCA's 75th anniversary theme was "Discovering New Horizons" or better phrased in Japanese, *aoide kansha mukaete yakushin*. It meant: with reverence and gratitude, we progress into the future. Tsuji-*sensei* certainly lived that outlook throughout his life. It is our challenge and responsibility as

Buddhists to implement and advance Tsuji-*sensei's* vision and dream.

His lifetime work may be simply described as *yasashiku, fukaku* and *hiroku*, or the spreading of the Dharma to all people simply, deeply and widely. This was the way of our great Nembutsu Buddhist, Rennyo Shonin, as credited by popular Japanese writer, Hiroyuki Utsuki. This description certainly aptly describes the life of our esteemed Rev. Tsuji. He knew that the challenge of spreading Dharma and Nembutsu in this country is monumental considering our numbers, however he knew that the message of Buddha and Shinran are truly real and applicable to all people. His legacy has been published in the BCA centennial history book as follows: "No Jodo Shinshu minister has surpassed him; the broad vision for American Buddhism that he expressed so fervently and frequently during his 13 years as bishop has continued at the Ekoji Temple which he helped to establish in the nation's capital."

Sensei was truly a man not only of vision, spiritual faith and dedication, but also a person who wore many hats. He was a bishop of the Buddhist Churches of America, a fellow colleague and traveler, president of the Institute of Buddhist Studies and the World Conference on Religion and Peace, Buddhist innovator and pioneer, translator, author, a dynamic spokesperson, film maker… too numerous to mention. To Sakaye-san, his wife, he was a devoted and loving husband of 58 years; to five daughters and their spouses, a great father; to his six grandchildren, a wonderful grandfather. I believe, however, that *sensei's* wonderful attributes were planted and sprouted in the sweat and toil on his parents' farm and thrived as he grew up in Canada and the family proudly sent its youngest son to Japan to study Buddhism. Their family's dream bore fruit through the guidance of teachers and friends at Ryukoku University in Kyoto.

Sensei was appreciated as a man of humor. As humor is defined as recognition of our frail human mind, he was able to joke and laugh at our imperfections. There is a Japanese Buddhist term *"gyakuen"* or seeing wisdom in our imperfections and failures. Sensei was able to laugh at his and our faults and limitations and not be critical, negative or downcast by them. He may be characterized as a Buddhist optimist. He was able to see the lotus that grows out of murky mud. His daughters had another view of their father. They referred to his humor and jokes as downright corny. Mrs. Tsuji told me that one of his favorite jokes or comments was to refer to her as a Bodhisattva because she was always acting and talking *"butsu butsu."* For those you who do not understand this comment, this is a play on the word *"butsu"* which means Buddha... but *"butsu butsu"* commonly means to complain or nag constantly.

This versatile man of wisdom once told his granddaughter Maya for a school interview of her grandfather these words, referring to the forced evacuation of both the Japanese Canadians and Japanese Americans in 1942: "... everyone was bitter, but I was not... my Buddhist upbringing made it possible for me to face all kinds of difficulties without fear, anxiety or hopelessness and to make [the] best of a difficult situation."

My personal memory of Tsuji-*sensei*? It was his constant fervor to communicate the Jodo Shinshu Buddhist teachings into an understandable and spiritually uplifting way in the English language. Among his many contributions as translator, his simple but effective translation of Namu Amida Butsu, the central theme of Jodo Shinshu as "I am one with Buddha" is one I like best.

His life was *Namo Amida Butsu*. Our being here to remember *sensei* is *Namo Amida Butsu*. Our BCA stands for *Namo Amida Butsu*.

I would like to close with an excerpt from Tsuji-*sensei's* writings included in his recent book, *The Heart of the Buddha-Dharma:*

Namu Amida Butsu

The Nembutsu is the sound of the universe.
It is the sound of the wind
as it rustles the leaves;
It is the roar of the waves
as they rush toward the shore;
It is the song of the robin, the whippoorwill
and the chorus of cicadas on a summer evening.

The Nembutsu is naturalness...
The first cry of the baby
as it emerges into the world
from the darkness of the mother's womb;
It is the powerful cry of independence
of individuality, of selfhood;
But it is also the great cry of awakening
to its dependence on something greater than self...
for its sustenance.

The Nembutsu is the proclamation of the Buddha...
"Above heaven and below heaven,
I alone am the World Honored One."
It is the ultimate declaration of life;
I alone hold my destiny in my hand
leading to perfect Buddhahood.

When I touch the heart of reality,
It is *Namu Amida Butsu:*
What else can I say?
When I truly share someone's happiness,
it is *Namu Amida Butsu;*
And in that moment of deep grief
over a loved one's death,
it is just *Namu Amida Butsu.*

Namu Amida Butsu
it is the sound of gratitude
not of my finding the Buddha,
but Buddha finding me.

BCA in the 21st Century

I gave this talk at the Tacoma Buddhist Temple as part of the Rev. Sunya Pratt Lecture Series on November 15, 2003, reiterating a perspective I had been sharing over the years.

I humbly offer my assessment of the issues facing the churches affiliated with Buddhist Churches of America (BCA). This assessment is based upon my 43 years of active ministry with three Northern California churches and with BCA organizations. The purpose of this outline is to offer my views of the institution and its leadership so that our BCA Sangha can thrive and grow here in the United States and the world.

I have divided this general subject into four categories: Buddhism and Jodo Shinshu Buddhism; institution (Nishi Hongwanji and BCA); Buddhist education and propagation; and the future of the BCA.

Buddhism and Jodo Shinshu Buddhism

Is the true spirit of Jodo Shinshu being expressed and practiced as it is found in the *Jodo Shinshu no seikatsu shinjo*? Is our religion relevant to the needs and signs of the times? Doctrinally, why is Jodo Shinshu Buddhism, as a Mahayana Pure Land Buddhist school, not able to address and emphasize the doctrines of Buddha Nature and Bodhisattva ideal? The future of BCA propagation depends on how Jodo Shinshu can address these doctrinal issues (*kyoso hanjaku* in Japanese).

The Institution (Nishi Hongwanji and BCA)

More than 100 years have elapsed since our teaching was transmitted to the mainland USA. And yet, compared to other Buddhist sects and schools (Theravada, Chinese, Zen and Nichiren Soshu), the institution has been primarily Japanese and Japanese American in its vision, scope, activities and goals.

The most important area of Buddhist Education (Dharma school, services, study classes, church library, seminars, ministers' sabbatical leave, etc.) has played a lesser and secondary role and priority as compared to other activities.

Many churches are isolated from the larger community. Community participation is oftentimes regarded as "unnecessary, unimportant and not church business." There is a vital need for more programs such as the *Nishi Hongwanji Dobo Undo* (anti-discrimination program), *Vihara* program (care for the sick and elderly) and Hawaii's Project Dana (care for the elderly). It is encouraging that some churches and temples have initiated these vital programs.

Shortage of BCA ministers and the problems and difficulties of attracting young people (and older people) are major BCA issues. How can we make this profession more "attractive and challenging"? Utilizing able retired ministers and lay ministers and assistants becomes vital.

Buddhist Education and Propagation

In order to teach and propagate effectively in this changing society, our traditional teaching method of relying primarily on ministers must change. BCA ministry will be greatly enhanced by utilizing the expertise and study of modern disciplines of science, technology, music, arts, literature, psychology, politics, business, medicine, media and even sports in an interdisciplinary approach.

Buddhist history has been rich with inspired Buddhist leaders such as King Ashoka of India, Shotoku Taishi, various Buddhist masters, Shinran, Rennyo and Lady Takeko Kujo of Japan.

Taiki seppo is a Japanese Buddhist expression meaning to teach the Dharma in accordance to the needs and capacities of the person(s). This idea is very important even outside the confines of the temple such as the Zen Buddhist hospice in San Francisco, Buddhist chaplaincy, Buddhist social work, youth counselors (for drug and alcohol, suicide, homeless, prison, schools, etc.), and even church athletic activities with more emphasis on Buddhist values understood and exhibited by coaches, parents and players.

As the saying goes: "I cannot do it alone but if I do not start it, nothing will be done." Or, to borrow from President Kennedy's famous statement: "Ask not what the Sangha can do for me, ask what I can do for the Sangha."

Future of our BCA?

No one can predict the future of our BCA 50 or 100 years from now. However, much will be determined by the vision and support of the members and leaders on the following issues:

1. Enlistment of more ministers and lay leaders

2. Membership and friends of the churches from the wider community

3. The creation of a contemporary and global culture for the new IBS Jodo Shinshu Center in Berkeley by working closely with the Graduate Theological Union

4. The ability of local church leadership to be fluid with all ages, gender and ethnic backgrounds, not focused on mere administration and fundraising, but on personal Dharma understanding and Dharma propagation (*jinshin kyo nin shin*—to teach the Dharma by first developing personal faith)

5. Church services open to new ideas while honoring the tradition of the past. For example, what will be the altar of the future church? Is there not room for research and study to have the *omyogo* (Namu Amida Butsu) in English or horizontally rather than vertically in Japanese?

6. The assumption of some ministerial duties by lay members so that the ministers may be able to visit, conduct outreach and teach rather than be confined to the office for administrative duties.

7. Interfaith participation, cooperation and dialogue

8. Publication, audio-visual and media outreach of both general interest and academic materials

9. Support and use of the Internet

Unexpected Joy in Mexico

This article I wrote was published in the January 2004 issue of Wheel of Dharma. See group photo in this book.

In December, my wife and I joined a 16-day tour visiting Colonial and Aztec Mexico. Because of this trip, we returned with greater respect and appreciation for the history and culture of Mexico and its people.

We've accumulated unforgettable memories of the great history-telling mural paintings of Diego Rivera, magnificent Cathedrals, outstanding museums, climbing to the top of the Pyramid of the Sun, colorful religious parades, our first bull fight, statues and monuments everywhere of Mexican and world-wide heroes, etc. Blessed with daily spring-like weather, we were thoroughly impressed!

Although our travel experiences were uniquely educational and pleasurable, they could not compare with the joy that I felt in a fairly unassuming place in Mexico City, the most populous city in the world (more than 15 million). The site was the Jodo Shinshu Buddhist temple called "Templo Budista Ekoji" headed by Rev. Gimyo Takemura, formerly of the BCA (most recently of Seattle Buddhist Betsuin). I expected a gathering similar to a BCA temple comprised mostly of *Nikkei* (people of Japanese descent), or in this case, Japanese Mexicans. Rev. Takemura had not told me anything about his temple or its membership when I had originally requested to meet his Sangha. Therefore, it was a complete surprise to be joined by nearly 40, mostly young, Mexican adults! The only persons of Japanese ancestry in the half tatami and half Western style *hondo* were the four ministers (including two who spoke Spanish, the Revs. Masao Ishii and Koiichi Todaka) and my wife, Helen.

At 7 pm we began by chanting the Nembutsu Wasan in Japanese and read its translation in Spanish from an attractive service book entitled *Jodo Shinshu Libro De Servicio* (published in May 2001). During the chanting, I was unable to hold back tears of joy and gratitude that the voices of these Mexican people reverberated the incomparable sound of Oneness, transcending language and culture with people from a historically Catholic background. The three-and-a-half-hour evening program included my short Dharma talk, a meditation period with music, Rev. Todaka's Dharma remarks in Spanish, Rev. Ishii's Dharma talk in Spanish and a brief Mexican potluck dinner. A lively question/answer/discussion period with excellent translation by young Mexican members followed another short Dharma talk on my part. The entire group sat in a large circle and participated in meditation with an ojuzu made with giant beads, and Rev. Takemura gave words of self-reflection.

I was especially impressed by nine members who were called upon to individually recite, in Spanish, "The Golden Chain." In our BCA temples, we would delegate such a task to Dharma School children, but these adults recited it most earnestly. I was touched by the beautiful *sunao* (child-like innocence or, as some Buddhist traditions call it, "beginner's mind") attitude of these individuals who to me exemplify "what it takes" to walk the Nembutsu path. Some of the members seem to have been searching for an alternative to the Catholic religion and expressed their happiness at finding a place that embraced them without barriers or expectations, a place where they felt comfortable and peaceful.

This unforgettable Buddhist evening of inspiration has re-affirmed my faith and belief that the messages of Shakyamuni Buddha and Shinran Shonin are truly universal. May the doors to our temples and churches be more widely open so that all who are searching for a Way may be given the opportunity to hear the Dharma in the spirit of *metta* (loving-kindness).

The Unforgettable Earthquake

These thoughts, offered a year after the October 2004 earthquake shocked Japan, remain relevant in the face of natural disasters that continue to rock the world.

The way we learn and grow in life is varied. Buddhist learning and appreciation is just that way. The fact that Buddhism is a "way of life" rather than a creed or dogma was clearly displayed to me by last year's earthquake.

The day was more than just a 6.9-scale shock. It graphically brought out the Buddhist message (which most of us do not ordinarily think about) that:

1. Life is impermanent: our possessions can be lost suddenly; uncertainty is the only certainty in life.

2. There is really nothing in life that we can call a permanent possession or even existence—the teaching of non-self or non-entity (*anatman*).

4. Life is characterized by constant suffering, frustrations and disappointment. Our human happiness is short-lived happiness (at best).

5. True happiness (peace of mind) is found only in deep awareness (understanding) of self, life and Buddha. This happiness is inexplicable, beyond our intellect, Nirvana.

The earthquake reinforced my conviction that the Buddha Dharma (teachings) is alive, real and ever-relevant. If we would but understand and practice it, our sufferings would surely be lessened. We would be like the bamboo, which has the ability to weather almost any windstorm (perhaps even an 8.0 earthquake). Let us live the life of true Buddhists, having our understanding of the Dharma reflect in our human relationships and experiences at home, at work and at play. Let us live the life of gratitude, for Shinran Shonin tells us that all we possess, even our own lives, are merely gifts from outside of ourselves that we are temporarily allowed to use.

Tule Lake Pilgrimage: A Meaningful Service

I had the privilege of participating in an interfaith memorial service at the site of the Tule Lake Relocation Center of World War II on the weekend of July 1–4, 2006. Because I was among the 18,000 who called it home for a few years (1942–1945), I was invited to speak.

The theme of the year's pilgrimage program was "Dignity and Survival in a Divided Community." Tule Lake, in Northern California, was the site selected to incarcerate those who refused to pledge loyalty to the United States government. The theme refers to the fact that for over 50 years, details concerning the "no-nos"[60] and "yes-yeses" have been discussed and debated. However, that is another (very important) story.

The memorial service was held, not at a usual "cemetery site," but on bare unidentifiable ground among sagebrush and tumbleweed. This was once the camp's cemetery site, located off a county road, next to State Highway 139 near the Oregon border. The interfaith service was co-officiated by Rev. Saburo Masada, a former ministerial colleague of mine from my Stockton Buddhist Church years when he was the pastor of the local Presbyterian church.

The "central altar" was ably constructed by Jimi Yamaichi (Tule Lake committee president and member of San Jose Buddhist Betsuin). It included wooden replicas of Castle Rock (a nostalgic mountain for Tule Lake people), a guard tower and barracks; candles were set in the front. On one side of this table was a portable Buddhist *omyogo (Namu Amida Butsu)* shrine with incense burner, flower vase and candle, while on the other side was a Christian cross.

During the chanting, I could not help but turn back the clock some 60 years when my late minister father and other BCA ministers had done the same chanting for many of the 331 persons who died there during those camp years. War Relocation Authority records show that only 11 of 331 persons were buried at Linkville Cemetery in nearby Klamath Falls, Oregon. It is also stated that some families cremated their loved ones and kept their remains. Today, there is nothing left at the site to remember and honor those who were actually buried here. In 2005, an archeological survey indicated that the site was excavated sometime in the past decade. The location of the remains of many of the people are therefore unknown. This gave me a great sense of regret and sadness. I am certain that the many who offered incense after the service shared similar feelings.

---

[60] The term "no-nos" refers to those who answered "no" to questions 27 and 28, the so-called "loyalty questions," on the War Department's Application for Leave Clearance form. The no-nos were sent to Tule Lake.

From my perspective, such public memorial services have deeper meaning and significance than what most of the 260 attendees might have imagined. *Mu en Hoyo* (memorial service for unknown persons) describes the focus of the service. *Mu en Hoyo*, a major annual service conducted at the Seattle Buddhist Betsuin, was originally held to remember fishermen lost at sea; it reminds us that true compassion embraces all these unknown persons whose contributions make our lives possible. The more traditional Obon service is another example of this all-embracing ideal of compassion to all living beings. Also, *Eitaikyo* (Perpetual Memorial Service) is conducted by temples in memory of deceased members who may have been forgotten by family and friends with the passage of time.

The service at Tule Lake on the unidentifiable plot of land had similar significance; this time, in solemn remembrance of those who passed away when the Japanese were suddenly uprooted and transported to desolate unknown lands.

As a former Tulean, the oldest of five boys (ages 2 to 12), with a minister father and his wife, accompanying and serving their many members who had traveled with them from the Sacramento Buddhist Church congregation, I asked myself, "How did they do it?" With their future unknown and for the many hardships endured by my parents, other *senseis*, leaders and all who were incarcerated, I can only express humble admiration and gratitude. The issues with which they had to deal daily must have brought forth great feelings such as helplessness, shame, pain, sorrow, humiliation, anger, fear, betrayal.

Therefore, the emotions I experienced cannot be described by inadequate words such as "gratitude," "thankfulness" or "appreciation." The Japanese language has more meaningful expressions such as *gokuro sama* (which acknowledges the pains and sacrifices to raise me), *sumimasen* (gratitude expressed as self-repentance and inadequacy for not doing more) and *okagesama* (acknowledgment of countless unseen karma causes).

The Japanese who emigrated from their native country brought with them the spirit of *gaman* (patience, tolerance or self-restraint), which did help them endure during those difficult, uncertain years.

All these expressions, I believe, are expressed by utterance of the Nembutsu (*Namu Amida Butsu*) "thank you" for allowing me to live with all of life's ups and downs with peace of mind within the wisdom and compassion of our ageless Dharma.

Our religious/spiritual way allows us to look at the pilgrimage theme of Dignity and Survival from this viewpoint. The history of the Japanese Americans has shown that we have been able to endure with dignity despite this black spot on our nation's history.

From conversations with many who traveled the long five-hour bus ride, I found that each person and family had their own reasons for making the pilgrimage; a karmic push (or pull). They ranged from nostalgia, wish for closure, education, curiosity, fellowship and the wish to honor our common history. Our pilgrimage together gave me a sense of community with all who attended, and I feel that this trip certainly fulfilled my wish to honor those who lived, died and survived in Tule Lake.

Namu Amida Butsu.

Second Trip to India

In 2006, I traveled to India for the second time (my first pilgrimage was in 1954-55), in a tour group led by Rev. Jim Yanagihara. Especially today, when travel is so easy, I believe all practicing Buddhists should conduct a trip to India—not just for tourism, but rather as a Buddhist pilgrimage. This journey can be an act of devotion, to better understand your own Buddhist heritage, which all started in India. If you're a Jodo Shinshu, going to Japan is important as well.

During this trip to India, the whole group spontaneously sang "Lumbini's Garden" in Lumbini's Garden. It was so much more meaningful than singing the *gatha* (verses) in church. I started leading the song and everybody followed. It was so inspirational. Visiting India makes the sites of the Buddha more than just names in a history book.

In addition, as a Jodo Shinshu Buddhist, I can better understand the specific history of Pureland Buddhism by going to India. Shinran, founder of Jodo Shinshu, went to Mount Hiei to study basic Buddhism, prior to his further spiritual development on the Nembutsu path.

I had the opportunity to go to the Mahabodhi temple in Bodh Gaya, where the Buddha attained enlightenment. There, I also did prostration practice, touching my forehead, elbows, knees and legs to the floor in the utmost *gassho* or physical prostration worship of Buddha. Similarly, priests and lay people prostrate from one place to another, circling the temple structure.

Seeing these pilgrims prostrating on the floor makes our standing *gassho* (hands joined together in a spirit of worship) appear incomplete and lacking what we wish to express to our Buddha.

My Dharma Friend, Rev. Toshio Murakami
I contributed this piece to the October 2008 Buddhist Churches of America Wheel of Dharma.

It saddens me to again bid a fond physical farewell to a fellow Dharma minister friend. The passing of Rev. Toshio Murakami on May 26 (age 76) while still actively serving the Pearl City Hongwanji Mission Temple in Oahu, Hawaii, is another major loss for our Nembutsu propagation. I was able to see Rev. and Mrs. Murakami in Pearl City just this past March, so the shock of the truth of impermanence seemed more real to me. When he came to pick me up for his church's seminar, he seemed quite physically frail in comparison to my previous contact with him. *Sensei* was a man of short physical stature and scholarly appearance but with much energy and humor. A dinner photo I had taken with Rev. and Mrs. Murakami shows him with palms together; he appears to be sincerely telling the world that he is happy to live and ready to die.

My personal friendship with Murakami-*sensei* began in the 1950s during my student years in Tokyo when he was the winner at a special *Bukkyo Eigo Kenkyukai Hanashi Taikai* (English-language Buddhist Research Association oratorical contest); I was one of the judges. Although I do not recall the content of his speech, the title was easy to remember: "Peanuts." From that time on, I often affectionately called him "Peanuts-*sensei*." Through his proficient linguistic abilities, he became one of the most fluent bilingual speaking ministers from Japan.

As a son of a minister of Eishoji Temple in Fukuoka, Japan, he came to the United States (Berkeley, California) as his dream-come-true mission in what he stated was "the new world, as a messenger of Jodo Shinshu Nembutsu Dharma." He wrote, in part, some of his thoughts in a collection of essays by Jodo Shinshu ministers in America entitled *Insight* (1980). His essay, "We Died for Their Tomorrow," pointed out, with actual examples of the feelings of dying soldiers in times of war, that we can live in some semblance of peace because of the sacrifice of countless others:

We must remember the wishes and aspirations of those who sacrificed their lives for peace and happiness. We must not negate this yearning. The yearning for perfection and the way opened by the Bodhisattvas coming together in the mind-of-enlightenment and manifest as Namu Amida Butsu, called Nembutsu.

Rev. Murakami's joy and dedication to the Dharma not only reached the many churches that he had served in the Buddhist Churches of America, Buddhist Churches of Canada (as bishop), Honpa Hongwanji Mission of Hawaii and even to far-away Australia, but most importantly to his two daughters, Mari and Rumi. The wisdom and compassion of Amida Buddha (through Nembutsu) in particular was a great source of peace and comfort to Mari, who became visually impaired at the youthful age of 17. Rumi expressed, in her eulogy at Sensei's funeral service in Honolulu Betsuin, these touching words: "It was as if she (Mari) was not alone, with Dad walking into the darkness with her. During his final days before passing, he told us, '*Mari, anta ichiban wakaru*' (Mari, because of your blindness, you understand the best)..." I feel like I am approaching physical incapacity, but I see myself mindfully and spiritually awakened with *Namo Amida Butsu*. These words alone do not fully express Rev. Murakami's life dedication to the Nembutsu Dharma, but it is a glimpse into his very personal life of Nembutsu.

I will also cherish the many personal memories and friendship with him... his likeable and often humorous side, everything from his first oratorical speech in Tokyo, the many meetings we attended together (often as roommates), the fun and frolic of ministers' post-meeting dinner parties, his eloquent bilingual sermons and lectures, and many other happy, funny and ordinary times, too numerous to mention.

In remembrance of Rev. Murakami's lifetime of service as a minister in many places, I liberally rephrase the title from his Insight essay from "We Died for Their Tomorrow" to "You Lived for Our Tomorrow." I will miss you, my dear *zenchishiki* (good Dharma teacher) friend.

Reflections on My 80th Birthday

I have been blessed with good karma. I have had a good life and have outlived my father (who died in 1972 at the age of 68) and mother (who died in 1985 at the age of 74).

I am now retired, but keep busy as a guest speaker and minister helping out with different churches, especially in Palo Alto and San Mateo. I have also been participating in various school reunions (a sign of getting old), bigger public Tule Lake reunions (three times) and the more intimate Northern California former Young Buddhist Association member reunions (three, four times).[61]

Life has been good to me—just as good or better than the richest men in the world. I have had good ancestors, parents, wife, children, grandchildren and friends.[62] I have been able to travel and enjoy good food. I have financial security on my own level. Bill Gates and Warren Buffet have more fame, but that doesn't bother me. Everyone has a story to tell; everyone should write a book based on their different life experiences, different karma.

Am I ready to die? I think I am. My only regret is I may not see my grandchildren get older and become adults. Jared, my oldest grandchild, may get married some 15 years from now, and that would make me 95. Am I afraid to die? I don't think I am, but you never know until you're told you only have a little time left. I might easily change my attitude.

On my 80th birthday, I still feel great! I go swimming Monday and Wednesday nights at 4 a.m. I don't like to swim in the three-lane pool when it is too busy and crowded. I still very occasionally garden, but I can't pull weeds like my wife, Helen. Last June, I did hurt my right leg. I was at the San Francisco airport and they announced my name, saying my flight was at a different gate. I ran, and that's when I pulled my leg. As I was pulling my suitcase in a Tokyo station stairway, a Japanese lady helped me—then I felt my age.

I am more appreciative of life now compared to when I was 70. Speakers at Jodo Shinshu center are very good now, when they used to put me to sleep during my younger years. I find the lectures more relevant, meaningful and inspirational now... again, due to my age and, hopefully, maturity.

When I was a teenager I remember calling 40-year-olds *"ojisan"* or "mister." Now I'm 80, I suppose I'm a "double mister."

---

61 The Placer County reunion is my most "historical" reunion, in that it goes the furthest back. This reunion brings together surviving Japanese American persons who attended schools in Placer County—including towns such as Penryn, Loomis, Newcastle, Rocklin, Auburn and Lincoln—in the '30s and '40s. I fall into this category, as I attended Penryn Elementary School in 1936–1939 when my late father was the minister of Placer Buddhist Church.

62 My father-in-law was lucky enough to have 26 great-grandchildren.

In Memoriam: Dr. Kenneth Inada, Buddhist Scholar

Dr. Kenneth Inada (1923–2011), a native of Honolulu, Hawaii, and distinguished Buddhist scholar, passed away in Honolulu on March 26, 2011, at the age of 87.

Dr. Inada, former Buddhist professor at University of Hawaii (1959–1969) and New York State University, Buffalo (1969–1997), was a leading Buddhist scholar in the field of Madhyamika Buddhist philosophy. His many publications included *Nagarjuna: a Translation of his Mulamadhyamakakarika with an Introductory Essay, The Ultimate Ground of Buddhist Purification,* and *Buddhism and American Thinkers*. He was the first Japanese American to receive a doctoral degree in Buddhist studies from Tokyo University (1960).

He served in the U.S. Army from 1943–1945 and was wounded in action in France as a member of the famous 442nd Infantry Battalion. It was the tragedy of war and human losses that led him to study Buddhism. This path led him to study under Dr. Daisetsu Suzuki and Dr. Shoson Miyamoto of Tokyo University.

Dr. Taitetsu Unno, a former classmate, provides this remembrance:

"Professor Inada was trained in both Western philosophy and Buddhist studies and contributed to the advancement of comparative philosophy. He was one of the leading figures in clarifying Buddhist thought from a philosophical perspective, but he also published a translation of Nagarjuna's Middle Way philosophy. His leadership in comparative philosophy will be difficult to replace. Active in academic circles, he nurtured the growth of younger scholars and had many friends in both East and West. Since my knowledge of Western philosophy was limited, I relied on him for guidance on philosophical matters."

His leadership after retirement with the Las Vegas Buddhist Sangha, a fellowship of the Buddhist Churches of America where he served as president in 2004, is gratefully remembered with these words:

"Dr. Ken Inada was a quiet but strong leader for our Las Vegas Buddhist Sangha. Actually, we wonder how we were so lucky to have had him as a member of the Sangha and especially as vice president and then president.

During those days, we only met once a month, but Dr. Inada was gracious and generous with his time to put together the course work for us to learn more about Buddhism and its relationship to other Asian religions. Also, during this time in Las Vegas, Dr. Inada was involved with the 442 reunions and made time for lectures about his role in that historical group of soldiers."

As for me, also a former classmate of Dr. Inada at Tokyo University in the 1950s, I personally regard his passing as a great loss for Buddhism. After his retirement from college teaching, I was able to meet him occasionally when he and his wife lived in Henderson, Nevada, from 1997 until 2010. He was not only a person deeply knowledgeable in Buddhist philosophy, but a person who practiced Buddhism with the Bodhisattva spirit of compassion and caring for others as a person and as an activist war veteran. It was with a deep feeling of sadness that I had the opportunity to visit him in a Honolulu military hospital four days before he passed away.

His memorial service was held on April 17, led by a minister of the Hompa Hongwanji Mission of Hawaii in Honolulu. He was to be interred at the Punchbowl National Cemetery.

Dr. Kenneth Inada is survived by his wife, Masako, and son, Ernest.

Me with Cancer?? No Way!

It was April 20, 2011, when Helen, Rina, her baby, Odin, and I drove back to the Bay Area from Southern California, and, upon returning home, I listened to the messages on my answering machine. Much to my surprise, I heard the voice of my Kaiser physician—and she was telling me to go to the emergency room! I said to myself, "Is this a real message?" I played the message again and heard the doctor say I was anemic and needed to get some tests.

I followed directions and went to the emergency room, where they performed a cardiogram and other inspections. I was then immediately sent to another section of the hospital to get a blood transfusion. I received two pints from some person to whom I feel deeply indebted. I wish I could thank the person for giving me the health to continue my life.

Following this transfusion, I visited another specialist, Dr. Ghandi, who discovered a potential malignancy in my colon based on a colonoscopy I had three years earlier. To confirm the discovery, a series of tests was recommended. So I had another colonoscopy, followed by a CAT scan and MRI, all of which confirmed the cancerous spot in my colon.

"Me with cancer? No way!" I thought at first. To many of us the word "cancer" sounds like a death sentence.

After the initial shock of the news, my many Buddhist seeds started to sprout. In some ways, it was not the best time for quiet reflection because I was quite busy. I was assisting with many memorial and funeral services for Rev. Ron Kobata of Buddhist Church of San Francisco, who had requested my help because he was scheduled to go to Japan for a special 750th memorial service for Shinran Shonin. I had also been asked to conduct a funeral service for the Palo Alto temple. And I was scheduled as speaker at various other Buddhist temples.

However, I found time to reflect upon my Buddhist faith and its teachings, which became more real and relevant with my serious medical illness. The teaching that human life is one of "birth, old age, sickness and death" called *sho ro byo shi*, became especially real. The Buddhist reading displayed at the home of my wife's cousin (Dr. Takuya Sato in Indianapolis) provided true peace of mind for me. I do not know who wrote or rewrote this Buddhist wisdom, but I would like to share it with the reader:

> *I am of the nature to grow old. There is no way to escape growing old.*
>
> *I am of the nature to have ill health. There is no way to escape ill health.*
>
> *I am of the nature to die. There is no way to escape death.*
>
> *All that is dear to me and everyone I love are of the nature to change. There is no way to escape being separated from them.*
>
> *My actions are my only true belongings. I cannot escape the consequences of my actions. My actions are the ground upon which I stand.*

It is a good coincidence that as I was writing these thoughts, I received a "get well card" from a San Francisco church member, Masako Iwase. The wording on the card impressed me. It read: "Don't think of it as being sick—think of it as being 'wellness challenged.'" These short words were Buddhist wisdom in disguise and so well said. My reinterpretation of the message was: it's like Buddha asking a person, "Are you sick or are you really well, as you think you are? If you are truly well, you have no need to listen to me.[63] If you are not truly well, you need to hear me, so you can cope with your life wisely, peacefully, gratefully and compassionately."

Surgery

Trying to maintain a Buddhist frame of mind, I met with my surgeon to discuss the immediate procedure she would recommend. Upon studying the various test results, my wife and I accepted her recommendation we proceed with surgery. The idea of surgery can give rise to all kinds of thoughts and feelings, on topics ranging from fear, insecurity, death and dying, pain, etc. My thought was singular—not fear, not insecurity, not death and dying, but pain... Will I be knocked out completely so I feel no pain or post-surgical pain? I am a pain scaredy-cat. I even tell my dentist to make sure the Novocain is effective because I am not the kind of highly disciplined Buddhist monk who can walk on hot coals.

Back to the real world of the surgery on May 25. Some of my family members were present, but we did not know what would be happening. To ease the tension and mystery of the situation, one of my sons just jokingly said "Bye, Dad" and laughed with a laugh that was not really a laugh (almost laughing and crying at the same time). It was just his way to cope with the uncertainty of the situation.

This surgery was technically my third. During my teenage years in Sacramento, I was hit in my stomach during horseplay boxing, rupturing the jejunum segment of my small intestine and requiring surgery. My second surgery was a single bypass operation at Seton Medical Hospital in 1991, my second year at the Buddhist Church of San Francisco. I am embarrassed I do not remember the surgeon who gave me an extended life, but I do remember it was an active medical doctor and church member, Dr. Kent Matsuda, who first diagnosed my health problem as angina. During this second surgery, I still vaguely remember hearing the conversation of the surgical team during the

---

[63] Some people don't know they are not all well; that's a challenge.

operation. It was kind of scary when I was not knocked out as completely as I was supposed to be. It is no wonder I was somewhat concerned about whether I would be completely anesthetized for the third surgery.

The new surgical team successfully knocked me out, and I became conscious the next day. However, I was immediately told I needed additional surgery on the same colon because there was still some internal bleeding!!! I asked myself if my delicate stomach would be able to cope with another incision. It's rather humorous to think that night I had trouble watching DVD of a bloody Japanese samurai movie, *13 Assassins*, which my wife brought for me. Especially difficult was a realistic-looking *seppuku (harakiri)*, the traditional Japanese self-immolation conducted by cutting open a stomach with a suicide knife. This pain "scaredy-cat" who would normally watch such a scene could not do so between surgeries.

The unexpected additional surgery was pronounced completely successful and, better yet, I was told my cancer problem had been discovered at an early stage so it was completely removed and had not spread to other bodily parts. But I was tangled in all kinds of tubes, including a mucous-removing breathing tube deep in my throat that prevented me from speaking. Curious about everything that was happening to me, I had to write out my questions. This was very frustrating to say the least.

It became hell on earth when the aide tried to remove the mucous and I had to exhale until I was practically out of breath. It was probably only due to my swimming conditioning that I was able to last as long as I did. It was like I was drowning and gasping for air—what I imagined a drowning person would experience before death. To make matters worse, my hands were tied to the bed so I would not accidentally (or purposely) take off the many tubes around my face and arms. This experience was not just hell but Black Hell like the Buddhist work of *Ojoyoshu*—a collection called *The Essentials of Rebirth in the Pure Land*, best known in Japan for its vivid description of various hells—that I was familiar with from my graduate studies in Tokyo.

At the risk of scaring future patients, I would like to share my other post-surgery experiences. One problem was the ordinary daily situation of moving the bowels. As I was barely able to move because of the sensitive aftermath of the incision on my stomach, it was difficult to get out of the bed. As I was urged to move and go to the bathroom on my own power, I did my best to do so. But in the process I could not control my bowels. A major disaster did happen. As I was slowly getting off the bed, my diarrhea-like bowel movement went from the bed, onto the floor, and into the toilet. Blackened due to my iron pill medication, the bowel movement spattered onto the bed, my robe and the white floor, making a trail to the nearby toilet. It was a major embarrassment to me. The hospital nurse aide looked at it and without any hesitation helped me by cleaning me up, as if a mother was changing a baby's diaper. My embarrassment disappeared as this helpful and kind aide cleaned up the mess. Yes, I felt totally dependent on these hard-working hospital staff members and most grateful for their dedication to help patients like me. Again, my feeling of *okagesama* was different from the usual gratitude for receiving a more usual act of kindness. Providing that kind of hospital care is a thankless task that requires a tremendous amount of patience, experience and dedication.

At the same time that I felt grateful for the wonderful hospital care given to me, I also asked myself, "What happens to the countless number of people who cannot or are unable to pay for such medical service and care?" Yes, President Obama had a most difficult task in convincing the nation that everyone should be given the same level of care that my health plan provided me.

There is more to the hospital experience. It is also a most valuable time when simple little things become appreciated. When things are normal and we are healthy, we take simple things for granted. I thoroughly enjoyed and welcomed a cup of ice so I could enjoy the coolness and refreshing thirst-quenching taste. I once read a personal Buddhist appreciation of someone reciting the Nembutsu after each bowel movement, after each urination. That is exactly the kind of feeling one can experience with even the simplest ordinary human activity. The feeling of satisfaction and appreciation when one is able to release his stomach gas without making a mess or seeing loose bowels hardening into a normal form were part of the experience.

The hospital experience was also valuable because it provided much-needed time for myself. In these modern times, there is not much time for such important human conduct. Dharma wisdom teaches us that life begins and ends with yourself alone. You can have a wonderful family, as I have, and yet, one is born alone, lives alone and dies alone. The Buddhist experience is very private and personal. It does not begin at church or with a church membership but originates from oneself. This is where the real Buddhist experience begins and ends.

Going Home

Following the 10 days of kind help from hospital staff members, it was a wonderful feeling of gratitude to be discharged. While many people of the world have no medical institution or are required to travel a great distance to reach it, we lived most conveniently only a few miles from the hospital and it was easy to return home.

I returned to a REAL home with all of its comforts... familiar food, drink, reading material, TV programs, comfortable sofas, a reclining chair (a new purchase), privacy, etc.

I must gratefully acknowledge the love and support of my wife of 49 years, Helen. As I write this, if all goes as planned, we will celebrate our 50th year of marriage next year. Although I oftentimes complain about every little thing, these are the actions of a foolish person. Yes, it is foolishness to only appreciate a person or a thing when it is missing. This is so true for everything we have, from the simplest thing to those much more important. We foolishly seek more and more of whatever we want and are never fully satisfied. Without my wife, who would help me during my period of recovery? Hired help? Friends? Siblings? I do not think so.

During this period of rehabilitation, one of my joys at home was watching our San Francisco baseball team, the Giants. The previous year's world championship was out of this world for me and my family—aptly described in a baseball magazine as a year of "torture to rapture." It was torture because the games were mostly very close and undecided to the ninth or some extra inning; rapture, because the team ended up winning the World Series.

This description reminded me of the Japanese Buddhist expression that explains in four short words the meaning or purpose of Buddhism: *bak ku yo raku* (remove suffering and joy begins). Buddhist joy becomes deeper and fuller with use *(mujin,*[64] unlike gasoline that burns and disappears, the more you use Buddhist wisdom, the fuller and deeper it becomes) and is a stage of experience that "will not fall back or retrogress" (*futai*).

It was the same way for the 2010 baseball season, but with one major difference: the baseball "rapture" became the source of "torture" the next season. Would it not be a miracle if this could happen to our dear Giants—season after season of championships without end? But that is not baseball, which is only a human creation providing temporary and occasional joy/excitement that

---

[64] See photo of "Mujin" calligraphy scroll by D.T. Suzuki, which was a farewell gift from Rev. Gido Undo, former tutor of both Abbot Kosho Ohtani and me.

we, foolish human beings, enjoy.

The Buddha does not laugh at us but just smiles. Buddhism is such a wise, patient, caring religion that I am happy to call myself a Buddhist. I can only respond by saying, "Thank you, Buddha, *Namu Amida Butsu*."

My Perspective on Good Health

Health is a vital subject for all of us. Without good health, our outlook on life changes. I remember a good minister friend of mine who said that all your ambitions, goals and dreams go down the drain with an unexpected change in health. It is perhaps only a minority of people who can utilize this type of problem as a way to become "more spiritual." (In Buddhism, it is called "reverse karma" when a person can take "negative karma," such as a sudden illness, and make it into something positive or spiritually advancing.) For most of us, a sudden or even gradual change of health becomes most challenging or possibly devastating. Most people become depressed, but some people can change that.

What, then, brings forth good health? It seems most people believe that good health comes only from good eating habits and exercise. To me, this is but one third of what comprises good health. The other commonly neglected elements are one's heredity from parents and ancestors, as well as the ability to cope with psychological or emotional stress.

I believe the Buddhist way of life can positively affect many aspects of health. A Buddhist understanding that one's life is given by parents and ancestors in what we may broadly call past karma can encourage a person to adopt good eating habits and exercise. Karma is the cause and/or effect of the conduct of body, mind and speech. The traditional Buddhist practice of *shojin* (commonly called vegetarian cooking, but the word does not literally mean vegetarian but "right effort" as in the six *paramitas*). *Shojin Ryori* (vegetarian cooking style) was and is the traditional way of eating for Buddhist practitioners.

As for heredity, some of us have inherited good health and some of us, normal or weak health, and there is not much we can do about that. However, if our parents and ancestors followed the way of Buddhism, it may have positively affected them and the karma we received. What if one is not fortunate enough to have good ancestors? I still remember seeing a movie called *Bad Seed,* a scary movie about an innocent-looking young girl who was a child murderer because she had inherited the "bad seed" of a murderous ancestor. Although it was just a Hollywood movie, it certainly had elements of what I am addressing. Thich Nhat Hanh, the brilliant Vietnamese Buddhist author/activist/scholar, aptly described this human state of heredity as follows: "Some seeds are innate, handed down by our ancestors. Some were sown while we were still in the womb, others were sown when we were children."

As for the ability to cope with stress, the central focus or goal of Buddhism is to alleviate or eliminate suffering. How can Buddhism help relieve our stress? It gives us the knowledge that everything is dependent on your mindfulness/outlook—how your own mind copes with a particular problem. If you have a strong foundation, your outlook will be different than someone whose mind is based on ignorance/lack of understanding. For good health, we have to change our minds from foolishness to wisdom/compassion/goodness.

Suicide, My Personal View

Professionally and personally, I have known friends, church members and relatives who have committed suicide. To me, such a death is tragic and unforgettable. Many studies have indicated that suicide is the leading cause of death among teenagers and adults 35 years and younger. This is a staggering statistic and difficult to comprehend when we stereotype young people as fun-loving, carefree and totally unconcerned about death and dying.

In the Japanese American community of years past, people only whispered behind people's backs when someone died by taking his or her own life. However, with education we have become more open and honest about this subject.

I remember one particular year when five of my Buddhist acquaintances took their own lives. They committed suicide for different reasons—a triangular love affair; poor health and financial distress; boredom. In the past, Japan was known for "lovers' suicides," sparked by unwanted pregnancy, parental disapproval, public shame, etc.

But other than the "suicide bombers" of current world politics and war, such as the World War II "kamikaze pilots," and traditional Japanese *seppuku* (a suicide ritual by cutting open the stomach), suicides seem to have one main underlying cause—to stop pain or what Buddhism calls *dukkha* (bodily and mental suffering). Wanting to stop pain is natural, especially when pain can become unbearable.

What is the Buddhist view of suicide? Although there is no one set view of this tragic human situation, I believe Buddhism leads us to the view that suicide can be prevented by understanding human life with the wisdom of the Dharma. The Buddhist way teaches it is possible to remove suffering and unveil wisdom, that suffering rooted in ignorance can be changed into joy. We may also view suicide as a sad path of one's karma or simply with sympathetic compassion.[65]

What a Relief! It Was Only a Nightmare

Stress affects health, even for ministers, Buddhist or not. We all dream and have nightmares. Lately, in my 80s, my nightmares are becoming more frequent. I wonder if this is connected with age, a guilty conscience, or ministerial frustrations due to high expectations of church members.

In many of my dreams, I am frustrated by trying to locate my parked car. In more recent dreams, I am trying to find a car to drive to a funeral I am to officiate. Other ministers living in a big city with congested traffic will probably be able to relate. Sometimes, I dream I am unable to find the appropriate minister's funeral robe to wear to a funeral service.

Another common nightmare is that I arrive just in time to conduct a service, only to find that the flowers in the altar vases are wilted and the floor is soiled. Fortunately, the uncared-for, drooping flowers are behind the altar curtain. I yell at my wife to change the old flowers, while I quickly try to sweep the floor—not using the vacuum cleaner so the congregation waiting in the chapel does not hear the cleanup. I am also trying to find an excuse for the delay in the service. Can you imagine the predicament? It causes high blood pressure, rapid heartbeat and maybe even a nose bleed. This terrifying situation is suddenly gone when I wake up and realize it was another nightmare of a retired minister. What great relief to know it was just another bad dream.

I can ask a psychiatrist, "What does this all mean? Is this a sign of guilt? Was I a careless and irresponsible minister?" Although I have never experienced such a situation in real life, it is saying something; the power of karma on my life as a minister is always there. The nightmares are real even if they did not happen. They are real fears for me and perhaps for other ministers as well.

Compassionate understanding by a church's lay members will certain-

---

[65] Some people from the Catholic tradition have deeply appreciated Buddhist funeral services that offered compassion, rather than judgment, for those who died by their own hand.

ly make the life of a minister and his or her family easier and less stressful. I hope that our members will understand that we ministers, as our Jodo Shinshu Buddhist teaching tells us, are foolish, non-perfect human beings no different from the lay members, and their stress can be relieved with understanding. The only difference between ministers and lay people is that we ministers have been blessed to meet, hear and have more Dharma teachers and Dharma friends. In our Jodo Shinshu teaching, ministers are therefore called "*kaikyoshi*" in Japanese— literally, "servant who spreads the teaching" (not master/teacher as in other Buddhist sects).

Tell Me About My Monshu Father

It was during his first official visit to the United States around 1950 that I had the rare honor of personally getting to know the Abbot Kosho Ohtani, the father of Abbot Koshin Ohtani and grandfather of the present Abbot Kojun Ohtani. This special relationship was made possible because my late father, Rev. Sensho Sasaki, was the minister of Sacramento Buddhist Church (now called Betsuin temple).

As the son of the minister, I was probably a convenient choice to drive him around for various unofficial errands and visits. The then-young abbot (who was maybe 40 years old) seemed to like having a young guy like me show him around Sacramento and nearby towns.

As a former Sacramento Young Buddhist Association (YBA) president, I gave the abbot a gift of our YBA basketball jersey and trunks with "Sacramento YBA 8-ball" on them. Without any knowledge of Hongwanji protocol, I asked him if he wanted to shoot some basketball in the Sacramento *kaikan* gym. He consented, so we shot some basketball with a church photographer taking some photos. I sent this basketball photo to his son, Abbot Koshin Ohtani, who was so pleased to receive this rare picture of his father that he asked me to visit him in Kyoto to tell him more about his late father's younger years.

Following up on this invitation, I arranged an informal meeting with the abbot on April 4, 2012, in Kyoto's Nishi Hongwanji Temple, with the assistance of Rev. Kiribayashi, the director of Nishi Hongwanji International Center. My wife, Helen, and eldest daughter, Sharon, with her husband and two young daughters, Zoe and Ava (then ages nine and seven), were also able to attend.

Our meeting was nearly cancelled due to a heavy wind storm that stopped all the trains in Japan the day before the scheduled appointment. We were fortunate to catch the first train from Fukui to Kyoto on the day of our meeting, but our honored guest had to wait for us for almost an hour as we frantically caught a cab from the Kyoto station to the vast, recently renovated historic temple. Upon arrival, the anxiously awaiting Rev. Kiribayashi rushed us to the official lounge.

We were privileged that Lady Noriko Ohtani could also join us and she was gracious in receiving us. My concern was how my young granddaughters were going to behave, as they were unaware they were meeting such a distinguished couple of historical importance and prestige. By way of comparison, it was like meeting the pope in Rome.

The abbot and lady entered the lounge after we were positioned to take certain seats to greet them. As the customary tea and sweets were served, we awkwardly did not know when and how to have the tea. We did catch on to the etiquette as the abbot said, "*Dozo* [please], have the tea." It was slightly embarrassing to see the granddaughters taste the unfamiliar Japanese sweets and enjoy them as if they were having ice cream.

The abbot asked me to share some of my memories of his late Monshu (spiritual leader) father, and I told him a story about his family name, Ohtani. When I drove his father to the then-very modern El Rancho Motel in Sacramento and he was asked to register, I saw him sign the register book as "Kosho Otani." Observing this, I had the innocent boldness to tell him that "Otani" was an incorrect way to spell his name in English. I suggested an "h" be added before the "t" to make it sound and read as his family name was pronounced in Japanese. Believe it or not, he and his son, the current abbot, have signed their family name "Ohtani" and not "Otani" ever since then.

I also recounted other memories of his father's younger years. His father loved sports, particularly golf. He was such an avid golfer that he organized his own golf group and tournament with his temple members. I can still recall the time when some of us BCA golfer ministers, including Revs. Junjo Tsumura and Kosho Yukawa, took him to a beautiful golf course in the San Francisco Bay Area. I had the privilege of riding in the same cart and was amazed he was such a rule-observing golfer. He would hit the ball even if the ball was in the gully—unlike our usual practice of moving the ball and taking no penalty. I would also like to mention the incident that day during lunch, when a green worm was found in his salad! We were so embarrassed that I do not recall what we did or said other than to have the salad returned.

He also loved to borrow one church member's Cadillac. He would drive and I would sit next to him as a passenger. He would often stop the car and take photos of commercial road signs. We once even had lunch at the then-popular Stan's Drive-In Restaurant with a car hop lady who would bring the meal to the tray attached to the car door. At that time, there was probably no such drive-in restaurant in Japan. I was kindly scolded for these informal unscheduled activities with this most important Buddhist person, who could have been injured playing basketball or gotten sick from eating at a drive-in restaurant.

We once went to shop for a Lionel electric train for his young son and Rice Krispies for his family. This kind of activity showed me a rare view of the human side of the abbot—his caring and loving attitude toward his family.
I had the privilege to see and experience the whole person. Perhaps it was this kind of friendship that inspired him to write me personal letters when I was a student at Tokyo University in the 1950s. He would write asking how I was getting along with my Buddhist studies.

Thinking about it now, this was truly a most privileged and unforgettable relationship that could not happen even in the next life. It was also a great honor I was able to share the memories of this most important spiritual leader of our historical Buddhist faith with his distinguished son.

To recite *Namu Amida Butsu* is the only way to express my gratitude.

Shousei Hanayama's Farewell Message

Rev. Shousei Hanayama passed away on July 15, 2016, at the age of 52.

I had known Shousei from the time his parents brought the family to the USA for a visit some 40-plus years ago. Shousei was like his dad—sociable, likeable, friendly and energetic beyond his size. As a minister, he was known for his loud chanting and Nembutsu recitation that sounded as if he had a built-in mic in his throat.

As in the wonderful photo with his farewell message (in Japanese) in the August *Horin (Wheel of Dharma)*, it is difficult to fully comprehend that he is no longer with his family, his Sangha and me.

His final words (below) truly reflect who he was—very human, very devout, very reflecting and very caring.

Shousei, however, will be where his father and grandfather are, in the Pure Land, and buried near them at the Shoheiji Temple cemetery in Tokorozawa, Saitama.

We call this *"kueissho"* (to unite in the same Pure Land), in the Japanese Buddhist expression.

We, too, will join him eventually. *Namu Amida Butsu.*

The late Rev. Shousei Hanayama posted this message (translated by L. Sasaki for BCA Wheel of Dharma newsletter) on his Facebook page on May 15, 2016, the day before he left Watsonville for his residence in Higashi Kurume, Tokyo, Japan.

> *"Hoping (or thinking) that there is a tomorrow is like hoping that wilting cherry blossoms will not fall in an evening storm."*
>
> *I have always been inspired by these words spoken by the young nine-year-old Matsuwakamaro (Shinran's childhood name) when advised he would be ordained as a priest the following day. His firm determination to enter the Dharma path could not wait.*
>
> *I feel a deep sense of shame and guilt to have to admit to myself that I could have done so much more as a minister and person since coming to Watsonville in 2002. However, I feel very happy and grateful that I did come to Watsonville.*
>
> *It may seem odd for a person about to die to admit that my good life would not have been possible if I had not come to Watsonville. It is here that I was married, blessed with a good family and really had whatever I desired. And yet, it is pitiful that my selfishness prevented me from fully recognizing this blessing.*
>
> *Again, it may be odd for a dying person to say this, but I would never have imagined that I would be dying with the same illness and suffering that my father (Shoyu Hanayama) experienced. His parting words,*

"Let me go (to the Pure Land)," constantly comes to my mind. Dying or death is probably the same for everyone, but I never thought that it would be so tough; it is like being in hell.

This dukkha (suffering) diminishes somewhat when I feel with gratitude that Pure Land exists; soon my pain and hardship will be gone. This awareness allows my suffering to gradually change to joy. Suffering, then, is vital and necessary. Without suffering, there is no motivation to live a true life.

To my dear friends, I express my gratitude to you. I truly appreciate your friendship. I wish I could have done more for all of you. However, I guess this must be it for now.

I, however, will return to this world as Buddha to lead you to enlightenment. Until then, please give me a call. I will be with you in a matter of time—soon or later.

Even my incurable pancreatic cancer will be gone. For now, I will continue my dialogue discussion, "Buddhism and World Peace," with my Dad.

I apologize to you for not letting you know of my terminal illness and not allowing your visitation. If I had seen you all, I would not have been able to comply with my mother's request to be cremated in Japan.

I had always hoped to meet many of you, but this became difficult due to my health issue and difficulty in speaking. It became very painful to sit up on my bed.

I do regret the fact that I could not meet you with my typical smile, laughter and joking personality.

Gassho,
Shousei Katsukiyo Hanayama

White Bones... So REAL

"As we deeply observe the changing form of human life, we realize that in this world, from the beginning to end, what is momentary and passing is the illusory course of human life." These are the opening words of Rennyo's *Hakkotsu no Gobunsho (Letters on the White Ashes)* that we hear at our BCA funeral services. This may not evoke emotion for those who have not recently lost a loved one. However, for those who have, the words are more real and probably are taken very personally.

Rennyo's words of wisdom were again made real to me in a span of just two months, when I had to bid a physical farewell to two dear friends in the persons of an active BCA minister Reverend Shousei Hanayama of Watsonville Buddhist Temple (52 years of age) and former "Mr. Universe"/Olympic weightlifting great Tommy Kono of Aiea, Hawaii. Rev. Hanayama was, like his late father, a former BCA minister/Buddhist scholar and an energetic and outgoing minister. In his prime, Tommy was considered as a physically perfect human person. They are now gone and have become white ashes.

My wife, Helen, and I were able to witness the reality of Rennyo's haunting words in Japan.

We were scheduled to meet the terminally ill Rev. Hanayama at his residence, because we had planned a trip to Japan in July. We had made a "date" to meet at his home on July 21st in Higashi Kurume, outside of Tokyo. Although we were able to visit him in Watsonville four days before his family's departure to Japan in late May, it was sad that our meeting in Japan had to be in the form of his funeral service. Re-scheduling our itinerary in Japan, we attended the service called *"kokubetsu shiki"* (farewell service) on July 19 in Tokorozawa City, Saitama Prefecture. The service in the Bekkan Hall of Shoheiji Hongwanji Temple was conducted by the head priest Rev. Tohyama and three other Buddhist priests; they included Rev. Shousei's brother minister, his cousin and his mother's former temple priest.

This "first service"—with the enshrined Ingo and Homyo (posthumous Buddhist title) of *"Kaizo In Shaku Shosei" (Storehouse of the Ocean and Purity Supreme)*—was similar to our BCA funeral service. The four priests chanted the "Shoshinge" ("Hymn of True Faith") and all were asked to burn incense. I represented the BCA in an incense offering before Rev. Shousei's wooden casket, which was placed in front of the flower-bedecked altar. The program included a eulogy and Dharma message. At the end of the service, all attendees placed flowers into Rev. Hanayama's casket until it was completely filled (leaving room for his face).

Following this first service and light refreshments, all who were invited boarded a bus that followed the hearse and took us to the crematorium where the casket was put on a moving cart. A "second service" was conducted in front of the crematory furnace. As the body was being cremated, we had light refreshments in a separate room. After the body was cremated, a female employee brought the cremated white bones in a metal container on a cart and, gently and carefully, explained the procedure to follow. She pointed out and demonstrated that the bones were placed in the cart in a special way; among them were parts of the thigh bone, rib, jaw, teeth and skull cap. There was a round porcelain container on the end of the cart where the bones were to be placed. She first asked Mrs. Keiko Hanayama and her two young children, Shoren, 12, and daughter Ehren, 8, to place the white bones into the urn. Metal chopsticks were used, with two persons, taking turns picking up a piece of bone, on each side of the cart. The person in charge pushed down the bone that had been transferred into the urn so that it would turn to ashes. This ritual continued until all those involved had participated in the transfer. At the end of the ceremony, even the few ashes that remained were brushed together onto a pan and placed into the urn. The attendant sealed the cover that topped the urn. Mrs. Keiko Hanayama held the urn in her arms, Shoren held his father's large framed photo, and we all returned to the temple on the bus.

The day was concluded with the "third service," the Seventh Day Memorial Service followed by *otoki* (lunch).

This entire farewell ritual from the outset was most touching and so different from what we are accustomed to in the United States. Although I had once before observed a funeral procession and service in Japan in the 1950s, I do not recall it being such a vivid event. This time it was an eye-opening Buddhist experience to observe this way of saying good-bye. I have never heard of this being done in the United States, where a funeral home is usually contacted to pick up the person's body, prepare the body for any services to be held (pillow, wake, funeral) and cremate the body without the family present.

From my experience, the great majority of Americans tend to fear, deny or wish not to deal with the subject of death. The rituals are not attended and avoided at many levels. As for myself, I felt that the Japanese tradition provided a very gentle and meaningful way to bid farewell to a loved one. It was, indeed, a privilege to be involved. I also believe that the Hanayamas felt a sense of true closure to observe the White Ashes ritual. Even the children were calm and seemed to be okay.

The late Rev. Shousei Hanayama has become a spiritual teacher to me by his life and death, making the words of Rennyo's wisdom real. I can only recite the Nembutsu... *Namu Amida Butsu.*

"Jabu Jabu Jiichan" for 13 Grandchildren

One my fondest memories of my fast-growing and grown grandchildren is giving them baths (hopefully also remembered by them). With this experience, I credit myself as their first swim coach—I got them to become unafraid of the water by teaching them to blow bubbles with their faces in the mysterious liquid.

The title of this article is *"Jabu Jabu Jiichan,"* from my version of Japanese. I call the sound of water splashing and fooling around in the bathtub water *"jabu jabu,"* and *"jiichan"* is an affectionate expression for grandfather in Japanese.

My second fond remembrance is taking the grandkids to visit our San Bruno neighborhood dog, Kelly. Kelly was once a very playful and energetic large dog who loved to have the ball thrown in her yard so she could retrieve it and return it by standing up on the fence. Kelly is now old and sadly no longer able to do this. While she barely walks, she still has the appetite to eat the dog food snacks I bring her. My love of dogs also extends to Koko (Sharon's family dog), Taro (Ellen's dog) and Lucky and Dunkin' (Stanton's dogs).

As a Buddhist, an important memory is our periodic *omairi* (family service) before the home *obutsudan* (Buddhist shrine). This has been a family tradition beginning from the years at the Mountain View Buddhist Temple, when the grandchildren's parents were still young. We now do not rotate being the *doshi* (informal chanting officiant), but still continue chanting the popular Buddhist *"Juseige"* (gatha on Amida Buddha's vows) and former Bishop Tsuji's poem, *"Gassho* to Amida." The chanting is followed by our favorite children's Buddhist song, "Buddha Loves You," referring to the Buddha's love of animals—birds, dogs, cats and fish.... It's always humorous to conclude the song by mimicking the sound of a fish gulping (breathing?) in water. The service ends with the offering (burning) of incense. Probably because it reminds them of blowing out birthday candles, the young ones love to be selected to extinguish the candle. I taught them the Buddhist etiquette of blowing out the candle with a fan and not your mouth. The Buddhist reason I was taught for this was so the purity of light (wisdom) was not extinguished by an "impure person of many defilements."

We have been blessed with "lucky 13" grandchildren. This good fortune is a result of good karma inherited from what my late father Sensho had always preached to us, that our present life is a result (good, bad or neither) of the "four gratitudes" described earlier in this book.

As of now, we have five grandsons and eight granddaughters, ranging from ages one to 17. We have been fortunate they have all been good students and healthy, athletic, caring and decent people. Health-wise, they have had one sports accident (relatively major) and one hospitalized illness of short duration. So far, Helen and I have also taken or plan to take 10 out of 13 grandchildren to Japan, so they can learn and appreciate their Japanese cultural heritage, meet their relatives in Japan, and visit the generational Sasaki Buddhist temple, Kozenji, in Fukui Prefecture. I am also most grateful that all of them are attending or have attended Dharma schools in their respective Buddhist churches.

From Helen and my perspective, we can summarize our general impressions of each of them as follows:

> **Bodhi:** He has started to walk. He surprised me by going to our family home shrine (*obutsudan*) and ringing the Buddhist bell with the stick. He must have observed this when we have our family *omairi* short services. Last but not least, as a Buddhist, I was pleasantly surprised (and extremely delighted) when Rina and Eric named him "Bodhi" (enlightened one)!

> **Odin:** He has impressed me with his patience to learn by observation. Even as a five-year-old youngster, he can sit through a nine-inning baseball game! He can patiently observe, with much curiosity, a TV show of a Japanese person playing the *koto* musical instrument. He also loves to hit a plastic baseball and shoot basketball, pretending to be a "dunker." I'm also happy that his full name is Odin Sasaki Vignola.

Mitchell Toru: He tries hard to please us whenever we visit Elk Grove by straightening out his bedroom (our Elk Grove bedroom) and bed, so we can enjoy the comforts of our second home… and also by serving coffee to me. Mitchell expresses his love and interests when ever we watch documentary TV shows about the planet and life on earth. Might he become a scientist or enter a profession related to a scientific or technological pursuit?

Ava Harumi: When we attended her promotion ceremony from elementary to middle school, it was a source of joy to see her enjoying herself with her peers, as well as being recognized for her math and science studies (perhaps her Ph.D. father's influence). Her Japanese middle name, "Harumi" (beautiful spring), appropriately comes from her mother's Japanese name "Hiromi" (beautiful ocean) and the fact she was born in March.

Molly Kinuko: Kinuko is my mother's name. As we are geographically closer to the Masebas in Northern California, we see them more often than our Southern California grandchildren. Molly is what we popularly describe as an all-around person. Be it study or sports, her enthusiasm shows. She is very artistic… future illustrator?

Zoe Toshie: My first impression of Zoe was that she was a studious kind of person. She's also very athletic. In her younger years she impressed me climbing up poles. She has also now turned out to be a good "point guard" in basketball. Her Japanese middle name comes from my wife Helen's Japanese name ("Toshiko" or intelligent child), as well as her grandmother Irene's Japanese name, Sumie.

Chad Senyo: When he was younger, I thought he was a "rascal" *(yancha* in Japanese). He has turned out to be a much steadier grandson. I may be prejudiced, as his Japanese middle name is my first name (Senyo, or 1,000 oceans). Am I wrong to keep reminding (influencing) him to become the 27th-generation Sasaki Buddhist minister?

Jenna Sayoko: Although she and Chad are twins, they look different. Chad has a definite "Tomiyama look," while Jenna has her father's Sasaki looks. She is the fastest runner on her basketball team. Is her energy from being a "rice lover"?

Emily Yukiko: Her love for the Japanese language probably came from visiting Japan in 2015. I am proud and grateful when she tries to use her Japanese phrases on me. She is a good "child-sitter," especially with her cousins, Odin and Bodhi. She's also popular with boys, but I caution her to distinguish "bad boys" and "good boys."

Katelyn Rumiko: The lasting memory I cherish of Katelyn is a short time I was able to spend with her out in a wetland wildlife refuge when we both drew the natural scene. Even if it was only for a brief period, it was a time of "bonding" together for a grandfather who usually does not measure up to a grandmother. I am proud she has been a good student leader in her school and one of the better players in volleyball.

Hailey Sachiko: She's the only vegetarian in the Sasaki family. And yet, amazingly, she is a good distance runner. I wrongly thought that you need to eat meat to be strong and healthy. As a Buddhist, I should have known better. Why? Theravada Buddhist priests, the majority of whom are vegetarians, are generally strong and healthy. I am happy that she is the current Buddhist Temple of San Diego YBA (Young Buddhist Association) president and even interested in United Nations affairs.

Lindsey Yuriko: I've probably spent the most time with her among all of the grandchildren, because our daughter Ellen would leave baby Lindsey, their first child, at our home when she went to teach at Westlake Elementary School in Daly City. I can still remember the times I bathed her and the times we ate popsicles in the front yard while watching the jets fly from nearby San Francisco International Airport to the corners of the world. Lindsey has grown up to be a fine young lady. She is what young people call a "cool person," socially poised with good friends.

Jared Sensho: He certainly is the tallest of the grandchildren... an amazing 6'5". This undoubtedly came from 6'3" father Stanton and 5'10" mother Lisa. That's DNA karma. I arm-wrestled with him when he was two to three feet shorter, but now it's impossible to compete. He's also a good student with a friendly, likable personality. I am grateful they gave him my father's first name of Sensho (1,000 elephants).

My professional book writer/editor, Mika Ono, asked me the questions, "What kind of world do you think they will be living in? And what are your hopes and fears for them?"

All in all, I am very grateful that they have all become good kids, but, as we popularly say, "knock on wood," as we do not know what possible bad karma may affect their futures. To summarize in a few words, I truly think the "four gratitudes" of the past will probably determine a good future for them. Therefore, as we always say in Japanese, *okagesamade* (gratitude to the good karma which has been mostly hidden and of which we are unaware).

My Pleasant, Satisfying and Fulfilling Relationship with LaVerne Sasaki

Rev. Richard T. Schellhase, a clergyman in the Evangelical and Reformed Church, and its successor, the United Church of Christ, shared some reflections.

I strain to find suitable words to describe my high admiration, personal fondness and deep respect for LaVerne Sasaki. As a person he is direct, non-judgmental and joyful. Completely without dissimulation. He loves life and wears on his sleeve his acceptance and compassion for all living creatures, helping us by his example to find purpose, meaning and joy in our own lives.

When I came to work for the Buddhist Churches of America on "The Campaign for Buddhism in America" in 1983, I immediately sought to meet him for his support, since he had been elected by his peers (for a second term) chairman of the BCA Ministerial Association. I phoned for an appointment and he advised, "Bring your bathing suit."

Everything thereafter went swimmingly!

At our first meeting, LaVerne impressed me with his progressive views and ardent enthusiasm for spreading the Buddha-Dharma and letting the force of its truth become a significant element in American culture. He used his position, vision and influence to speak up for the future of his religion and to make Shin Buddhism relevant in today's world and in mainstream America.

As a member of the Rotary Club and by his involvement in United Way and the Boy Scouts, he put his body where his convictions were. His inter-religious interests were expressed through his leadership as president of the local Ministerial Association of more than 50 area clergy, and through his founding of a Japanese Buddhist-Christian Clergy Discussion Group.

Not only was LaVerne an enthusiastic supporter of the Institute of Buddhist Studies, but he also envisioned its place among the other nine theological seminaries (the Graduate Theological Union) in Berkeley, California.

In the early 1980s, LaVerne attended (you might say "infiltrated") a meeting of the Santa Clara Chapter of the Conference of Christians and Jews. There, a serendipitous circumstance put him in conversation with Gordon Weber, a graduate of Harvard Law School, a prominent attorney in a San Francisco law firm and (not incidentally) the president of the Board of Trustees of the Graduate Theological Union. (He also spoke Japanese and in fact died in Japan in 1983.)

There, in that chance meeting with Gordon Weber, LaVerne played a key role in moving forward the affiliation of IBS with the GTU.

In this personal account of my relationship with LaVerne, I am compelled to admit my utter astonishment and intimidation upon learning that he was preceded by 26 generations of Jodo Shinshu priests. (My own ministerial genealogy began with my father and ended with me!) His priestly heritage is hard to live up to and, perhaps, even more difficult to live down. But LaVerne wore his generational mantle with grace, good humor and personal competence.

Perhaps the finest gift LaVerne gave to me over the years is his sense of gratitude, which he himself has woven so seamlessly into his own persona. Some years ago, at my request, he sent me nine or ten Japanese words that are used to express the feeling of gratitude. I always resonated with the word *okagesama*. In that spirit LaVerne lived his life, and I struggle daily better to emulate his good example.

LaVerne and I are still bosom-buddies and have occasional meals together. With eager anticipation, I always look forward to his annual New

Year's greeting and the accompanying family photo that keeps me abreast of his ever-enlarging and increasingly good-looking family.

Traces of a Key Dharmaic Trait in the Life of Rev. LaVerne Senyo Sasaki
By Rev. Tetsuo Unno

To define what is meant by "key Dharmaic trait," we first turn to the Zen Master Yamada, Mumon. That is, when a philosophy student from the prestigious Kyoto University asked Yamada, "What is the ultimate goal of Buddhism?" Yamada responded, "To play… just play… even Buddhas are always at play. To them, even the saving of sentient beings is nothing but play."

The Zen Master Sawaki Kodo poses and answers his own question. He asks, "What makes Ryokan so great?" And in response, he affirms, "What's great about Ryokan is that he's always at play." (Ryokan was an enlightened Zen monk of extraordinary genius as a poet and calligrapher who chose to live the simplest of lives. He is famous for being fully engrossed when he played with the village children.)

In Shin Buddhism, we have the example of the *myokonin*, or, in translation, "marvelously good people (of absolute faith)." *Myokonins*, for the most part, are either illiterate or semi-literate. And yet, being One with the Absolute; that is, with Amida Tathagata, they unfailingly exhibit a sense of Freedom, Spontaneity, Egolessness and Playfulness[66] that is both stunning and unbelievable.

For example, there's the *Myokonin Shomatsu*. Once with his Dharmaic friend Kikuzo, Shomatsu visited the Shogaku Temple in the village of Sanbonmatsu. Once there, Shomatsu went into the Main Hall and lay down on the *tatami* [mat]. Whereupon Kikuzo chided Shomatsu for his disrespectful behavior. To which Shomatsu said, "Look, this is our *oya's* house"—*oya*, meaning "parent," referring to Amida Tathagata—so there's no need to hold back. Anyone who talks like you must be a stepchild!"

Whether in the front of his friend Kikuzo, a spiteful and jealous priest, a local governor, or even the abbot, Shomatsu, without fail, exhibited that same sense of freedom and playfulness.

As for the Myokoni Asahara Saichi, although only semi-literate, Saichi wrote well over 5,000 poems, all of them manifestations of his Oneness with the Amida Tathagata. That Oneness, in turn, manifested itself as the playful-

---

[66] Rev. Unno notes that playfulness is the quality of being unselfconscious and unselfconcerned, while being fully conscious and concerned regarding the welfare of one's fellow beings.

ness, for example, of a child that is One with its Parent. What follows is three of such poems by Saichi:

> *Nyorai-san*
> *Let's you and me*
> *Do "Sumo" wrestling*
> *(Oh) I lost! I lost! I lost! I lost!*
> *I lost and was taken in by my "Namuamidabutsu"*
> *[Nyorai-san and Namuamidabutsu are alternative Names of Amidā Tathagata]*
>
> *Nyorai-san*
> *Let's you and me*
> *Play house*
> *I rejoice over this gift*
> *(Of being able) to play house with you*
> *Namuamidabutsu.*
>
> *Nyorai-san*
> *You think I'm cute*
> *(Well) I think about you (in the same way) too*
> *Namuamidabutsu; Namuamidabutsu.*

It's this very Dharmic trait of always being at "play" that, I believe, manifested itself in varying degrees of breadth and depth throughout the life of Reverend LaVerne Senyo Sasaki (hereafter referred to as LaVerne).

This belief is based on a number of experiences that I shared with La Verne. For example, when we underwent the two stages of our ordination into priesthood, which demands strict adherence to rules and regulations, La Verne, I recall, was among all the fellow candidates, the most at ease and relaxed.

Even at Tokyo University's Department of Indian Philosophy and Sanskrit Philology, where LaVerne and I were graduate students, there existed unspoken but strict rules of protocol. Even in this tradition-bound university, La Verne moved with, I thought, exceptional naturalness and freedom, easily making friends with his fellow students. He did so, it goes without saying and in the words of Confucius, "without transgressing what was right."

Or, to recount one specific shared experience, shortly after arriving in Tokyo, LaVerne suggested that, together with dates, we might attend a dance party being held at the *gakushuin* (college). Having some idea of *gakushuin's* illustrious past; for example, that it had been founded for the purpose of educating the children of nobility, I was somewhat surprised at finding ourselves headed for this ultra-elite college.

Not yet able to speak Japanese with the required fluency and taken aback by a number of contradictions—the fact of my being at this elite campus, the "rich" atmosphere of the whole event, despite the fact that Japan had yet to fully recover from the devastation of WWII and so forth—I simply sat back and "took in" the whole affair. At the same time, however, I noticed that La Verne was fully enjoying the evening, talking to our dates and to the *gakushuin* students etc. [I understand that the word "play," is related to the Dutch word "pleien" which, in turn, connotes "jumping for joy."]

This trait also showed itself at other gatherings. Such as those at the Tsukiji Honganji, where La Verne and I, together with the Reverends Yamashita, Iwamoto and Hata, took turns delivering the Sunday English sermons, after which we gathered together with those in attendance for refreshments and a chance to socialize. Suffice it to say, whatever the nature of the gathering, when LaVerne happened to be present, to some indefinable degree, there was a shift from formality to informality, from a certain tenseness to a more relaxed atmosphere or from being constrained by various forms (*kata*) of idealized behavior to simply enjoying a given event.

Finally, on a more mundane matter, I'd like to take this opportunity to thank LaVerne for ceding his dormitory room (which had originally been occupied by my brother, Taitetsu) to me upon his return to the U.S. At that time, he also handed over his bedding, a *kotatsu*,[67] a solid desk, a stately portable closet, a swivel chair and so forth, all of which helped materially in my effort to complete my master's thesis. This help was especially crucial, since due to circumstances, the thesis needed to be finished within an exceedingly short span of time.

There are other details that, without doubt, deserve mention; however, due to the limitations of space, this brief remembrance comes to an end at this point. May Reverend LaVerne Senyo Sasaki, however, continue on without

---

[67] A low, wooden table, which is heated and draped with bedding; this piece of furniture is used to stay warm and is often the center of domestic life, especially in the winter.

end to "play" and thereby serve to lighten the lives of his fellow beings, in both this and all other future worlds.

A Reflection on My Life

It is 4:30 a.m. in my San Bruno home as I quietly reflect upon my 87 years of life. It is my daily practice to go to bed early and get up early. To me, it is the best time to read and reflect. I am reminded of the late Rev. Nagatani of Visalia, who did all his church work and Buddhist reading when most people were asleep. It is also the time when my wife is asleep and I don't need to respond to her. It is no wonder that Theravada priests are single.

My mind is fresh in the morning so many thoughts arise, such as my barber friend telling me that, despite my recent colon cancer surgery, I will live for another 15 to 20 years... That would make me 95 or 100 years old, but I do not want to live that long.

I think of my father-in-law, Frank Yokoi, who lived to almost 97. Although he was able to see and receive visits from his faithful and devoted children, grandchildren and 26 great-grandchildren, he was lonely most of his days without his wife and most of his personal friends. I vividly remember he merely sat on his couch, staring at the outdoor garden and contemplating his life. However, he was comforted by the most dependable source of peace, his Buddhist faith. Whenever my wife and I would visit him at his senior residential care home in Foster City, he would appreciate the short service I would conduct with his home Buddhist shrine (*obutsudan*). His eyes seemed teary whenever we would sing the popular Japanese Buddhist song "Ondokusan" (song of praise to infinite Buddha). I think of him and my late parents whenever I sing that particular song. It was so human of him to cry and say he did not want to die.

This sentiment was echoed by the technology giant/icon/inventor Steve Jobs in his famous 2005 Stanford University commencement speech: "No one wants to die... and yet death is the destination we all share. No one has ever escaped it. And this is as it should be, because Death is very likely the single best invention of life." I was happy to read his life was profoundly influenced by his Buddhist faith and philosophy. [68]

My days are also numbered. We hardly think about these issues when

---

[68] An article in *U.S.A. Today* dated October 19, 2011, featured an opinion article by a British psychiatrist named Russell Razzaque, who wrote a fascinating article on Steve Jobs as a Buddhist. Although Apple was his technological palette, Buddhist philosophy defined Steve Jobs, showing how "ancient Buddhist philosophy" has become more alive, relevant and contemporary in the 21st century.

we are young and, on the rare occasion we do, it seems in the distant future. With this in mind, we spend most of our time, energy and money for a "secure and happy life in the future." We are like the hamsters my children had when they were young, running on a revolving wheel. While some would call it exercise, it always appeared to me the hamster was chasing happiness that never was to be.

I also ask myself, "Did I do my best with what I was given?" I tell myself probably not, because I did not focus totally on the important things in life, but instead many times on lesser things that interested me or gave me pleasure. Would my life have been different if I were not a minister? Would my life have been different if I did not marry this wife of mine? What if I had been born in Japan and became a business person in Tokyo? Perhaps, I could have been a wealthy person living in some fancy home in a high-class residential area... Would I have had a life similar to the one I am presently living?

Life's "karma ball" bounces more like an unpredictably bouncing football than a predictably bouncing basketball. While some of life can be directed with greater predictability, like a basketball, life is often inconsistent and unpredictable, like the bounce of a football.

Considering these factors, I can say my life was good because I was blessed with much good karma from my ancestors, parents, teachers, friends and family, and by the fact I was born here in the United States. The running theme of the "four gratitudes" (to the Buddha, your parents and other ancestors, your teachers, and your country/world) is a basic and simple teaching from my father that has been so true for me. As we commonly recite in the "Three Treasures" of Buddha, Dharma and Sangha, life's offerings are difficult to receive, and yet I have been fortunate to be given these rare and incomparable gifts. My life has been rich in ways that exceed the wealth of money, fame and security.

The Jodo Shinshu words found in the brief teaching called *"Jodo Shinshu no seikatsu shinjo"* (Jodo Shinshu Buddhist faith in daily living) has truly provided me with the necessary motivation and spiritual energy to cope with many challenges and frustrations. The four short paragraphs in this popular religious service reading express the entire teaching and philosophy of Shinran Shonin, the founder of our Buddhist denomination. It was remarkable that the scholars and leaders were able to summarize the vast doctrine in such a faithful and succinct manner.

The first paragraph emphasizes the importance of entrusting faith and its outcome of spiritual strength, beauty and joy, similar to the popular saying, "out of the mud grows the lotus." While people often misinterpret Buddhism as a pessimistic religion due to its fundamental starting point of life as suffering, there is nothing more optimistic.

The second paragraph brings out the life of gratitude one can receive when Buddha's wisdom casts the light necessary to understand one's true human nature. Without this light of wisdom, most of us will continue to depend on unreliable and limited human reasoning and logical thinking.

The third paragraph of this Jodo Shinshu Buddhist reading emphasizes the fact that the Buddhist way of life can be easily misunderstood if we don't listen to it completely and thoroughly. This implies the true way of Buddhist understanding and practice requires much patience and understanding.

The fourth and last passage teaches that people following the true Buddhist way of a life of joy will be inspired to respect and help all people and to build a better community. This kind of teaching has motivated me to become involved with the community via various social agencies.

A late *Nisei* Buddhist educator from Hilo, Hawaii, gave a lecture in which she appropriately and refreshingly described the Jodo Shinshu Buddhist way of life as a way to humbly return in gratitude what the world has given in more ways than she can return. This is the Jodo Shinshu Buddhist practice of gratitude in daily living. If more people can realize this kind of gift, the world will truly become a better place.

May this way of life become a reality for our church members and for my family members and friends. As it is said commonly in conversation, it is not how long you live, but how well you live this one short life.

Namu Amida Butsu.

ACKNOWLEDGMENTS

My father regularly spoke on *shion* (four gratitudes) in his sermons, mentioned several times in this book. These words summarize my whole life and publication of this book.

This book is not a comprehensive biography. I wish I could include names and remembrances of every person who has helped, supported, taught, watched over me and given of their precious time, energy, emotions and material gifts for my benefit. Unfortunately, this wasn't possible. To all the teachers, family members, friends, temple members and acquaintances who were my Bodhisattvas but are not mentioned on these pages, I hope you will accept my sincere apology.

This book would not have been possible without the support of many friends and colleagues who I am so fortunate to know and to whom am I so grateful. Thank you to those who took time from their very busy schedules to contribute wonderful new writings for this book: Bishop Kodo Umezu, the late Rev. Fumihiko Sakow, the late Kimi Hisatsune, Rev. Dr. Kenneth K. Tanaka, the late Rev. Junjo Tsumura, Mrs. Takaye Hanayama, Mr. Hiroji Kariya and Rev. Tetsuo Unno.

Thank you so much, Dr. Nobuo Haneda and Ms. Haruka Beppu, for providing your time, effort and expertise to translate articles from the difficult original Japanese.

Thank you to additional contributors Rev. Richard T. Schellhase, Sumi Uyeda, Della Bruens, Fumiya Sakow, Rev. Joen Amagishi, the late Rev. Shousei Hanayama, and Rev. Shudo Takahatake, whose writings are in this book, and Bill Teague, for advising us on book publishing.

Last but not least, I express gratitude to my parents; my wife, Helen; the family (especially daughter Sharon for assisting with this book project); writer Mika Ono, who devoted many hours from her busy schedule to turn my remembrances into readable narrative; graphic designer Michael Sherman; and the many teachers and friends who gave me this good life. Mika is the granddaughter of Rev. Jotetsu Kunimatsu Ohno (1900–1970). In 1948, Rev. Ohno was briefly assigned to assist my father at Sacramento Buddhist Church. I met him then and even remember teaching him to drive. It was another good karma that Sharon found Mika to edit this book.

Namu Amida Butsu.

APPENDIX

About the First Overseas Minister, Senjū Sasaki
This series was written by Rev. Shudo Takahatake 高畑崇導, *an overseas minister of the Montreal Buddhist Church, on the occasion of the 80th anniversary of Buddhism in Canada, counted from my grandfather's arrival in Vancouver in 1905.*

(I)

Senjū Sasaki was born in Shinshū Hongwanji-ha, Kōzenji 高善寺, in Fukui Prefecture. This temple has a long and distinguished history in Jōdo Shinshū. The founder was Zeshō 是証, who met Shinran during his exile to Echigo from Kyoto; Zeshō took refuge in Shinran. Kakuwa 覚和, the 50th head minister of Amidain 阿弥陀院, which followed the Shingon 真言 tradition, took refuge in Zeshō and converted this temple to Jōdo Shinshū. Senjū was the 24th generation minister after Zeshō.

The head ministers in Kōzenji have been resolute and undauntable. Zekū, the 14th generation minister, 是空, supported the Hongwanji [Jōdo Shinshū leadership] with its followers for more than 20 years when they were fighting with Oda Nobunaga 織田信長 [a powerful *daimyo* in the late 16th century who attempted to unify Japan]. As a matter of fact, the Hongwanji had a huge number of followers—more than half the population of Japan at that time. Some temples in the countryside were exceedingly wealthy. For instance, a head minister of Honzeiji 本誓寺, Chōken 超賢, contributed resources, such as *ikkan* of gold, 1,500 *hyō* of rice, 90 *hyō* of barley, 10 barrels of oil, 80 barrels of miso and 150 *han* of cotton for Kennyo 顕如. It was preparation fit for a military commander. Nobunaga needed to suppress the temples of the countryside as well as the Hongwanji due to this kind of support.

Nobunaga attacked and defeated the city of Echizen 越前, where

Kōzenji is located, subjugating the Hongwanji. Echizen was like "Hongwanji's hand and foot," indicating the power of the head minister of Kōzenji at that time. Moreover, it is told that Sasaki Kojirō 佐々木小次郎, who was the sixth son of Munekazu 宗寿, the 18th generation of Kōzenji, fought a duel with Miyamoto Musashi 宮本武蔵 in Ganryūjima 巌流島....

Senjū was born in Kōzenji in 1871. Japan had just entered a new era, Meiji 4 [a period of modernization]. The construction of public schools started during this year. Fukui was a particularly progressive place, sending students overseas to study abroad, inviting teachers from America early on and using the book *Self Help*, written by Karl Marx, and *Seiyō jijō* 西洋事情 as textbooks.

At the same time, this was a trying period due to *Haibutsu Kishaku* 廃仏毀釈 [the advocacy of expelling Buddhism from Japan]. As part of the anti-Buddhist movement, the government had a policy of abolishing Buddhism and temples. However, precisely because of this movement, Senjū's father, Shinkū 信空, sent him to not only junior high school, but also to the Hongwanji, the highest educational institution at that time. This was because he wanted Senjū to be "tough on himself," so he could endure such an era and be capable of overcoming difficulties.

But Kōzenji was quite poor, so at school Senjū had to use a straw rope as his belt. Senjū learned the heart of caring and loving from his parents, who, because they wanted to give high education to their child, squeezed out school tuition from their savings. This experience formed Senjū's character, "tough on himself" and "gentle to others." Later on, his character became a key factor in his accomplishments as an overseas minister.

(II)

Senjū was 16 the summer he entered the Hongwanji Bungakuryō 文学寮 for advanced education. At that time, important people in the Hongwanji included Shimaji Mokurai 島地黙雷, who went to Europe as the first Japanese Buddhist minister, and Akamatsu Renjō 赤松連城, who was capable of speaking about the Jōdo Shinshū doctrine in English. Ōtani Kōzui 大谷光瑞, who eventually became Monshu 門主 of the Hongwanji, overcame a challenge by *Haibutsu Kishaku*.

There were great teachers there, including Lafcadio Hearn, who is known as Koizumi Yakumo 小泉八雲, and Sugimura Kōtarō Sojinkan 杉村広太郎楚人冠 who eventually moved to the Asahi Newspaper and took a leading role in shaping Japanese public opinion. There were excellent students as well, including several two or three years ahead of Senjū: Takakusu Junjirō 高楠順次郎, who became a great Buddhist scholar, Sakō Egan 酒生慧眼, who became the first president of Bukkyō University at the age of 39 and eventually became Senjū's step brother, and Imamura Emyō 今村恵猛, who served the head minister of the Hawaii district and who later provided Donald Keene an opportunity to become a great Buddhist scholar at Columbia University.

However, the Hongwanji recorded that they were troublesome students. They bothered the Hongwanji with their demonstrations, which appealed for the improvement of the school and the reformation of the Hongwanji. Furthermore, they joined the temperance movement; Senjū also became the part of the temperance movement and never had alcohol. These students also published the magazine, *Hanseikai Zasshi* 反省会雑誌. During the year of Senjū's commencement, this publication moved its hub office to Tokyo and was renamed "Chūō Kōron 中央口論," which it is called to the current day.

(III)

Two years after Senjū graduated from Bungakuryō, he married Tomie, a sister of Sakō Egan. Soon after, he headed off to travel to India and Europe to gain a new perspective on the situation in Japan; in the early Meiji era, many in Japan believed in the supremacy of Western civilization. At the end of this trip, Senjū was assigned to be an overseas minister in Singapore. He ended up staying there for six years.

At that time, Singapore was a British colony—a miserable situation for the country, as is typically the case. Also in the 1890s, this land was "an anchor site for connecting with the East and Europe," "the industrial center of the world for rubber production" and "the base of Eastern Fleet of the British Navy." In 1904, during the Russo-Japanese War, a Japanese Buddhist minister found a Baltic Fleet on the coast of Singapore and sent a telegram to Japan. It is believed this minister was Senjū.

On another note, it is said that Singapore had a population of 250,000, half of which was "*Karayuki-san*" (prostitutes). Senjū's wife, Tomie, brought those girls to their temple and taught them sewing, manners and writing. Senjū and Tomie had their first son, Sengaku 千嶽, who passed away when he was very young, so their next child, Sensho 千象, was called their first son. They named him Sensho (whose Chinese characters mean 1,000 elephants) because he was conceived during their trip in India.

[See also the next article, "Singapore Report," in this appendix for Senju's own observations from this period.]

(IV)

Senjū received the assignment of first overseas minister of Canada when he was in Singapore. He briefly returned to Japan, then moved to Vancouver on October 12, 1905. His wife, Tomie, and Sensho, who was then two years old, accompanied him. Two months after that, on December 26, their first daughter, Fumie, was born. Senjū's mission started with the happy event of his daughter's birth. But not all events were so propitious: two years after their arrival in Canada, there were riots in Vancouver.

Senjū stayed in Vancouver for eight years, during which time he had three daughters and one son and designed and built the new Buddhist church with 650 members. There are so many stories about Senjū during these years. Here, we will focus on how Senjū spread Buddhism, lived his life as an immigrant outside of Japan and developed his thinking about the world. Now, let's look at his work in Vancouver.

Senjū accomplished many great achievements in Canada. He served in an important post in the "National school," which followed the policies of the Imperial Rescript on Education. He was pushed into the Canadian anti-assimilation group and got involved in the publication of the newspaper, *Tairiku Nippō* 大陸日報, although a student who attended one of Senjū's English classes was recruited by the Canadian pro-assimilation group. On one occasion, Senjū tried to address the fact that only the graves of the Japanese were not cleaned in a cemetery; however, when he went to visit, the grave keeper would not let him in. Another time, a Japanese man was executed and Senjū witnessed the execution, reading sūtras as if he was practicing asceticism. These incidents illustrate the fact that Senjū shared the difficulties of immigrants during that time and supported others.

The following story also tells us where Senjū was looking for a fundamental path to help overcome such difficulties. In May 1909, a training squad ron of Aso 阿蘇 and Sōya 宗谷 called at the port of Vancouver. Senjū delivered a welcome speech, "Japanese immigrants receive prejudice from Canada because we are not understood by the world."[73] He also appealed to the Navy officer cadet who eventually became a leader in Japan to "display national prestige." In other words, Japan would be dominated by the Western world as long as Japanese didn't recognize the strong bond between Japan (the nation) and the Japanese (the citizens).

Senjū left his position in Vancouver in November 1913. Senjū was 43 and his wife, Tomie, was 39.

(V)

By the time Senjū returned to Japan, the Taishō 2 era had begun. Japan was catching up with the great Western powers and was about to display national pride, dovetailing with Senjū's affirmation of the lasting bond between Japan and Japanese citizens. Also, the trend toward democracy was about to emerge. Unfortunately, displaying national prestige outside of Japan turned out to involve aggression and imperialism, and intellectuals who were educated in Taishō democracy fell short in dealing with the difficulties of society. In this contradiction, there was evidence that Senjū engaged in "Seikyōsha 政教社," an association that defined an enlightened nationalism and retention of the bond between Japan and Japanese citizens; this movement was organized by Shimaji Mokurai 島地黙雷, who was its patron and a teacher in Hongwanji, Moyake Setsurei 三宅雪嶺 and Shiga Shigetaka 志賀重昂.

Five years after Senjū's return to Japan, in 1918, the Hongwanji ordered him to become a missionary in the Siberian army. In addition to Senjū, a few other civilians stayed with the soldiers and experienced hardships in the extreme cold: one minister of the Sōtō 曹洞 school, another minister of the Jōdo 浄土 school and three journalists. Senjū was only the one who went back to Japan after serving his two years as a missionary in the army. It is said that the completion of one's thoughts begins in one's late 40s. In this respect, Senjū's experience serving in the military at ages 48 and 49 was a prompt to stick to his beliefs to overcome the tension between Japanese politics in the Taishō era and the ideal of society. And it was time for Senjū to gain the idea of nationalism.

---

[73] About 10 years before Senjū got to this post, a consul, Nose Tatsugorō 能勢辰五郎 reported to the first Japanese president, Itō Hirobumi 伊藤博文 who went to England via Canada that, "Japanese are ostracized because of Japanese immigrants' poor behavior in daily life." This idea is completely different from Senjū's. There is no life experience as an immigrant in Nose's statement.

(VI)

Four years after Senjū came back from Siberia, he was assigned as an overseas minister in Canada again. He turned 53 in February 1923. He brought his first daughter, Fumie, with him. She was born in Vancouver and was 17 at the time of their return. In later years, Senjū told her that the reason why he brought her was not only because he wanted her to take care of him but also because he wanted her to see another country. At the time, the Buddhist church of Vancouver had fractured into two groups, including ministers. Senjū's job was to clear up the confusion.

During this time, a woman came to visit Senjū at Vancouver's Patricia Hotel, where he was staying. She had been a prostitute but had changed and raised a family. She came to see Senjū to let him know how her life had changed. She took Fumie home and took care of her as a gesture of gratitude to Senjū and Tomie. Even now, Fumie can remember this woman's name and the ocean-view room on the second floor where Fumie stayed. We can see part of Senjū's impact in Vancouver through this story.

Senjū's visit to Vancouver ended within two months. The Hongwanji ordered him to become a head minister of the Buddhist Church of America. Senjū moved to America and served there for two years, from 1923 to 1925, when he was 53 to 55 years old. During that time, the second generation of Japanese Americans were school-age children. At the same time, Senjū couldn't have insulated himself from the fact that a strong Asian exclusion movement was afoot.

Buddhist churches in America started establishing dormitories to take care of members' children and educate the second generation of Japanese Americans. Two years later, Senjū communicated this circumstance to Ōtani Sonyu 大谷尊由 of the Hongwanji. Consequently, Sonyu visited Canada, America and Hawaii in November 1926. It was the first time for a Hongwanji Monshu to travel to these countries for the sole purpose of visiting overseas district temples.

(VII)

After three years, Senjū came back from America. It was in Shōwa 2 (1927) and he was 57.

Upon his return, he was surprised by the seriousness of his wife's rheumatism. Her difficulty walking was worrying. Senjū traveled slowly with his wife to Zenkōji 善光寺, Nara and Kyoto. There is a picture of them: Tomie is sitting on a chair and Senjū is standing by her side and a few deer are surrounding them. The picture must have been taken in the deer park in Nara.

The Hongwanji ordered him to serve Rinban 輪番 as an alternating head minister of a temple of Otaru. He left his wife, Tomie, behind and went to his new post with his second daughter, Chiyoko, who was then 22.

His time in Otaru was memorable. Senjū's first son, Sensho, who was serving as an overseas minister in America, came back to Japan to get married. It was early in his post in Otaru, but Senjū went back to Fukui to celebrate the wedding.

Sensho married Kinuko 絹子, who was a daughter of Hōkyō Hachirōemon 宝鏡八郎衛門 of Ōno 大野 in Fukui. Hōkyō was a family with a long history in Ōno and their Hōonkō 報恩講 tradition was to gather in Hōkyō's house and perform a Hōonkō service. Also, Kinuko's grandmother was from a temple family. Hachirōemon served as a chairman of the prefectural assembly for three terms. Kinuko was the fourth of nine children and the second daughter in her family. One of her older brothers, Terashi 晃, allied with Hatoyama Ichirō 鳩山一郎 and joined in the establishment of the Liberal Party.

In Senjū's position, one of his duties was to promote the Futaba 双葉 Technical girls' school to a girls' high school. He involved his step brother, Sakō Egan, in the project. Egan became the first president of Takanawa Buddhism University at the age of 39. However, he left the position and went back to Fukui because he was affected by tuberculosis. Shortly after that, Ōtani Kōzui, who was the Hongwanji Monshu, decided to close down the university because its educational policy was too Western and for financial reasons. From his sick bed, Egan criticized the Hongwanji for its action, writing letters to ministers in all parts of Japan.

In response, the Hongwanji deprived Egan of his ministry and described his behavior as "a betrayal of the Hongwanji." A year and a half later,

Egan received his ministry back, but he passed away at the age of 46 in frustration over the university's closure. Senjū's passion for education came from his interactions with Egan.

After his seven-year mission in Otaru, what was waiting for Senjū was the reality that his wife, Tomie, had become bedridden. She went back to the Pure Land the next year, in 1935, as if she was waiting for Senjū's return. She was 61 and Senjū was 65.

(VIII)

Serving in Otaru was Senjū's last assignment outside of Fukui. From this point on, he started occasionally writing things down. For instance, going back in time somewhat, he recorded in detail the crisis in Fukui caused by heavy snow and titled it "Ōyuki kanmuryōshukyō 大雪感無量終郷" (Being Full of Emotion as I Realize My Hometown May End from Heavy Snow). Also, he recorded items such as the price of vegetables, which tree branch in his garden was broken and the appearance of houses in his village. The title of this record book was "Ōyuki niyotte kokyō ga shūen wo mukaerukamoshirenaikotowo tannjiteiru 大雪によって故郷が終焉をむかえるかも知れないことを歎じている" (Lament of the End of My Hometown Which May Occur from Heavy Snow). It seems like Senjū played on words in the title, "Ōyuki kanmuryōshukyō 大雪感無量終郷" and "Bussetsu kanmuryōjyukyō 仏説観無量寿経."

Also, Senjū suggested young people in the countryside adopt the custom of making chairs, which he believed would strengthen the Japanese physique. He made a chair of Fukui bamboo, which is well known as the "bamboo doll of Echizen," and showed it to people. It is said he dreamed of the improvement of the industry and the strengthening of children's physique in Fukui.

Senjū also became a chairman of an elementary school parents' association due to his rich experiences. He told stories to children about the world. He named himself Amame 天米, hearkening to his experiences going to India (Tenjiku 天竺) and the United States (Bēkoku 米国). He wrote those stories in Sanskrit or English if someone asked him to, signing his name "天米" in Kanji. However, this happy period did not last long. He started suffering from stomach cancer five years after he came back from Otaru. On December 8, 1941, the Pacific War [World War II] started, as if to add insult to injury. The hostile country was the United States, where he served two years of his public life as the representative head minister of Buddhist Churches of America. It was also the country where his first son, Sensho, his wife, Kinuko, and Senjū's grandsons, Senyo 千洋, Senpo 千峰 and Senrey 千玲, lived. Also in the United States were Senjū's youngest, Masako, her husband and Senjū's nephew, Shawshew 章秀, and Senjū's grandson, Fumiya 文弥. In addition, Senjū's other grandson, Fumihiko 文彦 (Shawshew's son), had been sent to Senjū to study at an elementary school and get an education on being a minister so he could take over his father's temple in the future.

Senjū had recommended Shawshew and Masako learn about America and had sent them there through Sensho and Kinuko. It can be easily imagined how difficult it was for Senjū to face the reality that Fumihiko might not be able to see his father again because of the war. It can be seen in his behavior. Even though he must have known it was likely to no avail, he begged every single post office in his village to send a letter to his children and grandchildren when all mail had been stopped between Japan and America because of the war.

There was more than five feet of snow in his hometown in Fukui on December 8, the day the war started. It is said that he looked absolutely exhausted, begging post offices to mail his letter to the US. He eventually fell ill from cancer. He told stories of the world to his grandson while his energy was fading. Or Senjū might tell him about the books he read when he was a child, such as Self Help by Smiles or Seiyō jijō 西洋事情 by Fukuzawa Yukichi 福沢諭吉. Senjū passed away on June 23, 1944 before he saw his children and other grandchildren again.

Conclusion

Senjū lived in the three eras, Meiji, Taishō and Shōwa. These multiple periods in history and society shaped his personality and his path in life. Meiji, the beginning of a new era, represented Senjū's childhood and his young adulthood. Taishō, a time of anti-Westernized policy in Japan, represented an important evolution in Senjū's thought. Shōwa, during which militarism was established, coincided with Senjū's sad final years and waste of much fruitful thought and experience he had built.

During these three eras, Japan was wavering, trying to make a decision to "accept," "reject" or "assimilate" Western civilization. For his part, Senjū saw the contradiction in such history through his experience in Western countries. He had been considering the issue his entire life. Senjū also saw the irony of his traditional role, which meant he had to focus only on Hongwanji affairs[74] even though he was so talented, raised in the socially developed and progressive Fukui, and possessing experience in the enlightened world. Also, he struggled with the master-disciple relationship of the Hongwanji and temples in the country. Some say it was Senjū's "identity crisis."

In other words, Senjū had many identities. He had been looking for a value and place he could truly rely on for thought and action in an era that kept changing dramatically. Also, as one of the typically smart ministers of the Hongwanji temple in the countryside, he was bound by a rigid societal structure.

Postscript

Senjū's first daughter, Matsuura Fumie of Tokyo, the second daughter, Sasaki Chiyoko of Fukui, and the first daughter, Sakow Masako of California, held a service with their relatives on September 24, 1983 at Kōzenji in Fukui to mark 40 years since Senjū's death and 50 years since Tomie's death. The writer visited Kōzenji the next day.

Also, it is well-known that Senjū's first son, Sensho's wife, Kinuko, and their first son, Senyo, are serving ministry and rejoicing in listening to the Dharma at Mountain View, where Sensho served as the first minister.

Singapore Report

These three reports, written by Rev. Senju Sasaki when he was stationed in Singapore, were published in the Singapore Times and subsequently The Journal of Kyokai-ichiran in 1900 and 1901. This report was translated by Dr. Nobuo Haneda of Maida Buddhist Center in Berkeley, California.

First Report (published in The Journal of Kyokai-ichiran on July 11, 1900)

Last year the newspaper *Strait Times*, one of the major newspapers in Singapore, introduced our Buddhist projects to the public with an article entitled "Converting Singapore [into Buddhism]." Since then, I have been re

---

[74] As an aside, Senjū never politically joined the Hongwanji. There are scholars who say that having vanity and being exhibitionist was "bad conduct," as ministers should never act in such a way. It can be said that Senjū was free from that "bad conduct."

ceiving requests from Japanese people who live in the towns and villages of Penang, Sumatra, Sulawes and Java. They asked me to visit their places to propagate Buddhism. Non-Japanese people have also sent me letters to inquire into what Japanese Buddhism is all about. Among them, Mr. Zeer Nyse (spelling?), an officer of the British government who lives in the city of Kuala Lumpure, has asked me serious questions about Japanese Buddhism. Although we are separated by a distance of several hundred *Ii* (one Ii being 25 miles) and have not yet seen each other, he swore to me in his mail that he is a Buddhist. Since then, he could not suppress his desire to visit Japan. Eventually in the second half of May this year he made up his mind to visit Japan. He traveled from his place to the port of Singapore and got on the Tokiwa-maru, a ship that was on its way back to Japan from Europe. He is already in Japan now; he must be enjoying his trip there. Mr. Nyse is a man of an excellent character. Since he is full of religious devotion, his main aim in this trip to Japan is to see the status of Japanese Buddhism and its academic institutions.

Next, I want to talk about a couple of projects with which I am currently involved. Singapore is not only the point that connects the East and the West, but also a focal point between the north and the south, between countries, such as Australia, Java and Myanmar. Hence various types of people, such as scholars, businessmen and politicians, visit. Currently, the Paris Great Exposition is being held here. Many people are visiting from Japan for this exposition alone. I am helping local Japanese to build a tea house that is designed to welcome every one of the Japanese visitors. I am not sure, though, if I am doing a good job for the tea house.

As far as my propagation and teaching activities are concerned, I give Buddhist talks to Japanese people who live in Singapore, twice a month, on the 15th and 28th. I donate Buddhist books for occasional visitors to our Propagation Center; I also give the Dharma talks to them. I conduct funeral services; and whenever people request, I chant Buddhist sutras. I am pretty busy with those ministerial works. At our school that is attached to our center, we have classes from 9 am to 4 pm. In total we have more than 30 students. I teach girls the three subjects—reading, calligraphy and mathematics. I give boys a level of education that is given at the public grammar schools in Japan. In addition, I make sure that I give boys a class of English. During the evenings, I have a Japanese class for Caucasian people and various Indian people. I am about to start an English class for Japanese youth who came from Japan. In addition to these classes, a group of young people has recently urged me to start a class on the Tendai teachings; they asked me to give lectures on them. I have heard that the group has already made preparations for it.

Besides these activities, I work as an interpreter. Since last year, some drifters from Okinawa have come here. All of them are penniless and impoverished. So I work as an official interpreter and report to the imperial consulate office.

Thus I am a man of many hats: I work as a teacher, a Buddhist minister, a worker for a tea house, "an elder (*ojiisan*, probably a nickname)," and an interpreter. Since my work keeps me quite busy, I feel a bit overwhelmed by my duties. However, concerning my two undertakings of education and propagation, I have a plan of expanding them. In case I get one or two more additional Buddhist ministers here, in addition to the propagation by correspondence I want to send a Buddhist minister to nearby islands so that his propagation of Buddhism satisfies the desire of local Shin followers. As far as the propagation of Buddhism around the Pacific Ocean alone is concerned, not to mention around the Atlantic Ocean, there are many difficulties before we will be able to establish an adequate propagation front!

On June 6, at 9 am, the group whose mission is receiving the Buddha's ashes in Thailand arrived at Singapore by the Hakata-maru. This group consisted of the representatives of various sects of Japanese Buddhism, such as the abbot in waiting of the Otani-ha, Rev. Ryotoku Fujishima representing the Honpa Hongwanji-ha, Rev, Mokusen Hioki representing the Soto sect, and Rev. Josetsu Maeda representing the Myoshinji (or Rinzai) sect. This group that consisted of 18 people stayed at the Raffles Hotel. On that day, I welcomed the group on the ship together with Mr. Nakayama, the imperial consulate. It was quite fortunate for the group that since the weather was favorable, their travel was quite smooth and all of the travelers were in good shape. Prior to their arrival, I had sent to the local newspapers an article about this group's visit. Thus several Catholic fathers came to see the arrival of the group consisting of Japanese monks. Those Catholic fathers who had come to the pier quite early were surprised to see the robes in gorgeous colors that were worn by Japanese monks. Previously they saw a similar tour group from Ceylon. The monks in that group were wearing humble mono-colored robes. The Japanese tour group gave the Catholic fathers an impression as if it were a tour group of aristocratic people. The group stayed at the hotel during the following two nights. Then, on the following day, at 8 am, they got on the ship Singapore and headed for Bangkok. They were lucky because the prince of Thailand, who was on his way back to his country, having finished his studies in Europe, happened to be on board the same ship.

Second Report (published in The Journal of Kyokai-ichiran on July 29, 1900)

June 24: The group (consisting of 18 people) whose mission is receiving the Buddha's ashes arrived at Singapore by the German ship *Koratt* at 4 pm and the group landed at 6:30 pm. The group had received the Buddha's ashes from the King of Thailand, left Bangkok on the German ship *Koratt*, and had come here. The Otani-ha representatives stayed at the Raffles Hotel. Rev. Hioki, representative of the Soto sect, and Rev. Maeda, representative of the Myoshinji (or Rinzai) sect, stayed at the Matsuo Inn. Rev. Fujishima, representative of our Hongwanji-ha, immediately came to our Propagation Center to stay.

June 25: The Otani-ha representatives visited our Propagation Center.

June 26: At 8 pm, the group of 18 people visited the botanical garden in the city. I guided the tour. After having spent several hours in the garden, we left there. On our way back, we encountered a heavy rain and immediately returned to hotels.

June 27: No activities.

June 28: At 1 pm, a lecture session was held at our Hongwanji Propagation Center. The three lecturers were Dr. Bunyu Nanjo, Rev. Mokusen Hioki of the Soto sect, and Rev. Ryoon Fujishima of our Hongwanji-ha. At the outset I gave an opening message in which I explained the significance of the lecture session. It was followed by Dr. Nanjo's lecture on the meaning of the Buddhist theory of causation. Rev. Hioki explained the meaning of the word "Buddha." Rev. Fujishima gave a talk on Shinran's *wasan* hymns. The audience of several hundred people was moved by their talks and deepened their devotion to the Buddha. We ended the session at 4:30 pm with joy.

June 29: The group got on the ship *Martha* to go back to Japan. On June 30 at 8 am, the ship left Singapore. However, Rev. Fujishima of our sect alone did not leave for Japan because the sectarian headquarters had asked him to attend the religious conference held in Paris, France. In order to wait for a ship that goes to France, he is currently staying at our Propagation Center. He will probably leave for France on board the ship *Ratis* on July 8.

Third Report (published in The Journal of Kyokai-ichiran on May 15, 1901)

As you know, the Tripitaka Master Gijo (Chinese I-ching) of the Tang dynastic period, the author of the *Nankai-kikiden (A Travel through the Southern Ocean)*, started the propagation of Buddhism some 1,200 years ago.
Since then, most of the Malaysian people (who lived in Java as the center and in all the Dutch-Indian colonies—the territories near the equator) became passionate Buddhists.

However, when those people faced the rapid propagation currents of Muslim believers, Buddhism ended up in total destruction. Since then, Malaysian people considered Buddhism "a teaching for the lazy," and regarded Islam "the true religion." I think the religious and historical examination of this transition, which is different from other religious transitions, is an interesting topic.

Concerning this religious transformation, what I deeply regret is this. Buddhism contributed to the creation of a wonderful art in the Southern Ocean. It gave impact to the creation of things, such as *pagoda* towers, temples, multistoried buildings, wonderful artifacts that are made of gold, silver and jewels, sculptures and pictures. But all of these totally disappeared together with Buddhism. They were all buried in the soil of the inland of Java. (Although it is said that one wealthy native person stored in one island many Buddha statues made of gold and silver in their original forms, I doubt if those statues actually exist.)

Christian missionaries of Europe and the United States, who are passionate adepts in missionary works, have so far been unable to convert Malaysians. This fact, I think, presents itself as a huge question in the history of the study of world religions, although I regard Islam as a misguided faith.

Concerning the fact that Malaysians considered Buddhism "a teaching for the lazy," I can, as a proof, talk about one astonishing word in the Malaysian language. It is the Malaysian word "*budo*" (used in Java) or "*podo*" (used in the areas near Singapore), which they use to mean "Buddha," an English word. They associate "a lazy person" with the word "*budo*" or "*podo*." Their view of the Buddha as a lazy person came from the following fact. When they looked at Shakyamuni's six years of ascetic practice at Mt. Himalaya, they thought that Shakyamuni abandoned all his responsibilities. Thus they formed an idea that Shakyamuni was the laziest one of all people, who taught the teaching of "no work and no knowledge." I cannot help being surprised by their mentality and thinking. Towards these intuitive people who lack understanding and imagination we, Buddhist propagators, must adopt special means of propagation.

In the following, I will list several words that the Malaysian people commonly use in their daily lives. These words will show how they generally think. For example, the sun is *mata-hari* (the eye of the day); a stream is *sunge-ana* (a child of the river); a police is *mata-mata* (the eye of eyes); a detective is *mata-grappu* (the eye in darkness); ice is *ai-pato* (a stone of water); and an eclipse is *saki-matahari* (a sickness of the sun). This way, they give names to things by comparing them to concrete things they find around them. This is something that children often do. Since their ideas are childish, it's no wonder that they consider Buddhism "a teaching of the lazy." It is deplorable and pitiable that they make fun of one of the greatest religions of the world because of their immature thinking. I, however, think that the Malaysian language possesses wonderful poetic beauty (as I have shown above); no other languages offer aesthetically wonderful materials to the study of literary expressions as the Malaysian language does. Thus, it makes sense that some Europeans called the Malaysian language "the Italian in the East."

I will further talk about their lifestyles and customs. First, as part of their religious ritual, they observe *poasa* around January and February every year, in which they strictly observe fasting for one month. During this one-month period, they eat little food in the morning and do not eat at all during the rest of the day. Thus, as a natural result of fasting, they feel weak and tired in their bodies. They cannot perform any duties; they just sleep under trees assuming the airs of people of great faith. I feel it pathetic.

The people here do not show any interest in foreigners, particularly in the monks and ministers of other religions. As a matter of fact, I have experienced one interesting episode. Once in order to learn about local customs and make friends with local people, I became a member of the Daru Adappu

Entertainment Club that they built. But soon after that, when they found out that I was a Japanese Buddhist minister, they stopped exchanging a word with me. It was a very strange experience.

Then, what kind of character do they have—they who despise Shakyamuni, one the greatest teachers of the world, and who are courageous enough to suppress the desire for eating, one of the most difficult desires to suppress? Here I must agree with the view that many people have entertained from ancient times: the tropical climate does not produce heroes and great human beings and it makes people lazy. Today many of them have become slaves of other races. They have lowly occupations. They do not aspire to make progress in their lives. When they learn about a job that offers six or seven *sen* a day, they immediately take it. When their appetite is satisfied, they are sleeping on roadsides or under trees until they get hungry. They are indeed people who ruin their country. They whom some people regard as animals are laboring under the scorching sun of the equator. Those who feel sorry for them cannot help shedding tears.

Next, I want to talk about religious activities of European people in Singapore. As a result of much hardship in running their churches for a number of years, Protestant and Catholic churches are rising towards the sky. The voice of singing hymns that is in harmony with a piano is heard all over the place. This shows the flourishing of Christian faith. Christians are also busy running various schools where they are educating many children. Although their faith is not like that of Malaysian Muslims, there are many similarities between them.

On the last February 2, all Christian churches in the city held solemn memorial services, which have never been heard of before, to commemorate the passing of the British king. The whole city of Singapore that is usually quite noisy with the sounds of people and carriages was very quiet. At the same time, at the entrance of St. Andrew Cathedral, the most famous of all cathedrals, they were distributing to every worshipper a program of entertainments that were being held in the city. It is also said that the amount of money that various brothels made on that night reached a record. I cannot help saying that there is a contradiction in the attitudes of those worshippers. I am just reporting this as an incredible fact.

The history of the activities of Japanese Buddhist monks here started a long time ago. However, I will make a report on some individuals who have been active in recent years. There is a man who calls himself a Japanese monk who belongs to the Soto sect. He has been living in Singapore for the last seven years. He is a guest and gate-keeper at a brothel. He is a troublesome monk who visits prostitutes, constantly drinking sake during day and night. He is always eager to conduct funeral services. He is spoiling the dignity of Japanese Buddhism. He is brazen and is an extreme embarrassment for us.

Four or five years ago, one individual who had a fake-identity as a Buddhist minister appeared in this city. He carried a name-card that identified himself as the chief representative of a faith group (named Tenka Bukkyo Ushin-ko) belonging to the Nishi Hongwanji in Japan. Immediately people found out that he had a fake-identity; he was actually an abductor of women who were illegally traveling by ship. At one place a woman stripped him of his robe. He was truly a shameless man.

Besides these individuals, Buddhist ministers, who claimed to be members of the Inspection Committee of the Southern Ocean organized by the Nishi Hongwanji, appeared one after another. Their motivation was to deceive people and steal their money in the form of donations. The fact that all of them claimed to be Buddhist ministers of the Nishi Hongwanji surprised me. It also created some difficulties for me. Recently these weird Buddhist ministers disappeared and the dignity of Japanese Buddhism has started to be restored. Since I started to contribute articles to the *Singapore Times* and reported on the propagation activities of the Nishi Hongwanji of Japan, people here started to pay attention to our activities.

Talking about the Buddhist activities that I am currently undertaking, I cannot say that I have made a full success in them because I am the only Shin Buddhist minister who is stationed in this huge district. However, I am giving regular Dharma talks on three occasions: the first Sunday, the 15th and the 28th. And occasionally I make propagation-trips to various towns and villages that are within the range of three or four hundred *Ii* (one *ii* being 25 miles). For example, this month I was invited to Kuala Lumpure, the ancient capital in the Malaysian Peninsula, by the Kotoku-kai group that Japanese people there started. I received a warm welcome. I believe that it is necessary to have a branch there one or two years from now. As far as the activities of the educational department that is attached to our Propagation Center are concerned, I teach, besides missionary work, over 40 boys and girls with Japanese, Chinese and other racial backgrounds for six hours. I teach them various subjects: I mainly teach English to Japanese children; I teach Japanese and English to Chinese children. My wife is in charge of the class of sewing. Since we have several students who study at night, we are truly busy day and night. We are spending day after day, hoping to repay even the slightest portion of the great benevolence of the Buddha. In a place that is only one and a half degrees separated from the equator, in the shade of coconut trees, we are engaged in Buddhist activities to express our gratitude to the Buddha and our teachers.

Family on Carnival Cruise. From top step (right to left) to bottom: Jared, Lisa, Stanton, Sharon, Robert, Eric, Rina, Bodhi, Katelyn, Brian, Lindsey, Chad, Lorin, Molly, Ellen, Jenna, Zoe, Hailey, me, Ava, Emily, Mitchell, Gus, Odin, Helen, November 2016